Design for
Outdoor Recreation

Design for Outdoor Recreation

Second edition

Simon Bell

Taylor & Francis
Taylor & Francis Group

First edition published 1997

This edition published 2008
by Taylor & Francis
2 Park Square, Milton Park, Abingdon, OX14 4RN
Simultaneously published in the USA and Canada
by Taylor & Francis Inc
270 Madison Avenue, New York, NY10016

*Taylor & Francis is an imprint of the Taylor & Francis Group,
an informa business*

© 1997, 2008 Simon Bell

Designed and typeset in Univers by Alex Lazarou, Surbiton
Printed and bound in Great Britain by The Cromwell Press,
Trowbridge, Wiltshire

British Library Cataloguing in Publication Data
A catalogue record for this book is available from the British Library

Library of Congress Cataloging-in-Publication Data
Bell, Simon, 1957 May 24-
  Design for outdoor recreation / Simon Bell. — 2nd ed.
      p. cm.
  Includes bibliographical references and index.
  1. Recreation areas—Design and construction. 2. Recreation
areas—Management. 3. Outdoor recreation. 4. Recreation areas—
Environmental aspects. I. Title.
  GV182.3.B45 2008
    711'.558—dc22   2008000258

ISBN10: 0-415-44172-2 (pbk)
ISBN13: 978-0-415-44172-8 (pbk)

Contents

Acknowledgements vii

Introduction 1

1 Recreation planning 9

2 Design concepts for outdoor recreation 25

3 The journey to the destination 33

4 Providing visitor information 45

5 Parking the car 53

6 Toilet facilities 69

7 Picnicking 79

8 Children's play 93

9 Trails 105

10 Water-based recreation 157

11 Wildlife viewing 167

12 Design for overnight visitors 173

13 Interpretation 197

14 Comprehensive site design 209

Bibliography 219

Index 225

Acknowledgements

This book is the fruit of a number of years spent working in and visiting places designed and managed for recreation, so my first debt of thanks is to all those who went before, creating and managing places where many people have enjoyed themselves in the outdoors. I hope they will look in a positive light on any criticism levelled at their work. As it is a second edition and there have been many more examples from more parts of the world added, the number of people whom I must thank has increased.

In particular, I must thank Duncan Campbell for his excellent and patient editing work on the early drafts of the first edition, which has continued into the second edition since much of the original material remains. Dean Apostol also gave comments and help on the first edition which is still in the second. Warren Bacon supplied me with numerous references and material on the Recreation Opportunity Spectrum and barrier-free access. As there is a lot of new material I need to thank lots of new people and organizations. I owe a debt to Yoji Aoki of the National Institute of Environmental Studies in Japan and to the Japan Society for the Promotion of Science for a fellowship which enabled me to travel the length and breadth of Japan looking at sites. The trip to Australia and New Zealand that yielded so much material was done under our own steam but I should thank Bruce Chetwynd in Tasmania and Simon Swaffield and Jenny Moore in New Zealand who put us up and pointed us in the right direction of some good examples – including some of Jenny's work. The COST office in Brussels, who manage the European Union COST programme (Cooperation in Science and Technology) have enabled me to chair the COST Action on Forest Recreation and Nature Tourism and to attend meetings in many parts of Europe which provided examples. My colleagues in the COST Action also deserve thanks, especially those who arranged meetings and supplied me with photographs. My work at the OPENspace Research Centre at Edinburgh College of Art has enabled me to update many sections of the book with the findings of our and other people's research and I thank my colleagues there for putting up with me.

The effort to bring out a second edition is not quite as great as the first so there was less work for my wife, Jacquie, and less disruption when preparing it, but she still deserves thanks for helping me keep it going.

Thank you all.

Simon Bell
Dunbar
2008

Introduction

What is recreation, and why is it important?

Outdoor recreation and its cousin, nature tourism, are the big growth areas in leisure and holiday activities today. As the populations of most countries develop and become more urbanized, and as most people's work becomes less and less connected with the land, many more people are seeking to regain some kind of connection with nature and with wild landscapes, even if it is only for short periods at infrequent intervals. There are many reasons for visiting and exploring the great outdoors: physical exercise, release from the stresses of city life, fresh air, getting closer to nature, enjoyment of the scenery, hunting and fishing, walking the dog, an occasion to meet family and friends … the list goes on. For most people it is probably a combination of reasons. The trends in how people spend their time change from year to year, but contain broadly the same ingredients: a chance to escape from the city, to be alone or to be with other people, to be close to nature, and to relax and enjoy oneself. The activities that people pursue range from strenuous hiking into wild mountainous areas, days from the nearest settlement, to a gentle stroll in a park or woodland within or a short distance out of town, enjoying a family barbecue or just sitting and looking at the view. Increasing numbers also seek an adrenaline rush from participating in more extreme activities.

Recreation is the term used mainly to refer to activities that are carried out not far from home and within the normal daily routines while the term nature tourism implies activities that are part of a holiday or vacation and which involve staying away from home. Clearly, some people using a particular area may be locals who come regularly while others may be tourists from another region or country. As well as undertaking an activity, many people are interested in learning more about the area they are visiting; the organization which manages the place may also have an interest in teaching visitors about it, partly to increase their enjoyment but also to help in its protection or management.

The term 'the outdoors', as used in this book, is an all-embracing one that covers all those places where people feel they can achieve that special feeling of being 'away from it all'. To some, born and bred in the city, it may be an area of urban green space, a local nature reserve or countryside near home. Urban forests, increasingly common in Europe and North America, can provide opportunities for solitude and quietness well within the city limits.

People may need to go further afield from time to time, such as to the emptier, less human-dominated landscapes of otherwise urbanized and populous countries such as the New Forest and the South Downs, a short distance from London; the Blue Ridge Mountains of Virginia, not too far away from Washington, DC; the Black Forest of Germany, within reach of many urban areas; the Blue Mountains of New South Wales, Australia a short distance inland from Sydney; Mount Fuji, reasonably accessible to the residents of Tokyo; Losiniy Ostrov (Elk Island) on the outskirts of Moscow. Many of the most densely populated countries still have emptier and remoter regions that are accessible on a longer trip of perhaps more than a day's duration: the Scottish Highlands in Britain, Mount Daisatsuzan in Hokkaido in Japan, upper New York State in the USA or the Sierra Nevada in California.

A well-known scene in the Blue Mountains of New South Wales, Australia. This is a national park very close to and accessible from the city of Sydney.

Lake Baikal, in Siberia, Russia. This is an example of a more remote and wild landscape which is becoming increasingly attractive to visit and explore. The huge lake has hardly any road access points and is mainly visited by boat.

Further away and offering an experience closer to the natural elements are central European mountain ranges above the settled valleys of the Alps, the Pyrenees or the Carpathians, the Southern Alps of New Zealand, the fells of Lapland, the Cascade Mountains of Oregon and Washington or the hills and forests around Lake Baikal in Siberia, where a few hours' hike from a road or village can take you into areas where nature dominates. Finally, there are truly wild, remote areas, accessible only by long hike, float plane or helicopter, boat or kayak, where civilization is utterly absent.

As well as the temperate regions, many tropical countries are increasingly visited by nature tourists (as well as for cultural or beach holidays). Jungle lodges and camps, treks on foot or perhaps by elephant, by boat or raft are ingredients for people who want to experience remote areas, nature and culture of native peoples. The participants may be very environmentally aware and keen to have as authentic an experience as possible.

In all these landscapes people can make their presence felt in large and small ways: creating paths and trails, leaving their rubbish behind, lighting fires that can cause serious damage, disturbing sensitive wildlife, and damaging crops. This may be through carelessness or ignorance. Some areas are so fragile that it takes only a few visitors to damage plant life and cause erosion that may take decades to heal. Other areas are more robust, but are so attractive to visitors that they start to wear out under the sheer weight of numbers. Visitors need managing if landscapes, habitats and wildlife are to survive, and if the enjoyment and purpose of the visit are to be fulfilled. The places that we visit generally need some help in order to cope with the pressure that we place on them, and we need facilities to help our enjoyment. Thus, we have to design and maintain a wide range of features in all but the wildest, remotest landscapes, where the absence of anything man-made is a key aspect of their attraction. We have to respect the landscapes we visit and avoid reducing their essential character and spirit of place. This is the greatest challenge to the designers and managers of recreation sites: how to avoid spoiling the very qualities that people have come to visit, while providing the facilities that are so necessary to the enjoyment, safety and hygiene of the visitors and the physical protection of the immediate site. Much depends on the scale and vulnerability of the landscape in question. The Grand Canyon is hardly going to wear out, but a small valley and waterfall might be more delicate.

We do not come to recreation design from first principles. Visiting the countryside, wild or scenic landscapes has quite a long history. Many of the places, the existing facilities and the expectations of what a visit to the great outdoors should consist of are almost traditional. Some wonderful designs of buildings in parks date from the nineteenth or early twentieth century. Some of the best were created by the Civilian Conservation Corps for the National Parks Service in the USA in the 1930s. These are now part of the landscape, and have helped to establish a character or style for site and artefact design: generous scale, use of local materials, and a generally 'rustic' appearance. This is echoed in most countries, which have borrowed the idioms from each other. We should appreciate this lineage, and consider the history of outdoor recreation so that we are worthy heirs of a great tradition.

The history of outdoor recreation

For most of the history of humankind, and still for huge numbers of people, the main goal of life has been to ensure their own survival and that of their families. At the same time, civilizations developed, allowing elites to arise who provided priestly, leadership or royal functions. Such individuals and their families can pursue other activities, as they are largely relieved of the task of obtaining food. Hunting and hawking have been important forms of recreation for the monarchy, from ancient times until the present. Thus it is obvious that civilizations must reach a certain level of economic and cultural development (usually quite advanced) before concepts such as 'recreation' or 'leisure' can be entertained.

Following the agricultural and industrial revolutions in the eighteenth and nineteenth centuries, particularly in Britain but subsequently in other countries, wealthy landowners and industrialists could afford to pursue outdoor recreation in field sports: hunting, shooting and fishing. Many also ventured on sightseeing tours, as an interest in scenery developed and became fashionable, especially with the 'picturesque' movement in Britain. Poets and painters celebrated nature, and philosophers pondered on 'natural' law and the 'noble savage'. Arduous tours were made across the Alps to view the scenery. Later, the English Lake District, the Scottish Highlands, the German Black Forest, the Finnish Lakeland, Niagara Falls and numerous other places became fashionable resorts, made more accessible by the advent of the new railways.

In North America, John Muir began to spread the message about the dramatic landscape of Yosemite and other wonders of nature, to campaign for their protection as places not just of beauty but also where the spirit might soar and where people might commune with nature. His efforts eventually bore fruit, and visitors made their way to the many new national parks of the USA founded in the later years of the nineteenth century and the early years of the twentieth.

In Canada, round about the same time, the railways across the Rocky Mountains were developed in close partnership with the resorts of Banff and Jasper. Mountain scenery, wilderness, thermal springs and modern amenities provided by resort hotels helped to promote the national park system of that country. Visitors to such areas were the forerunners of nature tourists – as many are today, driving to see the marvels of Yellowstone in Wyoming, the Grossglöckner Pass in Austria, the North Cape of Norway, Lake Baikal in Siberia or Uluru (Ayers Rock) in Australia.

The waterfalls at Yosemite National Park, California, USA. This is where it all began. The unsurpassed beauty of the place convinced John Muir that it should be protected as a place where people might get close to nature just as he had done. Nowadays the main threat to it is from too many people. In recent years the numbers of visitors have been restricted by the park authorities to avoid overloading the facilities.

During the Industrial Revolution, a new kind of recreational demand arose among the middle and lower classes. Urbanization of former rural populations provided the labour to operate the new industries, which hugely influenced the development of Europe and the eastern USA during the nineteenth century. Britain was one of the first, and still remains one of the most urbanized countries in terms of the percentage of its population living in cities. Later in the century, working people began to question the quality of their lives in grimy, smoky slums, and to desire freedom to escape from this poor environment. In cities such as Manchester or Sheffield, which expanded close to wild moorland landscapes, groups of people formed clubs to walk or bicycle into the countryside at weekends.

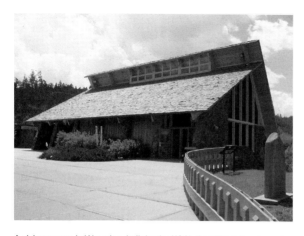

A visitor centre in Wyoming, built by the US National Park Service using modernistic approaches during the 'Mission 66' era. Although modern in form and function, this building also uses local and natural materials.

A viewing tower at the Great Smoky Mountains National Park in Tennessee, USA. This is an uncompromisingly modern construction, using concrete.

These people wanted the freedom to roam about the countryside, and this was perceived by private landowners to conflict with their interests. By the 1920s and 1930s, outdoor recreation in Britain, Europe and America had become an established pastime for many people. Day trips on the train or bus or by charabanc, picnics and walks, boating, swimming and nature study became common.

In America, the pioneering settlers migrating to the West and living off the land are an important aspect of the nation's folk history. Technology – paved roads, electricity, automobiles and radio – increased the nation's well-being, and brought people closer to each other because of better communications. As this developed, nostalgia grew for parts of the pioneer way of life which then became important as recreational activities to reinforce and maintain the old connections with the land and in some ways a sense of national identity. Hunting, hiking and trail-riding changed from survival activities into leisure pursuits.

The demand for recreation stimulated the designation of national parks, where scenery and to some extent wildlife protection were combined with opportunities for recreation. The work of the Civilian Conservation Corps in the 1930s to restore degraded areas like Shenandoah as parks in the USA, the establishment of national parks in Britain in the late 1940s and early 1950s, and similar developments elsewhere in Europe, Australia, New Zealand, Canada and Japan all reflected similar demands.

The next major impetus for recreation was the increase in car ownership and the freedom to travel

they afforded. The availability of mass-produced cars and good roads to drive them on was pioneered in the USA. In the 1950s and 1960s, the Interstate system of freeways and major highways brought previously remote areas within easy reach of a wide range of people with cars or trucks to go hunting, fishing or hiking. Camping was a cheap way of staying in an area, and still remains popular. In the USA, at the same time, in recognition of the huge post-Second World War increase in demand for access to national parks, a programme called 'Mission 66' was implemented. This led to a massive increase in the network of facilities such as car parks and trails established in the national park system. More than that, however, it developed the whole concept of the packaged visitor experience and invented the 'visitor centre' and 'visitor interpretation'. It also pioneered the use of modern design and construction methods and materials in wild and natural settings, something that is still seen as inappropriate in such locations by probably a majority of people.

In Western Europe, mass car ownership took longer to develop, although a road system already existed. By the early 1960s, places like the New Forest in England were beginning to disintegrate under the pressure of cars and visitors. Traffic jams became common in the Lake District, and convoys of trailer caravans – a favourite means of holiday transport in Britain and Europe – were regular sights during the summer months on many roads. In Eastern Europe and the Soviet Union, recreation was popular but car ownership was not so widespread. People made much more use of railway travel. In the decade and a half since the collapse of

A scene showing visitors to the New Forest in Hampshire, England, during the 1960s. Unrestricted access by car to many parts of the forest resulted in site damage, danger to people, litter and pollution. After planning and design, access was controlled, and facilities were installed that now allow visitors to enjoy the forest without seriously damaging it.

communism, car ownership has dramatically increased and the use of the car for recreation trips has become as common as elsewhere. The removal of the 'Iron Curtain' has also increased the scope for European travellers keen to explore all aspects of the parts of Europe that were inaccessible for 40 or so years.

The most recent trend in transport has been the enormous growth in cheap air travel. This has done for international travel for tourism what the boom in car ownership did in previous decades. As a result, people are more likely to travel to far-flung destinations for long trips, perhaps trekking or undertaking other nature tourism-based journeys as well as shorter weekend breaks. How long this trend can continue is anyone's guess; the main factors affecting its continued development are likely to be fuel prices, overall inflation and the effect of any 'green taxes' that may be imposed by different countries.

As access to the outdoors has become easier, and people have become more adventurous in what they can do there, a plethora of different activities have developed. Some, such as mountain or all-terrain bike riding, were unknown a couple of decades or so ago but are now not only very popular but have subdivided and developed into different varieties, each with their own sets of followers. A whole host of specialist, often seasonal, markets has been developed by enterprising people. These include white-water rafting trips, outfitting for guided back-country trail hikes, and heli-skiing, where skiers are flown to remote mountain locations by helicopter and dropped off to ski back to base.

Now that outdoor recreation is a well-established regular activity for millions of people every year, what precisely do they get out of it? What are the benefits of the great escape from the city? What does this tell us about the kinds of settings, sites and facilities that need to be provided?

Escaping from the city

In 1901, John Muir wrote:

> Thousands of tired, nerve shaken, overcivilized people are beginning to find out that going to the mountains is going home; that wilderness is a necessity; and that mountain parks and reservations are useful not only as fountains of timber and invigorating rivers, but as fountains of life.

From that time to this there has been a widely held belief that, although the rate of urbanization is increasing, cities are somehow bad for us, and that in order for a complete feeling of well-being we must be able to escape, to connect with nature, to 'get in touch with the nerve of Mother Earth', as John Muir phrased it. In recent years, there has been an increased research focus looking at the health benefits of nature. More and more evidence is now building a convincing case that visiting green areas (ranging from parks and gardens to more remote places) is good for our physical and mental health. As rates of stress increase and mental health levels decrease, the restorative qualities of natural settings are increasingly being seen by health providers as good alternatives to prescribing people with anti-depressants. Rates of obesity are increasing in all developed countries, mirrored by reduced rates of physical activity resulting from our sedentary lifestyles and associated with poor diets. It has also been noticed that the people who make the most frequent use of natural environments are not those who need help the most. Many sections of society living in poor conditions environmentally, socially and economically are also those with lowest accessibility to green spaces near home, let alone any places further afield. Creating the opportunities, and then the motivation, to visit green areas for both physical and mental health and well-being has become an element of public policy in most developed countries. Understanding the barriers to this is of paramount importance.

The benefits of physical exercise in nature are partly associated with the quality of the environment, as clean and unpolluted. What are the qualities of nature that offer mental health benefits? The mechanisms of this are not yet fully appreciated. It has been suggested that we become stressed in part because modern lifestyles require us to react to persistent unwanted discordant stimulations and by the constant need to concentrate on many activities simultaneously when living and working in cities, so that the harmonious sensations of nature provide stimulation where no effort is required. Even the colour of trees, water and sky, their greens and blues, can have a calming effect.

The knowledge that we can escape from the negative aspects of city life also appears to do some good, and there are obvious benefits in being able to visit a more natural area, close to home whenever we want, assuming that there are such places within easy reach of everybody.

However, to many people, wild landscapes – especially forested ones – present stressful and frightening aspects. Women especially are often afraid of being attacked if they are alone in woodlands. People from ethnic minorities may also associate nature with dangerous animals such as snakes or rabid feral dogs. This may be the result of exaggerated assessments of risk; or it may go deeper, to feelings arising from long-established cultural associations with forests expressed in legends and stories such as Little Red Riding Hood. Perhaps we have had some of our natural instincts for survival bred or tamed out of us, and like pet rabbits let loose, we are unable to cope with freedom.

The purpose of this book and its audience

Some of the themes discussed briefly above will be explored further in this book, because they pose real challenges for the designer. The major message is that the outdoors offers particular qualities and benefits for people, which have evolved and been recognized over the past two and a half centuries. Today's demands can also cause adverse effects on certain landscapes, habitats and wildlife where outdoor recreation and nature tourism occur, and can place burdens on those who use and manage land.

It is vital that designers and managers work to maintain a good balance between the qualities and special value of the outdoors, which offer such benefits to people, and the ways in which land is used. It is important to create and maintain opportunities for people to enjoy and understand nature, but recreation has to be sustainable. Future generations must be given the opportunity to experience Yosemite, the Lake District or the Alps just as we can, and preferably at an enhanced level. Past intervention, such as bad design and lack of management of sites or people, has damaged the special qualities of many places. We should seek to reverse that damage, and to design the features and facilities sensitively, allowing nature, not people, to be the dominant influence on how things ultimately shall be.

Outdoor recreation is provided by many people and organizations. Some of the major providers are national, federal, or local government bodies such as national park services, forest services, states, provinces, counties; there is also a vast array of private companies and individuals and, increasingly, non-governmental and voluntary bodies. Some operate huge areas with recreation as a primary objective; some fit recreation alongside utilitarian functions such as timber production or water management. Some are small businesses: campground operators, trail guides, horse and bicycle hirers, refreshment concessionaires. Some employ skilled recreation professionals, landscape architects and designers; others do it themselves. Some have distinct corporate styles and long traditions; others are newcomers who replicate what they like from others. It is to all these people that I offer this book.

It is not a bible or a cookbook; it is more a synthesis of what I believe, in the light of my experience of working for one of the major outdoor recreation providers in Britain, of researching into many aspects of access to the outdoors and of travelling widely around the world, to see the best and worst practice in the field of site and facility design.

It should help to stimulate the old hands, and give useful guidance to the newcomer. All sites benefit from a reappraisal, a spring-clean and some new ideas from time to time. The book is intended as a guide to the design factors that should be considered in order to achieve a good balance between the needs of the visitor, the site and the manager. Examples are drawn from a wide field representing several years of travel in Europe, North America, Russia, Australia, New Zealand, Japan and elsewhere.

One point that I wish to stress, which is often overlooked, is that of influencing the experience of the visit itself through the design process. Think of how visitors are likely to use the area, what they need, what they expect and how the design can be developed from this perspective. Planning the visit starts at home, often aided by media advertisements, travel programmes, the internet and literature, and with anticipation of the trip ahead. Images of the place fill the mind, and travelling to the area allows these expectations to build up. The experience of the arrival and the subsequent visit must fulfil these expectations as far as possible, making the most of the positive features and minimizing the negative ones. The journey home is usually where a note of sadness sets in, but recalling a good experience retains the positive values of the visit for a long time afterwards. In addition, such a good after-glow is essential to persuade the visitor to return, and to tell his or her friends to come. This is as important for the variety of commercial ventures as it is for the reputation of government agencies with multi-purpose objectives.

The approach is also worth using when refurbishing existing facilities and sites – a common activity for many providers. Often problems with existing layouts, the effects caused by changes in demand and wear and tear can be solved by a complete reappraisal of the site from the point of view of the user.

Owing to the wide range of countries and varieties of land managers with differing skills and resources available whom I hope will use the book, costs, while an important factor, are impossible to deal with in a meaningful way. One general rule, however, is that cheap construction frequently means expensive maintenance or repairs, while good quality, more expensive solutions will save much time and money in the long run.

It is also worth mentioning at this stage that a number of design examples shown in this book are proprietary makes or are otherwise covered by copyright. If anyone wishes to use or copy a design, they would be advised to consider this issue. The book is not meant to be a design catalogue but a stimulus to ideas and approaches for recreation design. Many of the photographs or illustrations give credit to their sources, and these are most likely to be copyright.

In addition to the comments on cost and copyright noted above, it is relevant for readers to consult their local sources of standards for construction, safety and quality, such as the British Standards Institution (BSI), the International Standards Organization (ISO), the German DIN (Deutsche Institut für Normung) or the American National Standards Institute (ANSI), together with the local planning, zoning, building, highways, pollution control and other regulations and codes that apply.

As the book covers practice in the USA, Canada, Europe and elsewhere, dimensions have been shown in metric and imperial units, converted from one to the other or vice versa unless local sizes are quoted. Normally metric is shown first followed by imperial.

Many of the names or terms used for structures and facilities vary from country to country, particularly between North America and Britain. In most cases, the British term is used, but the alternatives are shown in brackets when it is first introduced. Most terms are, in any case, commonly used and fairly interchangeable, so that a glossary is unnecessary.

Finally, I hope that readers are stimulated and excited by what they find within the following pages, so that design is accorded its rightful place in helping visitors to have a rewarding experience when they visit the outdoors. As this is the second edition, readers should find many features have been updated, fresh examples have been included, the coverage broadened and the results of research incorporated. The bibliography has also been extended. In the ten years since the book was first published, many developments have occurred which needed to be reflected in the contents. In particular, a European Union-funded networking project called a Cost Action (Cost stands for Cooperation in Science and Technology) allowed some 80 researchers and practitioners in forest recreation and nature tourism from 26 European countries to work together between 2004 and 2008 and many of the new ideas and examples were discovered through the opportunities offered by this project.

One

Recreation planning

Before designing sites and facilities it is important to put the right kinds in the right places. Site planning is essential if conflicts between different users, and between users and the landscape setting and wildlife, are to be minimized. Difficult or costly management and maintenance activities also have to be avoided. As with the development or marketing of any commodity, the operator has to match supply with demand. If this is not achieved, problems are likely to occur. Visitors may fail to get the most out of their experience; the setting or site may suffer undue wear and tear; expensive investments may be underused; other resource values such as habitats may be damaged unnecessarily.

Many of the organizations or individuals that provide recreation own or have access to a land base of varying extent. They are providers of opportunity. How much they provide depends on the demand from actual and potential visitors, the capacity of the site or land base to supply that demand without damage over time – that is, sustainably – and the resources available, including income from visitors, to provide and manage the necessary investments in facilities needed to meet the demand.

Recreation planning is about assessing the demand, both actual and potential; about assessing the capacity of the land base to meet that demand in a sustainable way; and about using available resources wisely to optimize the potential. Planning can be looked on as taking place at three levels.

The first planning level is strategic, where major decisions are made based on policies set by government, whether national, regional or local, the main demographic and demand factors operating at a macro-level. The

data that affects the development of these policies may include national surveys of recreation demand patterns as well as development planning issues surrounding urban growth trends, transport development and economic factors. Examples of strategic plans include the decision to develop a series of 'community forests' in England partly, to provide major new recreational resources near to where large numbers of people live; the plans of the Danish government to locate new forests on former farmland to provide new recreational areas; the new legislation developed in the UK to increase the rights of access to various types of private land such as forest, moorland and non-cultivated farmland. Countries with traditions of strong planning systems, such as many European countries, are generally more able to develop these kinds of strategies than countries such as the USA where strategic planning is only possible in Federal or State lands.

The second type of planning is where the policies and strategies are delivered on the ground at the level of the land management unit. If the recreational provider is a state institution such as a national forest service, it is likely that the policies will reflect very closely some or all aspects of the national policies and strategies; it may be one of the tasks of the organization to undertake a major initiative such as the expansion of forest in Denmark either directly or through fiscal incentives to the private sector. Assuming that it is developing the project directly, then the planning approach involves assessing the potential of the area to supply recreation goods, facilities and services to a defined market, perhaps the local and regional population within an hour or two's drive of the area. The data used to inform the planning will probably include an interpretation of the relevant demand, planning and other factors interpreted at a regional or sub-regional level. Without such data, any plans for an area are likely to be risky.

The third planning level is the site level, where a more localized area is to be developed as a specific site for particular activities, with car parking, information, toilets, trails, and so on. This may be one of several such sites in a single large recreational area. The general plan may zone the overall area for different activities or identify specific attractions to be developed. These specific site plans deliver the brief to the recreation planners and designers charged with the development of the site, its layout, facilities, construction details, information provision and everything else needed. Once constructed, the site is handed over to the managers who will operate it. Ideally the planners, designers and managers will work together as a team, ensuring that everything is dovetailed together from the outset.

This chapter mainly deals with the area planning stage, taking on board many of the major trends likely to affect recreation over time and then planning the distribution of recreational activities in space and time, providing the main specification to the designer of an individual site.

Trends in demand for outdoor recreation

Observers of recreation management over recent decades will have noticed two things: first, that demand for outdoor recreation has grown continuously, and shows no sign of stopping; and, second, that the types of recreation that people are using have changed in several ways.

This could mean that existing destinations may be having difficulty in coping with increased numbers of visitors, and that the facilities and opportunities provided may not be meeting people's desires and expectations. A car park built to accommodate 30 cars may have to be doubled or trebled in size if people are not to be turned away; the advent of a newer activity such as extreme mountain biking may mean that conflicts with existing users arise, and special trails may have to be created to segregate uses and reduce wear and tear on the ground.

There are a number of key trends shaping the changes in recreation demand in developed countries that can be identified and their influences analysed. Some of these are demographic trends, some are social or political, others are technological and economic and yet more are driven by lifestyles.

Older people are now one of the major user groups of the outdoors. Their requirements have to be considered, along with those of other groups, to ensure that they have a chance to gain the most from their visits.

Demography

The population structure of most developed countries is changing. The proportion of children and younger people is declining while that of older, retired people is expanding. Significantly, the proportion of women is increasing as they live longer than men on average. This trend is likely to increase during the lifetimes of everyone living today. Older people have more free time, which may extend up to 20 or even 30 years beyond working age, given greater life expectancy.

A recent phenomenon is that of 'agelessness', where people are willing to participate in activities that used to be associated with younger people. Thus, people are in one sense becoming younger, or at least do not consider themselves to be old until much later in life. This is partly associated with better health and, for the baby-boom generation at least, affluence. The economic power of this generation is well recognized by the advertising industry.

Of course, not all elderly people are affluent, fit or live in places where access to the outdoors is easy. They may not have cars. However, a great many take up at least some of the opportunities presented to them. Many are active walkers (with or without a dog), and may visit the same area up to twice a day. Many participate in nature-watching activities, enjoying driving into the countryside at any time of the week or season, and this helps to keep them active and feeling fulfilled. Senior citizens in great numbers go on coach trips to visit scenic attractions, and enjoy the chance to see wild and natural places, albeit briefly.

A family of Turkish people in a park in Berlin. These people come from a culture where visiting a park or green area is mainly an opportunity for a family outing.

As people become older, they also have particular requirements. They may need easier, smoother paths, shorter routes, more seats, more access to toilets and fewer steps or stiles. They may appreciate a chance to drive to a viewpoint rather than having to walk to it. They may prefer places where wardens or rangers are nearby to help them if they are worried about getting lost.

Increasing ethnic diversity

Migration of people is becoming a major feature of modern societies and a significant demographic factor in many countries. Migration may include within-country migration – from rural areas to cities, leading to rural depopulation, though this does not lead to increased ethnic diversity. Migration from one country to another, such as within Europe, is a major trend over recent years and this leads to different cultural and ethnic mixes. A good example is the large number of Polish people moving to live and work in Britain. As well as Polish delicatessens and increased attendances at Catholic churches, the Polish migrants have different traditions in the use of the outdoors. They are especially keen on mushroom collecting, for example, and in the mushroom seasons will visit forests for this purpose. In the USA recent trends have focused on the Hispanic, largely Mexican immigration to many areas, affecting the language of whole regions as well as other cultural aspects and recreation traditions.

Migration between continents has been taking place for many years, such as Turkish people going to Germany, people from the Caribbean and Indian sub-continent moving to Britain and Africans moving to France. This is increasing and new trends are emerging. Many of both the established and the new ethnic groups have very different attitudes to outdoor recreation and as a result their needs may not be recognized. In Britain, for example, people of Caribbean origin often prefer to visit a country park, if they visit at all, for a large celebratory family get-together rather than to go for a walk. In Germany, the same is typical for the Turkish community.

With the increase in ethnic diversity often comes an increase in language diversity, leading to a need to consider the way that information is provided. It may be necessary to use several different languages in order to help promote a site and to ensure that the widest possible community know about it.

Social changes

Nowadays there are fewer nuclear families of the variety once featured on most television commercials for breakfast cereal: married couples and their dependent children. More people are living singly, as child-free couples or as lone parents. Single people may be widowed or divorced as well as those who are unmarried. Multiple shared occupancy – where a number of single people share a house or apartment – is also increasingly common and not just among students.

The ways in which many of these new types of household use their free time to visit the outdoors are different from those of the heyday of car-borne family camping holidays or visits to the seaside. Single people may be more likely to find friends with similar tastes, perhaps of the same sex, to pursue particular types of activity. They may use leisure activities as a means to meet people, often using the internet (see 'Technology' below). Young people, especially, may favour more risky forms of recreation, and if they are reasonably affluent, this may require special equipment (see 'Specialized tastes' below). Childless married couples are freer to maintain the activity patterns of their youth, unencumbered by small children. They may pursue similar activities to single people, but favour those where mixed sexes can more easily share the experience.

Lone parents may present the most varied characteristics. Frequently, single-parent families are less affluent, less likely to possess a car, and less able to take up the opportunities available to other people or families. Because many are less affluent, such families may want to visit places nearer to where they live, where access need not be by car, and which are free or cheap to visit. If divorced or separated, non-custodial parents have access to their children at weekends or during holidays, they may want to make the most of such times by visits to special places.

Polarization of income

Social inclusion is another aspect that has become more important politically in recent years. Polarization of incomes has increased significantly in the past 10 years in most countries as the economies of developed and developing countries have grown substantially and tax regimes have been less progressive. In countries of the former Soviet Union or Eastern Bloc, economic growth is strong but polarization is dramatic.

Available leisure time and spending power have therefore both increased, but in different sectors of the population. With the changed economic patterns of many countries, higher-earning people tend to work harder and longer hours and have less leisure time, while the lower earners and unemployed have more enforced spare time but, in many cases, little cash for leisure spending.

If both these groups participate in outdoor recreation, then the highest earners are more likely to go for weekends at ski resorts or to take expensive long-haul holidays to exotic locations, where the most is made of the limited opportunity for leisure. Another feature is the demand for high-quality experiences and high-quality service by the more affluent.

Less affluent people may already live in less attractive residential areas, suffer from poorer diets, participate less in physical exercise and have poorer health, leading to a compound indicator of 'social deprivation' being used in social exclusion policy–making. In some countries there is a growing political will to address this and, as far as access to the outdoors is concerned, the need to bring areas suitable for recreation closer to where the least advantaged live has become an element of policy. In Scotland, for example, the term 'environmental justice' is used to describe the need for people to live in and have access to good environments.

Lifestyle changes

The way people live has also been changing rapidly. Changing work patterns mean that there is an increase in the number of people with part-time work or multiple jobs. Home working is also on the increase. Furthermore, there is an increase in the use of career breaks and 'gap' years or sabbaticals taken by everyone from school leavers and students to mature employees. The working week with fixed weekends is not as common so there is greater flexibility about when to participate

in recreation. There is a demand for a better work–life balance, in part reflected in European legislation like the Working Time Directive. This adds to the trend for recreation and nature tourism to be year-round activities, which can be good news for providers keen to expand their businesses from seasonal limitations.

The empowered consumer is also a feature. People are becoming harder to please, more demanding and have higher expectations. The quality of the recreational offer made by providers has to be high, products and services have to be special, not just ordinary and recreational experiences (places, activities and services) have to be provided to a high standard. This also leads to a need for the standard of design of facilities to be high.

Coming with the empowered consumer is the convenience culture. With the perceived lack of time noted above, convenience in everything is one means of making the most of limited time. Thus, people want activities that use their time well, they want them close to where they live, they want them easy to get to and to prepare for so that they can take whatever opportunity they have to fit them in.

Specialized tastes and the fragmentation of leisure

With increased experience and more activities to pursue, recreation consumers are becoming more sophisticated, and the market is diversifying in order to meet the wide range of specialist markets. There are now many 'communities of interest' who participate in specific activities, often requiring special areas, equipment or access during particular seasons. Success in leisure markets depends much more on identifying the

Adrenaline sports have become increasingly popular in recent years, albeit undertaken in a controlled environment with minimum physical risk.

specialisms or niche products. This poses great challenges for managers and designers, as special facilities may be needed with particular design requirements, such as segregation, zoning and other forms of management strategies in order to deal with potential conflicts.

As economies mature and the desire for material things is to a large extent satisfied, this is replaced by a desire for experiences. This is accompanied by the increase in interest in adrenaline sports and the outdoors becomes a place where such experiences can be authentically achieved. Recreation can be packaged and marketed as an experience.

Some activities tend to be fashionable and their period of popularity may be rather brief. Recreation managers need to be able to respond quickly to provide for these as the fashions develop and, equally, to drop them once the fashion fades.

The networked society

Society is always connected and networked 24 hours a day, seven days a week via the internet; increasing numbers of people of all ages possess mobile phones and are used to being able to plan their activities at the last minute. The internet has enabled the rise of virtual communities of almost any interest. Many exist for outdoor recreation, providing a means of meeting people, of participating in events, of planning to attend events, and so on. People therefore expect things to be available and places to be open at the last minute and all the time.

The mobile phone also gives people the sense that they are always contactable and therefore can summon help quickly. Coupled with hand-held global satellite positioning system receivers, it is now almost impossible to get lost, enabling people to direct help to a single location anywhere in the world. As a result, they may undertake riskier activities or do these with inadequate equipment, planning or preparation.

Changing perceptions of risk

Notwithstanding the comments made above about risk taking, generally there has been an increased perception of risk compared with the past. People are increasingly seeing higher risks involved in certain places or types of activity and also seem less capable of assessing risk themselves. This leads to a situation where a risk assessment by providers of recreation should show there to be no risk before some people are willing to participate in an activity. This has led to a demand for more formalized or regulated activities, in order for recreation providers to protect themselves.

Health and safety regulations have arguably tended to err too much on the side of demanding a low risk and failing to recognize the value of learning to assess and overcome risk as part of necessary life experiences. This increased perception is not universal. In many countries this has not occurred yet and even in places such as Britain or the USA where this is perhaps most developed, there are differences between urban and rural people's perceptions.

The risks of most concern are of those posed by criminal or anti-social behaviour, diseases such as Lyme's disease, beaver fever or tick-borne encephalitis, dangerous areas without safety barriers and trees falling down. This has led to women becoming fearful of going to places alone and of parents becoming unwilling to let their children out to play by themselves or in groups. In both cases but especially regarding children, this can lead not to increases in safety but perpetuates the inability to assess risks because this has to be learned through experience, especially when growing up (see Chapter 8).

Managers are therefore faced with a need to balance genuine concerns for people's safety with their own fear of litigation in the event of an accident and of designing or equipping places with so many safety features that they are completely uninteresting to visit.

Health concerns

The current health agendas of many countries are focusing on physical and mental health concerns – the 'epidemic of obesity' sweeping the USA and other countries; heart disease rates, the increases in mental health problems, the rates of prescribing of anti-depressants, and so on. The value of green areas as places to go to get more exercise and the value of nature in countering depression are now the focus of much research, as noted in the Introduction. This is likely to increase over time as the results of research work their way into the policy agendas of many countries. The challenge is how to persuade people to visit green areas regularly and to undertake exercise that is sufficiently aerobic as to have a positive effect. The ready availability of green areas close to home and work as well as the quality of those spaces, their level of management, sense of welcome and suitability in all weathers are probably all factors that will prove to be important.

Commercialization

In the past, many public-sector recreation providers allowed people free access, or charged for permits to control the amount or season for different activities such as fishing or horse riding. However, governments and other public agencies are finding that funding to maintain sites and facilities, and to cope with increased demand and wear and tear on the landscape, is becoming difficult to maintain. Opportunities to charge visitors for appropriate services to help offset these costs, or to upgrade old or provide new facilities, are being considered as one solution. This is a sensitive matter, as in many European countries free access for all people to the outdoors is a much cherished tradition or right. There is also an additional dilemma for public agencies where recreation facilities are already provided from public money, and it could be argued that the taxpayer is being charged twice. Thus, care is needed by public bodies to ensure that charges are only made for services that are clearly additional to the provision of free access.

Notwithstanding these reservations, many people are willing to pay for better facilities and better services. This in turn may persuade managers to develop more commercial opportunities at high-capacity, high-demand sites in key locations, such as gift shops, restaurants and unique attractions such as cable cars to scenic viewpoints. Equipment to collect money – such as ticket machines, pay booths and the need for increased security at commercial sites – all have an impact on design and management.

Environmental concerns

Governments and the public at large are displaying more concern for conservation, heritage and wider environmental issues. It may be easier to manage areas where excessive visitor demand endangers the landscape due to wear and tear, overloads sewage facilities or causes pollution from motor vehicles. People may also be more willing to be managed or even prevented from visiting areas that are fragile or damaged if the reasons are explained to them.

The demand for specific forms of recreation may increase, such as nature watching where rare species have captured the imagination of people through publicity or special projects. Another feature may be the use of sustainable materials in the design of facilities and artefacts, for instance, types of timber from renewable resources, rather than products made from finite resources or which depend on fossil fuel.

Transport infrastructures are becoming overwhelmed by traffic demands in many places. Traffic jams cause pollution, noise and stress and take away from the pleasure of a visit to a recreation area if they are part of the journey in one or both directions. Public transport is often a problem for reaching many places. This adds to the arguments for establishing or creating more accessible places closer to where people live as well as for considering transport issues in strategic planning.

Assessment of demand

It is worth finding out the pattern of demand for a particular destination, how it has changed in the past, and how it may change in the future. Areas that are within easy reach of large cities or centres of population may be the main local places to visit for day trips by certain groups in the population. In other places tourism might be the main market and the demand pattern for tourists may be more difficult to assess.

As part of the strategic planning process a number of countries or agencies within countries undertake regular assessments of the patterns of recreation to discover the various trends described above. Where these exist, they provide reliable information which can be interpreted for planning of areas. Tourism agencies may also undertake surveys of visitors to a country or region as well as of potential visitors from key countries, supplying some of the equivalent information for tourist visitors.

At the planning level, it is not too difficult a task to undertake a study of the demography of a particular area, using a relatively simple but effective questionnaire, for example. It is often a good idea to survey existing users on a fairly regular basis in order to see who is coming, how often, from where and for what purpose. Trends of the profile of the users will emerge and planning, design and management can be redirected to meet the changing demands. A wider survey should be able to identify potential as well as actual users of an area so that their demands can be built into the brief for the development of a new or redevelopment of an existing area.

More direct involvement with the various user groups is also advisable. This will enable planners, designers and managers to uncover ongoing issues concerning an existing area and can also be valuable for identifying key aspects to be taken into account when planning a new one. Each recreational activity is likely to have its own community of interest – horse riders, cyclists, bird watchers, climbers, disabled ramblers, and so on. Various participatory planning approaches are available depending on the scale and scope of the project. These methods are most useful for places where there is a local or regional demand for outdoor recreation.

A remoter location further away from larger centres of population may be more likely to attract tourists who want to spend more time there, perhaps overnight or for several days. Therefore the market may already be determined, by catering for those who can afford transport to get there and by the possibilities offered by the landscape setting.

It should also be borne in mind that demand can to some extent be created by marketing and publicity activities and also that demand may increase once people get to know about a new experience that is available. Publicity is vital for reaching key groups such as disabled people who are frequently unwilling to visit an area unless they know that they are able to participate in activities there. Publicity will therefore have an important effect on converting potential into actual demand. This may be counter-productive if the actual demand becomes too great for the site to cope with.

The landscape as a setting for recreation

While it is possible to take part in many activities in an artificial or unattractive environment – for example, climbing on an indoor artificial rock face, or fishing from the bank of a canal in a derelict industrial area – for most people the setting in which the recreation takes place is a very important part of the whole experience. In many instances it is the landscape that they have come to see, and often the facilities needed are only those that enable them to obtain the most enjoyment from a scenic view.

A landscape embracing habitats, wildlife, cultural heritage and different land uses may have the potential to supply the opportunities to meet some or all of the demand, by way of the type of recreation, by its carrying capacity or land use, or all three. However, because of its fragility it may have no potential for recreation. The activities, the carrying capacity and the quality of the setting in which they take place are considered together. As the market is highly differentiated, the recreation planner has to match the aspirations of different people with what the landscape has to offer and can accept. This depends on the extent of the land base and its current use, its variety and robustness, the climate and the alternative opportunities offered by other leisure operators working in the same vicinity.

Land base

The extent of the land base will determine how many visitors can be spread out so that some can find true solitude while others can enjoy more gregarious situations. For example, larger areas can allow potentially conflicting activities to be zoned in space: a large lake can be zoned so that dinghy sailors and speed-boats are kept separate, while each type of user has enough room to maximize the experience of the visit. Larger areas also mean more scope to move activities from place to place if wear and tear shows signs of getting serious, or if there is conflict with other land uses. In a managed forest, logging will move from place to place, and may have to disrupt the use of an area for certain recreation activities, such as orienteering, for a number of years. Larger areas also enable use to be dispersed instead of concentrated, so that the pressure of wear and tear can be spread out and reduced. This has implications for design, depending on what facilities are needed and how much recreation is amenable to dispersal. Also, the management and maintenance implications of shifting and dispersed use as well as the logistics needed should be assessed.

The existing land base might already be used for some recreational purpose. Proposed new developments might not be compatible with either the existing land use or recreation activity unless there is space to alter one or both and achieve a compromise.

Landscape variety

The variety of the landscape and its components can suggest what might be provided. A landscape of extreme topographic variation, such as a mountainous or hilly area, will probably offer more scenic attraction. It might also provide mountaineering, rock climbing, hill walking, hang-gliding and other pursuits not offered by flat terrain. A variety of vegetation types will provide different settings. For example, forests can hide a great many people: they have a high visual carrying capacity, and tend to be robust landscapes containing particular animals and birds. Meadows or grassland provide good walking country with open views, places to camp, and different wildlife. Sand dunes are fragile and easily damaged, and can tolerate only very light or controlled access. Bogs and marshes offer limited possibilities, an abundance of biting insects and very low carrying capacity.

Water is always an important element, and greatly increases the attractiveness of an area. Whether the water is flowing or still it has special attractions – reflection, movement, drama, the play of light, the sound the water makes, and its cooling effect. It is also a place where numerous recreation activities can take place, thus combining in a unique way the satisfaction of the activity with the beauty of the setting.

In general, the more varied the landforms and range of vegetation and associated wildlife the more attractive an area tends to be for scenic and wildlife viewing. There is a widely held view that variety tends to be preferred over monotony.

Carrying capacity

The robustness or fragility of the landscape, and of the habitats and wildlife it contains, is termed its ecological carrying capacity. The landscape's resilience to wear and tear, and its ability to recover from damage are key factors in determining what can or cannot be provided. There is also a social carrying capacity which might be the numbers of people encountered in a particular place which reduce the experience of solitude, for example. While the concept has been widely used, it also has its limitations. These, and an alternative, more measurable approach, are discussed later in the chapter. However, the concept is worth discussing in this section as it remains a valuable aspect to consider in planning.

Rock and soil are the first aspects to be considered. Hard rock is hard-wearing, but alluvial soils, scree and talus are fragile and easily dislodged. Wet soils, clays, soft rocks and peat are easily eroded, so that significant access is acceptable only if specially surfaced paths are constructed and maintained. Unrestricted trampling over peat moss in the English Peak District has shown how difficult it is to put right the serious effects of this type of damage. Sand dunes are the most vulnerable of all. Volcanic lava is very uncomfortable to walk over, even in tough boots, for any distance.

Vegetation is another important aspect to assess. In high alpine mountains or tundra regions, vegetation grows very slowly, and site recovery after damage is extremely slow. Hence significant access should be avoided. Pasture grass may be one of the most robust surfaces, but it can only stand so much wear and tear. Forest vegetation may be dense and impenetrable, but when opened by paths, offers opportunities for access without too much risk of people straying from the trail.

Constructed facilities

A major opportunity for managers to increase the physical carrying capacity of an area is to construct various facilities. Hard-wearing surfaces can improve the robustness of access and confine the visitor to predetermined locations, as many are disinclined to stray far from a trail. Such action requires investment, continuing management, maintenance and good design. Although built facilities can contribute to the robustness of a site, they can also stimulate increased demand and adversely affect the visual carrying capacity in certain circumstances. Nevertheless, built facilities are important in increasing the potential for barrier-free access for disabled people.

Climate

The climate is often a vital factor in the capacity of an area to supply a particular range of recreation opportunities. For example, it is obvious that snowy winters are needed in order to ski under natural conditions. Areas with more extreme climates – that is, hot summers and cold winters – tend to favour a concentration of recreation at certain times of the year: for example, the winter season for skiing and snow-mobiling or the summer for sailing, sunbathing, windsurfing and swimming. Oceanic temperate climates such as that of Britain, the coast of Oregon or parts of New Zealand facilitate a wide range of activities all year round.

Some climates pose risks to people outdoors. In mountains the weather can close in and become dangerous for less experienced hikers in areas where it can change very quickly, such as in Scotland or the Cascade Mountains of Oregon and Washington. Deserts can cause heat exhaustion and dehydration at the hottest times of the year. This limits the range of activities and the type of people who can cope unless special measures are taken – for example, waymarking of tracks in mountains, provision of shade and water in desert areas – so that others beside the young, fit and experienced can enjoy the area.

Seasonal changes are linked to the climate in many ways but also have different features. Some seasons such as autumn or spring are the prime times for scenic viewing, when the vegetation colours are at their best and wildlife is active. Many people prefer to visit forest landscapes during these seasons – New England is noted for the brilliance of its leaf colours in the Fall, for example. Seasons for fishing or hunting may be important in many areas, and hunting may cause potential conflicts with other users due either to disturbance of game or the risk to humans of being accidentally shot.

Alternative opportunities in the area

The major recreation providers, such as national parks and forest services in the USA and Canada, frequently have large tracts of land in locations where there are few if any alternatives provided by other operators. In more crowded countries such as Britain, the Netherlands or Germany there may be a wide variety of different

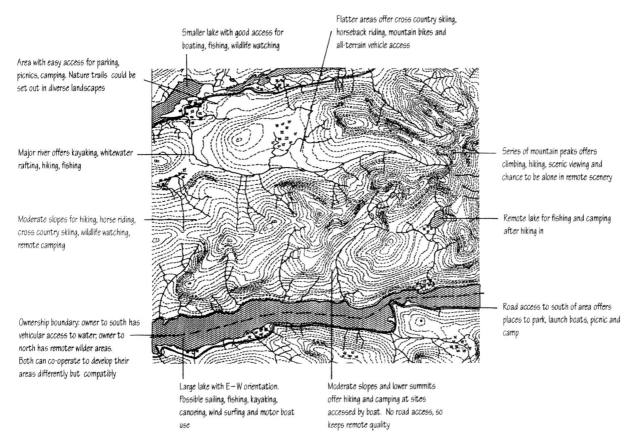

Area with easy access for parking, picnics, camping. Nature trails could be set out in diverse landscapes

Smaller lake with good access for boating, fishing, wildlife watching

Flatter areas offer cross country skiing, horseback riding, mountain bikes and all-terrain vehicle access

Major river offers kayaking, whitewater rafting, hiking, fishing

Series of mountain peaks offers climbing, hiking, scenic viewing and chance to be alone in remote scenery

Moderate slopes for hiking, horse riding, cross country skiing, wildlife watching, remote camping

Remote lake for fishing and camping after hiking in

Ownership boundary: owner to south has vehicular access to water; owner to north has remoter wilder areas. Both can co-operate to develop their areas differently but compatibly

Road access to south of area offers places to park, launch boats, picnic and camp

Large lake with E–W orientation. Possible sailing, fishing, kayaking, canoeing, wind surfing and motor boat use

Moderate slopes and lower summits offer hiking and camping at sites accessed by boat. No road access, so keeps remote quality

A plan showing the possible range of opportunities for recreation in a landscape. Co-operation with neighbouring owners should always be considered.

opportunities provided by a range of public and private operators. It is unnecessary in most cases for an operator to try to provide all of the potential activities if someone else is in a better position to do so. In many cases, as facilities may be provided free, particularly access, it is sensible to consider where respective strengths may lie. For instance, two neighbours might possess different types of landscape such as a lake or reservoir and a forest. In this case it is easy to provide different experiences such as sailing on the lake and hiking in the forest. It may furthermore be sensible for there to be one car park to serve both facilities instead of two separate ones, and for hiking trails to include access to the water at certain points. In another case, two adjoining owners might both possess lakes. Rather than each trying to satisfy demands for fishing and powerboats, it might be better for the landscape, wildlife management and the recreation experience if the lake best suited to fishing was solely used for that purpose and the other concentrated on powerboating.

In this way, the demand is catered for while the carrying capacity of the wider landscape is respected.

Appraisal of opportunities

As part of the initial recreation planning, a survey or inventory of the landscape should be carried out. The area can be classified into areas of particular visual characteristics based on the landform and vegetation types, presence of water, land use, cultural heritage, and so on. Special note should be made of sensitive places, those with fragile soils and vegetation, the presence of rare plants or wildlife that are easily disturbed, or where there are dangers of rock fall, avalanche or steep cliffs. Note should also be made of places with unique or prominent features which give them a strong identity or 'spirit of place', often termed *genius loci*. These might include hidden lakes, waterfalls, ravines, curious rock formations, areas of old-growth forest, places with dramatic or surprise views, or flat landscapes where the sky dominates.

STRENGTHS

Size of area gives high
carrying capacity

Presence of water in various forms and sizes

Varied topography gives range of landscapes

Road access to north and south

Undeveloped character

Diverse habitats and wildlife

WEAKNESSES

Core area is a long way from public access
by road

Lake to south is barrier to access

Peat bogs and marshes are unsuitable for
access or use

Climate and weather are unpredictable

Terrain is rough and steep

Water is cold

Insects are plentiful in summer

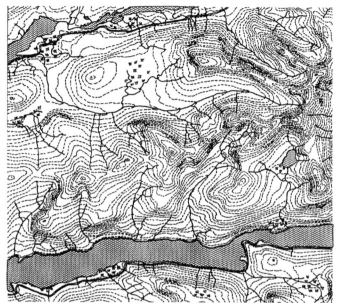

OPPORTUNITIES

To develop a range of recreation activities in
keeping with the landscape

To protect vulnerable habitats from development

To relieve recreation pressure from heavily used
areas nearby

To develop an integrated plan for management to
ensure minimal site degradation

To supply the demand for high quality facilities
and landscape settings

THREATS

Commercial exploitation of forested areas with
good access

Hydroelectric development to the southern lake

Forest fires, arson and vandalism

Uncontrolled access by motorized vehicles such
as boats, all-terrain vehicles and snowmobiles

Mineral exploration

A plan showing how the landscape has been appraised using a SWOT analysis.

On the basis of this inventory and the knowledge about the demand for various types of recreation, the places where different activities could take place can be identified. Sensitive areas can be avoided completely or, if this is difficult, special measures to prevent damage can be identified, such as a boardwalk across a boggy area. Potential conflicts between recreation activities can be identified using a matrix technique, and from this, solutions by design or management can be identified, for example, by activity zoning, according to carrying capacity and compatibility.

SWOT analysis

There are various ways of refining the analytical process following from the basic inventory. One is to evaluate each character area or landscape zone. SWOT analysis provides a useful method. SWOT stands for **S**trengths, **W**eaknesses, **O**pportunities and **T**hreats. It is usual to divide the analysis of an area into those factors that are aspects of the site itself (strengths and weaknesses), and those that affect it from outside (opportunities and threats). There are two ways of completing an analysis. The first method is to list the factors under the four headings on a sheet of paper using a matrix format. This has the advantage of making it possible to see the

relationships more easily, especially when factors can be both strengths and weaknesses at the same time. The second method is to identify the factors and record them on a map of the area. This helps to locate these factors and the way in which they are spatially related. It is of course possible to use both methods.

The advantage of a SWOT analysis is that it is quick, yet produces useful results and arranges them in a way that is of immediate use. The aim in design and management is to build on the strengths, minimize the weaknesses, take up as many of the opportunities as possible and avoid the threats. A useful method of initiating an analysis is to 'brainstorm' the issues: once a basic knowledge of the area has been gained from site visits, consider these, perhaps with other people or a project team, and classify all the issues into the various categories as they emerge from the discussion. Then sift them for importance and assess the implications of each for design and management.

If the area is used already and has some facilities, then the SWOT analysis can be used to appraise these so that they can be redesigned if necessary and improved to meet any new circumstances. The SWOT analysis can be very helpful in developing the brief for the designer on the range of issues that need

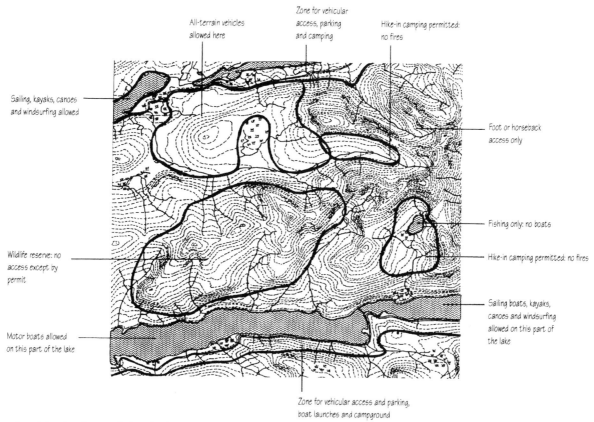

All-terrain vehicles allowed here

Zone for vehicular access, parking and camping

Hike-in camping permitted: no fires

Sailing, kayaks, canoes and windsurfing allowed

Foot or horseback access only

Fishing only: no boats

Wildlife reserve: no access except by permit

Hike-in camping permitted: no fires

Sailing boats, kayaks, canoes and windsurfing allowed on this part of the lake

Motor boats allowed on this part of the lake

Zone for vehicular access and parking, boat launches and campground

Examples of spatial zoning of use applied to a landscape.

to be solved in order to achieve the objectives of a project. The designer is then able to develop creative solutions in design and management terms that best fit the objectives and the requirements to sustain the characteristics of the landscape.

Zoning

As already mentioned, zoning is one of the major ways in which to resolve conflicts between different users and between users and the landscape. The inventory and analysis described above may simplify the job. Zoning identifies what is acceptable and where, although it can include more than just physical factors. Aesthetic considerations and expectations of the experience to be enjoyed can also be built into the exercise. Zones can be based on any convenient and comprehensible unit that helps to manage activities and the landscape in compatible ways.

Following the first coarse sieve of allocating activities to appropriate areas, more refined zones can set limits on what, how much and when activities can take place. Different scales might be employed, from the whole land ownership unit down to sub-zones within

broad categories. Zones might be based on areas: for example, a large zone for hiking might be subdivided into zones in which camping is permitted. The camping zone might be further sub-zoned into an area for tents and one for trailer caravans, and so on.

Zones can also be based on linear routes. Different trail systems might be sub-zoned, for example, by mode of use – horse, foot, cycle – or by degree of difficulty for people with various disabilities.

Zoning in time is another approach. This might be long term: for example, lease of an area for use by a particular interest group for a set period. Seasonal zoning is easy to administer, especially when particular weather is necessary, such as snowy conditions for skiing. Weekly or daily use can spread out and lessen the impacts of activities; examples are booking a permit to go fishing or for access into back country for a particular time duration. Once again, any convenient time interval can be adopted that meets the management objective.

The idea of zoning to meet aesthetic and aspirational needs is one that has been developed in particular by the US Forest Service, and is now used in various forms elsewhere. This is called the Recreation Opportunity

Spectrum or ROS. While designed for large tracts of landscape, the general principles can be adapted for the smaller areas more common in Britain and parts of Europe.

The Recreation Opportunity Spectrum (ROS)

The ROS takes as its major premise the fact that recreation is more than just the activity, such as hiking, fishing and camping, in which people participate. It also includes the quality of the specific setting in which that activity takes place. This was alluded to in the Introduction, and may seem to be common sense. Yet to incorporate this concept will not only raise the standard of experience gained by people but will help the designer and manager to refine the match of activities to appropriate landscape zones in space and time and avoid any conflicts that otherwise may arise. The concept therefore deserves further consideration.

The spectrum is one of **recreational experience** correlated to the **type of landscape setting** where that experience is most likely to be fulfilled. It ranges from the experience of solitude allied to a sense of challenge, some risk taking and the feeling of being self reliant, to the other extreme of feeling secure, comfortable and having a chance to socialize with other people. The spectrum is then divided into six categories, which describe the degree to which these experiences can be achieved. The terminology is chosen to be compatible with other aspects of land and resource management planning carried out in the US Forest Service. The names are not as important as the qualities that they are meant to convey. Each category can be broken down into three components: the activities most suitable, the character of the setting, and the expected experience to be gained.

The categories are summarized as follows.

1. **Primitive**: that is, natural areas unmodified by human activity and large enough so that visitors can find solitude and feel close to nature. The remoteness means that one has to be self reliant, using back-country survival skills, and thus experience challenge and some risk. The activities are all those using muscle power and basic equipment.
2. **Semi-primitive, non-motorized**. In this category are factors such as size of area, degree of human intervention or chance of meeting other people, which reduces slightly the primitive experience of the first category. Minimal site controls may be needed, but the overall experience should be similar to primitive. The same activities are appropriate.
3. **Semi-primitive, motorized**. This is essentially the same as the previous category, but because motorized activities such as motorboats, snow-mobiles or all-terrain vehicles are allowed, the qualities of quietness and absence of disturbance are likely to be impaired.
4. **Roaded, natural**. This category is mainly natural in character, although management activities may be present, and there will be more evidence of use, including roads that provide easier access. The experience will be some solitude and some social interaction but risk-taking and self-reliance aspects will be reduced in importance.
5. **Rural**. This is where human activities start to dominate over the natural character, although the landscape contains significant natural components. Thus solitude and closeness to nature are highly compromised, and there is little scope for risk-taking or for using backwoods skills. There is more chance to socialize, and as use is more concentrated there is a need for more facilities.
6. **Urban**. The widest range of activities is possible but the setting is more or less completely dominated by human activities, and generally constitutes

The Recreation Opportunity Spectrum relating activities, settings and facility designs together to provide the optimum experience.
Source: Courtesy Warren Bacon.

(Left) A part of the Amsterdamse Bos, in Holland, where it is busiest and crowded. (Right). A relatively remote, quieter area, contrasting with the busier section. The fact that it is possible to find solitude and escape in such a relatively small area subject to many urban influences shows the skill of the planners, designers and managers.

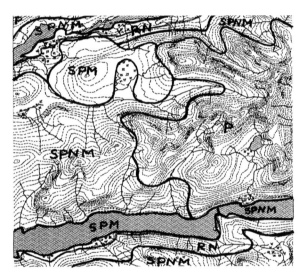

The application of the Recreation Opportunity Spectrum to an area, aiming to match the setting and activities to maximize the quality of the experience. P = primitive; SPNM = semi-primitive, non-motorized; SPM = semi-primitive, motorized; and RN = roaded, natural.

an urbanized environment. Consequently a large amount of design and management is required, as well as many facilities. The setting makes solitude difficult to accomplish although by good design and management some representation of this element may be possible. The need to find challenge and risk is not apparent in most users' minds.

This brief résumé of the ROS shows that it is possible to zone the landscape into the various categories depending on the settings present. Thus, in many US national forests, there will be everything from wilderness providing the primitive setting down to at least the roaded rural if not the urban setting. In Europe it may not be possible to have such a range in many countries. In the Netherlands – one of the most densely populated and managed landscapes – the major categories are probably rural and urban. However, it is possible to develop a miniature ROS within a land area by careful design and management. For example, in the Amsterdamse Bos – the city forest to the south of Amsterdam – the layout of the forest is such that even on busy days when certain areas are crowded it is possible to walk or cycle to empty places, with a good chance of feeling alone and close to nature. Of course, the sense of self-reliance is missing, and this landscape is far from being natural, but it is the relative degree of naturalness compared with other elements in a particular setting that is important.

A further use of the ROS is to help determine the amount and types of facilities and artefacts provided in each category, as these also affect the experience. For example, a primitive setting does not call for surfaced paths, which would be out of keeping and make it appear 'tame'. The general rule is that in the primitive area, only work to protect the site should be undertaken without any facilities being provided. Any materials should be local to the site so that they can blend in completely. If necessary, the semi-primitive, non-motorized areas can have some rudimentary facilities, but these should be rustic in nature and use locally native and natural materials. For the semi-primitive, motorized areas more site protection is probably needed, and more facilities could be appropriate, as many people will make their way into the landscape in a vehicle rather than hike in. The roaded natural and the rural areas are likely to require more facilities than either of the semi-primitive categories. As a reflection of the more managed character of the rural landscape, these facilities can be more highly finished, but should nevertheless aim to use natural materials and finishes as much as possible. In the urban setting there is nothing wrong with any of the previous levels of provision if the situation warrants it, but more facilities will be necessary to deal with greater demand, higher visitor expectation of ease of use and comfort, as well as provision for more formal activities. More robust artefacts may also be appropriate to stand up to the wear and tear and possibly vandalism.

For the designer, the ROS can help to determine the framework for the range, type and number of facilities and artefacts. It is another way of helping to develop the brief and for evaluating the design ideas put forward to meet its requirements.

The ROS can also be used to assess the amount of intervention necessary to minimize the impact of visitors on the landscape habitats and wildlife and in this sense can be used as a visitor management system as well as a planning tool. Ideally, the primitive areas should have a low, well-distributed use, while the urban areas can have high, concentrated use. However, sometimes wear and tear occurs that needs repair. Outside the most sensitive areas, where it may be appropriate to discourage access, the emphasis should not be on trying to prevent any impacts but on considering how much change can be allowed and what actions are appropriate for controlling it. This approach has been developed into a concept called **limits of acceptable change**, in which a range of people, including managers, experts in the landscape and ecology, and users, decide what change, if any, can be allowed. Some of the actions will be managerial, such as closing areas to allow them time to recover, and others will relate to design, such as provision of paths and boardwalks.

This technique was developed in response to perceived limitations in the original concept of carrying capacity. These limitations arise because it is difficult to establish exactly what a specific carrying capacity is from the measurement of impacts on soil, water, plants or animals. Different types of experience also tend to have different social carrying capacities and these may also vary for people depending on their culture and social background and expectations. It has proved to be difficult to establish a strong causal relationship between the amount of use and the level of impact.

Essentially, carrying capacity is a value judgement, not a scientific assessment. With visitor use, change of some sort is inevitable, therefore the questions should be: how much change is acceptable?; and what is the threshold or limit of acceptable change?

Thus, recreation planning should incorporate a system of measuring and responding to the changes that recreation inevitably brings to an area – a system of adaptive management based on formalized procedures. Management intervention should then be aimed at preventing change from going beyond that which is judged to be acceptable. A set of indicators is needed that can be measured cost effectively and which accurately reflect some relationship between the amount and type of use and the impact. These indicators should be related to concerns expressed by users and responsive to management activity. Indicators can be ecological, such as reduction in water quality, increase in soil compaction, changes to vegetation cover and composition or social, such as the number of encounters with other people on a trail or other signs of human presence such as amount of litter or the number of people at a given viewpoint at any one time. Standards can be set for each of these which if exceeded trigger a management response.

Planning to reduce negative factors and perceptions

While recreation managers try to meet the demands and expectations of people who want recreational experiences of various kinds, there are a number of factors not mentioned so far that, unless addressed, prevent many people from making the most of their visit. They are those things that tend to prevent people from enjoying themselves because they are uneasy or frightened, or feel at risk in some way. The main worries appear to be as follows.

1. **Are we allowed here?** This is fundamental in those countries where it is illegal to trespass on private property. People feel uneasy in case they meet an irate owner, occupier or employee. Signs and information help to reassure people, so that they can relax and enjoy themselves.
2. **Are we going to get lost?** Many people are not very good at map reading and worry about getting lost. Waymarking of trails helps, as does a pictorial map showing landmarks that are easy to identify.
3. **Am I going to break a leg/fall off a cliff/drown in a river?** In other words, safety is important to people, especially in less wild areas where fewer

risks are expected. The design of facilities should incorporate as much appropriate safety thinking as possible without taking away the quality of the experience.

4. **Am I going to be attacked by animals?** In some places people unfamiliar with an area may feel or be genuinely at risk from being bitten by snakes, attacked by grizzly bears or even bulls in a pasture. However, while the risks might be small, some thought is needed as to how people can be reassured and protected when necessary.

5. **Are the trails suitable for my level of ability or disability?** It is important that as much of the area is as accessible as possible for all abilities. This does not mean making paths up to the top of remote mountains for wheelchairs but it does mean thorough planning and design to develop the least restrictive access possible in the circumstances to help all people make the most out of their outdoor experience. The design of facilities to be free of barriers is an important topic, and the brief for the designer is best developed with the aid of people representing different types of disability, who can evaluate whether or not the proposals meet their needs.

6. **Am I likely to be attacked/mugged/raped?** This is a widespread fear, especially among women, not only in urban parks and forests, but also in other places. While this may only be a small risk, it does prevent a large sector of the population from making the most of their visit. Designers and managers of facilities can go some way to ensuring a greater feeling of security.

Research has explored issues of safety and fear. Much of the problem stems from the appearance of the recreation area: if it is untidy, poorly maintained, if litter and rubbish are dumped there, or if a lot of vandalism has occurred. This makes the area seem unmanaged, uncared for and likely to be the haunt of anti-social people. In urban fringe areas the need for solitude is not so widespread. People frequently visit in groups and prefer to see other people, giving them a sense of security or of help being available. Some strategies to be adopted in planning for recreation include different types of landscape that give different atmospheres, from visible open woodland or spaces to wilder areas that more confident people can choose to use. The same applies to routes, where the main paths should be designed for maximum visibility and with fewer places where people might feel trapped. Other paths

can be wilder, more winding and more enclosed. Signs and waymarking also increase confidence, as long as they are clearly understandable and easy to follow. Finally, the presence of wardens, rangers, workers and other staff in uniform or otherwise recognizable adds confidence, as visitors know that the area is being watched, and there is a source of help or policing.

Sustainable recreation

As far as possible, any recreation provision should be planned and designed with sustainability in mind. At its simplest, sustainability means that the present needs of the people and their environment should be met without compromising the ability of future generations to meet their own needs.

An example of how sustainability could be included in recreation planning is recent work by Scottish Natural Heritage, the government body with a responsibility for the landscape, nature conservation and outdoor recreation in Scotland. The following section is reproduced with their permission.

The approach is founded upon five main principles. These principles are based on common sense, and are designed to promote a sense of responsibility and understanding in how we all use the natural heritage. Enjoyment of the outdoors causes relatively little environmental damage, compared with major land-use impacts, but all the principles – as set out below – are relevant to access planning and design.

Wise use

Non-renewable resources should be used wisely and sparingly, at a rate that does not restrict the options of future generations. A major call on non-renewable resources (particularly hydrocarbons) by outdoor recreation activities is the use of the motor car. Use of the car is central to the freedom and flexibility with which people enjoy open-air recreation. But we should aim to be less dependent on the car, especially for the more frequent short and medium-length journeys. The provision of better local access, especially where this can be reached on foot or by public transport, will benefit both the environment and the natural heritage, and should therefore be a key objective.

Carrying capacity

Renewable resources should be used within the limits of their capacity for regeneration. Many areas of natural vegetation, and some wildlife, are inherently vulnerable to the impact of too much recreation. Scotland lies at northerly latitudes, with harsh winters and cool summers, both of which inhibit quick recovery of damage to natural vegetation on high ground. 'Carrying capacity' refers not just to the physical impacts of people on land, but also to the risk of causing undue disturbance to valued wildlife, and sometimes to the loss of a sense of wildness or solitude – the very qualities that attract people to remote places. The practical implication of this guidance is that there may be a need for restraint on the use of the most vulnerable areas.

Environmental quality

The quality of the natural heritage as a whole should be maintained and improved. Recreation is becoming a major user of land. As outdoor recreation continues to develop, its effects on the natural heritage will become more widespread. There is a need for greater commitment to resolve problems through management, through environmental education, and by strategic planning of the means of access in terms of roads, parking facilities and footpaths.

Precautionary principle

In situations of great complexity or uncertainty we should act in a precautionary manner. Access measures are sometimes concentrated on places that are ecologically or visually sensitive. Where there is reasonable doubt whether substantial or irreversible damage would be caused to places of special value, the management process should start much earlier, as soon as the problem starts to emerge, and it should seek to identify limits of acceptable change. Meanwhile it is only sensible to constrain and divert activities that might prove damaging to the health of the natural heritage.

Shared benefits

There should be an equitable distribution of the costs and benefits (material and nonmaterial) of any development. We are all 'land users' in our own ways. Access to the countryside confers great non-material benefits on those who can participate in outdoor recreation. But there can be drawbacks, which mainly affect local communities and those who manage land used by the public. Damage now should not compromise the future, either in reducing the enjoyment of generations to come or in creating problems for landowners and managers.

Hence it is important for recreation planners to consider the effects of their actions on the wider environment, on transport, on energy and on the local traditions and economy. Designers need to assess whether their work protects the site from damage, degradation and pollution. The use of materials has to be considered: for example, the implications of using timber from natural and sensitive tropical rain-forests; the effects of timber preservative leaching into the soil; effects on drainage systems; the impacts of construction; the ease of re-vegetation after site work; the ability to restore a site completely after use is finished. This may favour the simplest, most economical solutions, the use of local and native materials, a reluctance to construct anything too permanent, and an adherence to the principle of 'less is more'. This is a good principle, and is particularly valid when arguably one of the central concepts of design in the outdoors is to allow the landscape to maintain dominance over human activities.

At the conclusion of this chapter the designer should be able to assess the requirements of a comprehensive brief for the kind of recreation best suited to a particular place, its likely impact on the site, and the amount and location of constructed facilities and artefacts needed to limit site damage and provide for the safety, comfort and convenience of recreational visitors. The next step is to consider what concepts are appropriate for design, how these relate to different settings and, most importantly, how they will be used by the visitors themselves.

Two

Design concepts for outdoor recreation

In the last chapter, some of the trends in recreation demands and the expectations that people have when they visit the outdoors were examined. How to realize the opportunities that a landscape offers and how to zone or plan in order to meet the demand sustainably, were also considered. What emerged from this examination is that the quality of recreational experiences is significantly dependent on the quality of the setting in which the activity takes place. By this is meant the whole quality of the environment as perceived by the senses. When moving along a trail we see the landscape around us, we hear the sounds of birds, wind, water, feel the wind or warmth of the sun on our skin, we sense the path beneath our feet as it climbs or descends, twists and turns and we can reach out to feel tree bark, leaves or rock surfaces, inhale many smells and taste fruits as we pass. This means that special attention should be paid to the multi-sensory aesthetic qualities of the landscape setting, the facilities and artefacts provided, and the overall maintenance of areas that people visit.

Compared with most landscape architecture, which designs an entire space, in recreation design we primarily take a landscape that has many existing qualities that we wish to protect, and insert as sensitively as possible the minimum amount and number of facilities necessary to balance the anticipated use with the protection of the resource.

Quite often, a destination will be chosen because of its particular qualities as scenery or at least as a scenic backdrop in which to pursue a particular activity. The beauty of the landscape will be particularly important to the large numbers of people who visit areas repeatedly during the year. The anticipation of returning to an area is often heightened by a sense of expecting its beauty to be the same as the last time, with the exception of seasonal change. When there has been a change, perhaps due to a management activity such as logging or a natural event such as a fire, then expectations are disappointed, and anger or sadness can replace satisfaction.

It is impossible to keep any landscape from changing. However, some changes are slow and thus are barely noticed. It is the sudden and dramatic changes that are difficult to accept. Here lies the challenge to managers: to inform people about the dynamics of a particular landscape and prepare them for change, and to accomplish this – whenever possible – in such a way as to make the change either seem to be for the better or fit in so well that its impact is neutral. This requires design skills that are applied to large-scale landscapes. Such design is largely outwith the scope of this book, which is mainly concerned with facility and artefact design, but it does give a sense of the wider context.

Contrasts between city and wilderness

One of the major reasons why people go to the wilder, more natural areas is to escape the daily life of the city. As societies become more urbanized, and as people tend to work less in industries such as agriculture or forestry, they tend to lose the sense of connection to the land that such work brings. The life of a city dweller, culturally rich as it can be, for many people tends to be stressful in some way, dominated by hectic lifestyles and timetables of transport and work. The city is

A city view where human activities and structures dominate. The plan is based on a geometric grid, the buildings are rectangular, densely packed, and the whole is tightly controlled, as are traffic movement and the regulation of people's lives to some degree by timetables. New York.

A remote, uninhabited wilderness area, untouched by direct human activity. The mountains, glaciers and hard climate dominate. It is possible to wander freely and feel far from the urban world; to obtain solitude; and to use the skills of self-reliance when facing natural hazards. Alaska/Yukon border, USA/Canada.

crowded; this is not always a negative situation, given the gregariousness of the human species, but personal space is often limited. The city is also almost completely a human construction. In large metropolises, there may be very little remaining of the natural landscape that once existed. The layout of many cities is based on a giant grid. Landform, old tracks, small streams and former agricultural areas are dominated by this layout, which is relentless in its taming of nature. This is a reflection of the world-view dominant since the Age of Enlightenment in the seventeenth and eighteenth centuries, in which humans consider themselves above nature and consider it their destiny to tame it and bend it to their will. This view has had major consequences for the exploitation of the world's resources, and only recently has it had any kind of sustained challenge. Many people now believe that it is important to be able to escape from the city in order to reconnect ourselves to our roots in the wilderness, the forest, or the natural and semi-natural landscape of the countryside.

To many people, the city represents order, control, the geometric grid, noise, pollution and overcrowding, so they perceive its antithesis in the outdoors. The converse qualities of chaos, lack of control, absence of geometry, quiet, cleanliness and solitude are very important. They provide cues for the kind of landscapes and facilities that designers should consider.

At one extreme, parts of the 'wild' landscape of the English Lake District were spoiled by geometric gridded plantation forests, which seemed to reflect the philosophy of human domination over nature by creating

'factory forests' in natural places. At the other extreme in terms of scale is the urban style of car park, complete with concrete kerbs, white lines and ornamental shrubs in a remote moorland setting. This reduces the sense of contrast between the city and the outdoors, and removes the illusion that such landscapes are wild and unspoiled.

A design philosophy for the outdoors

Arguably, it is therefore important to maintain and reflect the character of the landscapes in the design of facilities and artefacts, while providing many functions that are the same as those needed at home, as well as reinforcing the contrast between the city and the more natural landscapes of the outdoors.

However, it is possible to develop designs that are more redolent of the stylized settings of Tolkien or Disney than those reflecting the real qualities of nature. This must be avoided, as must all forms of pastiche or superficial imitation, in favour of honest, robust, simple, unobtrusive designs, which serve to provide their function with the minimum of fuss. These must not upstage the greater landscape setting that people have come to enjoy.

At this point we can return to the Recreation Opportunity Spectrum (ROS) described in Chapter 1. This helps us to define the type of landscape setting and the most appropriate approach to facility and artefact design. In some locations the correct solution is no facilities, no artefacts, and only repair to physical

A design for a shelter, taken from the design manual prepared for the Civilian Conservation Corps and the National Parks Service of the USA in the 1930s. The style is simple and robust, and uses materials as close to their natural state as possible: round logs, wooden shingles and rough stone all left to weather naturally.

A sign in Tervete Nature Park in Latvia demonstrating another traditional skill in the use of wood.

damage. It is crucial to develop a modest approach, and to resist the need to make grandiose statements or to follow a flamboyant style more suited to pretentious office developments.

Before the early twentieth century there was no such thing as recreation design in the way we describe it nowadays. People visited areas, and in a few national parks in the USA some simple facilities had been built. In the Alps, where mountaineering and hiking had become popular, mountain huts of the type used by shepherds were pressed into use and a few special facilities such as funicular railways enabled well-dressed families to ascend mountains. It was largely in the 1920s that special recreational buildings and other structures came to be designed and then in the 1930s that a design idiom for national parks emerged which was adopted by other organizations. This was when the huge staff resources made possible by the Civilian Conservation Corps, the CCC, made hand-crafting of walls, buildings, shelters, signs and paths possible, using natural materials in a sturdy, simple way, reflecting their settings very well. The legacy of this era remains in many places and in comparison with what followed, does not seem to have dated.

The period of the 1950s and 1960s saw the Mission 66 expansion and development programme in the US national park system. This was aimed at coping with the huge increase in visitor numbers after the Second World War unleashed by the development of the system of Interstate freeways and mass car ownership. The adoption of modern architecture, industrialized construction and the use of steel, concrete and other materials represented a break with the hand-crafted tradition of the CCC days and, while undoubtedly efficiently dealing with the immense numbers of visitors who duly arrived as expected, shocked many people and caused a backlash. The facilities built in the CCC days were incapable of handling more visitors and the buildings would not comfortably scale up to those needed for the modern concepts of the visitor experience moderated by interpretation. Among the many modernistic constructions, however, are some that managed to form a close relationship with the landscape and which, for all their size, made a limited visual impact. Simple forms and earthy colours enable non-domestic building forms to reflect landforms, rock outcrops or other natural forms, at least from a distance. The details of kerbs, signs, toilet blocks and the interiors of the new 'visitor centres' did not perhaps stand up to scrutiny when compared with the more distant views.

Post-Mission 66 design in the USA went through a period of adding pastiche western façades to some of the modernistic buildings, a thoroughly failed strategy. Many of the original Mission 66 facilities are still functioning today but most look very dated, and while they might be considered period pieces worthy in their own way of preservation as representatives of an era, their design idiom has had its day.

The CCC idiom was heavily borrowed by the US Forest Service, which is also a major provider of recreation and had its own programme in the 1930s.

A hotel seen from across a lake in the High Tatra Mountains of Slovakia. This modernistic building was constructed during the Communist era for mass tourism to the area.

A viewing platform in Iriomote National Park on Iriomote Island in Japan. This strange construction is made entirely of concrete, painted to look like wood, giving an impression of something from a cartoon. It is highly inappropriate in this setting.

The approach was then taken up by many other places and it could be argued that a hybrid approach has developed, using much of the CCC look with local or regional additions yet also with an admixture of many aspects of the Mission 66 visitor experience concept and also the principles of site layout, functionality and attempt to minimize the impact of large structures in the landscape – something the CCC large hotels never tried to do.

In areas largely unaffected by the spread of American design ideas – notably the former Eastern bloc and the Soviet Union – recreation design also went through a modernistic phase. In popular areas, large modernistic hotels were built and trail networks constructed but the impact of the car was much less and the need for roads and car parks was limited. Folk art idioms also remained popular and have had something of a revival in recent years. Wood carving and craftsmanship have tended to survive and, when applied well, produce artefacts to an exceptionally high standard. It might also be said that people in these countries expect or are satisfied with lower standards of facilities so that simplicity and lower

impact designs should be possible. However, simplicity is also sometimes equated with crudeness and lack of follow-through in design and construction.

In Australia and New Zealand, it is fair to say that much of the design approach has learnt from the American experience. The materials and design idioms reflect colonial designs to some extent and the use of corrugated galvanized steel (corrugated iron) is a feature that reflects this tradition quite appropriately. Local timber species are also used, as are adaptations to the climate that are also necessary.

In Japan, which has a long tradition of construction with timber and a unique style, the urge to modernize has resulted in an eclectic mix of approaches. Some very Japanese elements can be found as well as good contemporary designs of no particular provenance together with some most inappropriate concrete concoctions designed and painted to resemble wood. These unfortunate structures look more at home in Disneyland. The use of concrete masquerading as wood is actually quite widespread, though sometimes it is difficult to say exactly what it is.

A more recent example from Germany uses natural stone, gravel and weathered rough sawn timber, which work together and fit their surroundings. Simplicity and good attention to the detail of construction make this a timeless solution.

(Top) The landscape at Glenveigh National Park, County Donegal, Ireland. The lake, bare mountains, subdued colours and natural textures present a character that should determine the use of materials and finishes. (Bottom) Part of the external landscape around the visitor centre, where urban materials and finishes used in a fussy design are out of keeping with the character of the landscape as a whole.

The following chapters will concentrate on the design of facilities and artefacts, but as a broad concept it is relevant here to consider the types of materials that might best suit use in the outdoors. Without doubt, a fundamental criterion should be to use as much local material as possible. Stone is best in rocky landscapes; timber is appropriate, especially in forests, but also in most other places. Artificial materials such as plastic, concrete or stainless steel are not always out of place, but should be used with care, in small amounts, for particular purposes, in relevant locations such as rural and urban settings, or associated with buildings, particularly their interiors. Some materials will work when least expected. Plastic-coated profile steel (a modern version of corrugated iron) works surprisingly well as a roofing material, usually in a range of dark colours. Dull iron or weathered, galvanized or 'Cor-ten' controlled-rusting steel does not look out of place in the countryside, and can be a useful protection against vandalism.

The use and appropriateness of various materials for use in the outdoors are best explored using a couple of examples. The visitor centre at Glenveigh National Park in Ireland, recently constructed for the Office of Public Works (OPW) to the designs of Tony O'Neill, offers some interesting contradictions. The setting is a majestic, bleak, barren, windswept, empty valley among dramatic bare mountains. The narrow public road that takes the visitor there passes through a similar, virtually uninhabited landscape for some miles. In order to respect the character of the landscape, the concept sensibly places the building low down among the landform, so that it barely impinges on the view. The building is composed of a number of circular concrete pods, and is roofed in turf, thus becoming almost a part of the landscape. It houses information, displays, toilets and offices to service the many visitors who come there, and acts as a gateway to the park.

The design of the external layout incorporates many elements that are somewhat urban in form and material. The use of black tarmac surfacing, concrete kerbs, paving setts and steps and tubular metal handrails is questionable in the landscape setting. All these artefacts would be completely at home in an urban park but probably not a wilder setting such as that found at Glenveigh. There is little of the contrast that would otherwise mark a distinct change in the experience from that of city or managed landscape to that of this wild area. What is accomplished in the architecture is less happily continued into the external treatment.

At the heart of all design concepts where we want the landscape to remain dominant is the need to identify and respect the *genius loci,* the spirit of the place. This intangible quality is what makes places individual and special. It is what marks them out in the first place, and what makes them attractive to visitors. The designer must take pains to identify the *genius loci* and use it as a source of inspiration. It must also be respected and not compromised by the facilities created to allow visitors access and to protect the site.

An example of the *genius loci* being taken into account is the set of simple facilities available at the Franz Josef Glacier in South Island, New Zealand, installed and managed by the Department for Conservation. The glacier descends down from the western slopes of Mount Cook into a wide valley whose floor is covered with boulders and rocks together with the river draining the meltwater away. The valley sides along this lower section are covered with temperate rainforest containing many trees such as southern beech species, tree ferns and other plants which are unique to New Zealand. A trail leads to the snout of the

(From top – a) The parking area at Franz Josef Glacier in New Zealand, showing the gravel surface and the large boulders. (b) Shows a toilet block sited well among the vegetation but open and welcoming, using traditional materials and colours. (c) The entrance to the trail leading to the glacier, with a sense of expectation raised by the fact it disappears into the forest. (d) The glacier, seen from the lower valley, the destination for the hiker.

glacier along this valley, which is very dynamic. Visitors are provided with a car park, toilets, information and the trail to the glacier, although the further reaches of this are unstable due to regular floods and so there is no specific surfaced trail, only a waymarked route. In keeping with the glacial environment, the rocks and the forest there, the facilities have been kept simple and mainly use local materials. The surfacing of the car park uses compacted gravel from the area exactly the colour and texture of the glacial material. The parking area is separated from the trailhead, bike racks and toilets by a line of huge boulders that give a little hint of what is to come. The toilet building is set in backing vegetation while remaining visible and easy to find, designed using a typical New Zealand style, materials and colour. Signs at the entrance and within the site use the Department of Conservation corporate design of dark green and yellow but these are kept to the minimum and generally give necessary safety information as well as the usual orientation and directional signs. The glacier remains out of sight at this point and only once the visitor has proceeded along the trail some way, leaving the car park behind, does it appear. This technique of providing surprise, of raising and then fulfilling expectations is a classic design approach skilfully exploited here, with the facilities very much in a subservient position to the main attraction, the glacier and its landscape. The route can be rather treacherous and difficult to follow, being rough and requiring the crossing of water courses without bridges but this adds to the special qualities and the absence of constructed trails leaves nature intact. Strategically placed warning signs continue to guide the visitor where necessary for health and safety.

The design of the visit

So far in this chapter the issue of design concepts most appropriate to the landscape setting has been considered, and how this contributes to the experience a visitor might expect. This issue should also be turned around and considered from the visitor's point of view. What do visitors expect from their visit to the outdoors, particularly in the facilities, help and information provided, to enable them to obtain the best experience and to persuade them to return? Many of the perceived problems that managers have are not from visitors behaving badly so much as their requirements being inadequately thought through, so that conflicts inadvertently occur. In this section the concept of 'designing the visit' as a sequence of events will be explored, together with actions and decisions made by the visitor, which can be helped or hindered by the manager. A typical example of the most common kind of visit – a day trip for picnic and walking to a particular place for the first time – will be used.

A visit to an outdoor recreation facility does not begin when the carload of passengers rolls past the entrance sign into the car park. It begins when, prior to the occasion, someone decides they will make the visit. After several suggestions they decide to go to one particular area. In order to make the decision they must obtain information from somewhere or someone. Perhaps they have a leaflet, or perhaps a friend suggested the place or they searched on the internet. Either way, they will have some kind of image in their minds and an expectation of a wonderful setting in which to have an enjoyable time.

The next stage of the visit is preparation: packing the kit, the picnic and setting off. The journey from the city to the outdoor destination will be marked by a changing landscape. The city will gradually be left behind, the roads will become less urban, and the rural or wild landscapes will eventually appear. At some point the visitors will start to look for signs to lead them to the area. These should help them to prepare for the arrival, and will also heighten the anticipation of what is in store. The absence of advance warning signs may make the family anxious: Are we lost? How far is it now? What if we overshoot the entrance? Signs that give good warning and allow a safe turn-off from the road in possibly heavy traffic are essential. The quality of the landscape along the route, especially the last mile or so, is particularly important: first impressions are those that count, and expectations rapidly fade if the general setting is of a poor standard.

At the entrance to the area, a sign reassuring the visitors that they are at the right place is important. A short drive into the area before arriving at the parking area helps them to wind down, and to become accustomed to the slower pace of the wilder landscape. This is especially valuable if the main highway was busy and fast. It also enables the driver to look out for the actual point of arrival: the threshold where something of the landscape can be glimpsed as well as the car park itself. At that point an orientation sign can be helpful: where are we and where do we go? This can either help to negotiate a large parking area or be present when the visitors first get out of the car.

On arrival, the first basic requirement may be a visit to a toilet, depending on the travelling distance, the age of the children and whether there are any elderly people. Is there one? Where is it? Is it clean? Does it smell?

are the common questions. The toilet is frequently considered an important amenity, whose absence or poor quality can greatly diminish the experience of a visit. After that, a chance to relax for a moment, stretch limbs cramped by the journey and let the children work off some pent-up energy (dogs as well) is often appreciated.

At this point the next thing usually needed is some information in the form of a display board, a leaflet or a person from whom the visitors can find out more on what there is to do. The information needs to be clear, accurate and brief, and conveyed in a friendly way that most people can understand. Symbols instead of words can be used to simplify the amount of material presented, while maps may be less meaningful than pictures for many people. If any of the visitors have disabilities, the information should be presented in ways suitable for them – tactile maps for those with visual impairment, for example.

If the visitors want to eat something, they may look for a picnic area. An attractive spot with some views but also with corners where a little bit of private territory can be established is ideal. Absence of litter, and possibly some picnic furniture that signals 'it is all right to eat here' and a choice of sun or shade will also help.

Once fed and relaxed, the visitors may perhaps wish to go off on a hike, or to try whatever other activities are available, or to just have a nap. Young children will usually need to be occupied if their parents want a longer rest. An area where they can explore and play safely can be helpful. This might involve active play, some learning through exploration and some social interaction with other children. Some families might use the visit especially for the purpose of adult rest and children's play.

If the visitors decide to go for a hike, they may be capable of using a map to navigate their own route to a landmark or viewpoint. Many other people usually prefer a trail set out for them, and along which they know they will not be in danger or liable to get lost. Information on the choice of routes, their length, the approximate time it will take to walk them and how strenuous they are, is important to help them plan the hike with consideration for the needs of young children, older relatives, baby buggies and wheelchairs. A pleasant day out can easily be spoiled if the hike turns out to be too long, too rough, too steep, or if some of the party get too tired.

The trail should incorporate views, rest stops and varied scenery so as to make walking it a journey of discovery and a rewarding experience. There may be explanatory or interpretative material available for those who want to know more about the area, but the pleasure of the walk itself will be enough for many people.

After the hike, refreshment and visits to the toilet, the visitors might decide that they are ready to go home. Hopefully they have had exercise for the body and stimulation for the mind, and are relaxed and happily tired (though not too tired to drive home safely!). The journey back and recollection of the visit, once at home, complete the experience. If they have had a good time, the visitors may tell a few of their friends. If they have had a bad time, it is possible they may tell more, advising people to stay away. If they picked up a leaflet, this might be shown to other people, used to remind them to visit again, or just to help them recall the pleasure of a nice day out.

All aspects of any visit to pursue other activities can be considered in the way described above, and also from the point of view of a range of visitors: old, young, fit, disabled, men, women, and so on. It is very interesting, if you are a professional recreation manager or designer, to visit an unfamiliar area and assess your experience stage by stage to see how well your needs are catered for in the design and management of the area. If you are a manager, you can develop a checklist and put yourself in someone else's shoes, visiting your own area for the first time. It is surprising how many items for improvement can usually be found!

Three

The journey to the destination

In the last chapter, several key concepts to be applied to the design of recreation sites, facilities and artefacts were considered. The need to reflect the character of the setting, to contrast and avoid urban qualities and therefore to use an appropriate and site-specific range of materials and finishes was emphasized. This concern for the setting and the experience that it helps to invoke was balanced with a concern for the needs of the visitors. The sequence of actions, decisions, impressions and feelings that actually constitute the experience of a visit are influenced by the setting, the facilities, the information and the ambience present in the visited destination. From this it is an easy and logical step to unite the needs of the setting and the needs of the visitors, and to look in detail at the layout, design and maintenance of the site facilities normally provided for each stage of a visit. Periodic monitoring of visitor reactions to facilities provided or charged is also important.

This chapter and the following 11 will cover all aspects of a typical day out in the outdoors. This day out will follow a similar pattern to the one described in the previous chapter. For reasons outlined in the Introduction, sheets detailing or specifying standard items will not be provided. Instead, the main considerations and examples of what to do and what not to do will be demonstrated.

Anticipation

As briefly explained in Chapter 2, the visit starts with planning and the anticipation of what enjoyment might be gained from the visit in prospect. Managers and designers can influence this through the quality of information that is made available to the prospective visitor. Leaflets that promote attractions are commonly provided at tourist information centres, in hotels, in libraries and at a number of other places. Tourists are frequently bombarded with a wide range of leaflets, so that the choice of where to go may depend on the impressions conveyed by the cover and main text.

Increasingly, too, the internet is being used to plan visits. Tourists from far afield can look at the websites of most recreational providers and plan their holidays or vacations from the information – and promotion – contained there. Some sites also allow people to rate or score destinations and to make comments on their experience, on the facilities, on the attitudes of staff, and so on. These are likely to be even more popular and advanced technologically in the future.

Disabled people are also using both printed information and websites to find out more about a place and whether it is likely to be suitable and worth going to. If there is no information for disabled visitors, they are unlikely to bother going because they probably do not want to risk being disappointed. Therefore, information about disabled parking, accessible toilets, the length, surfacing, slopes and other aspects of trails, on-site information presented in formats suitable for people with visual or hearing impairments, benches for resting, and so on, are vital if recreation providers are serious about welcoming everyone to their area. Printed materials and websites also need to be designed to be accessible. This primarily means using a non-serif font or typeface of at least 12 point size with a high contrast between text and background. Websites can also be designed so that different background colours can be

A collection of leaflets from various sources giving information about places to visit. They also promote their location. Some oversell their area, leading to an anticlimax when the destination fails to live up to its promise.

A webpage from the US National Park Service, providing details about Yosemite National Park.

selected by the user. Programmes that allow text to be read by the computer to blind or visually impaired people can also be used. Deaf people may use sign language first and be less familiar with the native spoken language of their nationality. Therefore simpler language should be chosen. Symbols and the use of several languages may also be helpful for all users, especially when international visitors constitute a major part of the market.

While wishing to present the destination in the best light in order to attract visitors, it is important to be honest in the information and images used. It is a terrible disappointment to be lured to a so-called attraction by information that overstates its charms. The letdown is something remembered for a long time, and is likely to discourage a return visit.

A big advantage of many of the destinations being considered here is their naturalness, their larger scale, and their scenic attractiveness. This can be put to advantage by using photos of seasonal colours and local features, which are often hard to overstate. However, the smaller-scale, more rural or urban fringe locations can be spoiled by badly designed and maintained facilities, which may be the first things seen on arrival.

On the road

The next stage of the visit is travelling to the destination. Most people travel to the outdoors by car. In many places the distances involved and the lack of alternative transport methods make this unavoidable. In some cases seaplanes or boats are also used. There are also places where access on foot, by bicycle, horseback or public transport is common, such as urban forests or country parks that are close to where people live. This is to be encouraged for environmental reasons wherever it is possible. Public transport is also preferable for those who cannot drive because of a disability or those who cannot afford a car. In countries such as the Netherlands and Denmark the networks of cycle tracks make it possible to reach many outdoor destinations without a car, perhaps directly or by taking a bike on a train and then cycling from the nearest station.

Where the car is the normal mode of transport, then the journey itself and the unfolding landscape seen at travelling speed are both part of the day out. If there is a choice, it is hoped that the visitors will take the most scenic route, and this should be encouraged by promoting scenic byways or specially signed tourist routes. However, direct control over the landscape is exercised by those who own or manage it. If the route passes through a reasonable stretch of land under the same ownership or management as the destination, then the sense of expectation can be influenced more directly, in the quality of the landscape seen along the route, and by the judicious use of signs.

The landscape along the route will change as the visitors progress through it. The change may be subtle

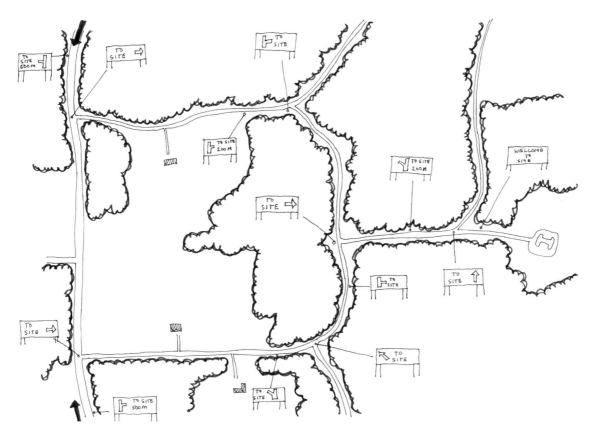

This plan shows the layout of signs along the approaches to a recreation area, using principles of wayfinding: at every point where a decision is needed, a sign is positioned.

and gradual, so that there is a slow realization that they are approaching the general area of the destination. This might be the case where the landscape is rural rather than wild, and the destination is an area set in this landscape. More commonly, there might be a distinct threshold where the landscape changes quite dramatically. This could be where the landform changes – the start of the mountains, the entrance to a narrow valley or the beginning of coastal scenery. It might be where the land use also changes – the entrance to a forest out of farmland, the change from managed to natural, undisturbed forest; the onset of heathland, coastal vegetation or open, unenclosed countryside from enclosed agriculture.

Wayfinding

It is also necessary to consider how the visitors will find their way to the destination. Map reading skills should not be assumed to be universal, and poorly placed and inadequate signs can be misleading. It is also frustrating

and a waste of time when visitors get lost on their way to a recreation destination. Wayfinding is partly a spatial task of understanding the route and partly of employing landmarks and signs at strategic places. If a route from a main road or highway leads through a twisty set of minor roads and junctions are not clearly signed, this is when problems are most likely to arise. Therefore it is advisable to follow the potential routes and to provide clear and unambiguous signs at every place where route choices have to be made. A wayfinding tool kit has been developed to help managers solve this problem.

Threshold signs

If the opportunity to manage the landscape begins at this threshold, or if influence can be exerted, then it may be a good idea to identify this in an appropriate way. This can be by using an obvious sign, such as is common in national parks, state-owned forests and other designated landscapes. The signs can be simple, merely announcing that a special area is being entered, or they can be used to advertise and promote the attributes of the area and the organization involved, where this is permitted in local regulations.

Many organizations have standard sign structures designed to be easily recognizable by their shape, symbols, logos and colours when seen from a moving vehicle. The typeface for the names is also usually of standard type. Variations may occur, but too much can confuse visitors if they do not recognize the name or logo of the organization and the destination. This aspect of corporate identity has three features. First, it maintains awareness of an organization as the provider of a particular product. Second, it gives messages about what kind of experience, its atmosphere and the quality of service are likely to be found at the destination. The third feature is a subliminal one: it could maintain the perception about a particular organization doing a good job, providing value for money and thereby worthy of continued support. Whatever the conclusions from the above observations, the design of a threshold sign should include the following features:

- It should be large enough to enable all the messages to be read at the average speed of passing vehicles. Table 3.1 shows the size of letters so that they can be read easily.
- The name of the destination or area should dominate over that of any organization.
- The structure should be simple and sturdy, and its size and shape should fit the setting; it may need specific components to resist high winds or to deter vandalism.
- The structure should be positioned against a simple, uncluttered backdrop with a clear, non-obscured foreground; it should not become an intrusive feature.
- Symbols or images of the landscape can be used to establish the identity of the area, but these need to be simple: almost caricatures of the salient points.
- The colours used for the structure of the sign should be chosen from the ranges found in the landscape, and should not be too bright or gaudy. Lettering needs to be contrasting, but structural components should be more subdued.
- Text and typography should be large, simple and clear, and should usually employ capitals and lower case in a non-serif typeface. The constant use of capital letters can be difficult to read. Text should be depicted in light, bright colours to contrast with the duller sign structure.

Table 3.1: Minimum sizes of letters for readability at different approach speeds and reading distances

Approach speed		Reading distance		Letter height (capitals)	
Km/h	Mi/h	m	yds	mm	in
80	50	120	130	300	12
80	50	90	97	225	9
50	30	60	65	150	6
30	18	45	49	115	4.5
15	9	30	32	75	3
15	9	23	25	56	2.25
0	0	15	16	38	1.5
0	0	11	12	28	1
0	0	8	8.5	19	0.75

(Top) The threshold sign at the start of the Blue Ridge Parkway in Virginia, USA, is a simple structure that relies on the silhouette of the landscape for impact, rather than the words. The name of the facility is more dominant than that of the organization. The siting of the sign against a simple backdrop of vegetation maintains its high impact. (Above) An example from a national park in Japan, where the name of the park is written in English as well as Japanese. The design has borrowings from the US National Park service styles.

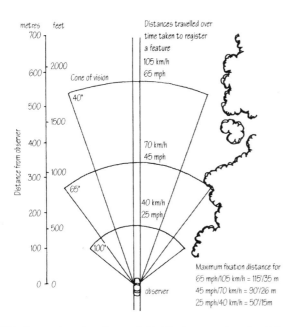

A road in Arizona, where the landscape is diverse in structure and spatial character. This is more interesting to drive along than a solid wall of trees.

This diagram shows how the speed of traffic along a road can be used to determine the scale of variation along the edge, the duration of views and the size of openings.

The landscape at the threshold can be managed so as to intensify the contrast and the sense of entering a special place – a 'pinch point'. A narrow, closed-in part of the forest; some large trees; massive rocks; a dramatic view of a landmark or portal feature – these are all examples of such thresholds.

Roadside landscape design

Beyond the threshold, the landscape on either side of the road can be developed. This might include creating and maintaining views towards attractive components of the landscape, and managing the edges along the road. If the approach is through a forest, there are opportunities to manage the trees: by thinning; by felling, to create spaces of different sizes and shapes; by pruning, to let light through; or by allowing sections to close in. In more open country the quality of the foreground in the vicinity of the road should not detract from the broader views. Fences, walls, earth banks, hedges or areas of trees should be well maintained. Occasional views towards focal points can heighten the visitors' sense that they nearing the destination, and that their expectations are about to be fulfilled.

The roadside landscape must be developed at the speed at which the motorist is expected to drive. This determines how far ahead it is possible to focus on the landscape, and at what angle from the car it is possible to see it. Also, open views need to be of a minimum width in order to be seen; the faster the speed of the car, the wider the view needs to be. For example, a 1-second duration at 60 mph (100 kmh) requires an opening of 30 yd (27 m), while at 25 mph (42 kmh) the space need be only 12 yd (9.6 m) wide. A survey of the road should be carried out by driving its length in both directions at a typical speed, noting features observable at that speed. A video recording is quite useful, because it can be used to check the location of features, and to time the duration of their appearance in view. If other vehicles, such as coaches or bicycles, or pedestrians use the same stretch of road, then similar surveys can be carried out. Coaches give better views over the tops of fences, walls, hedges and embankments than cars, while more detail is seen from a bicycle or by a pedestrian. If the general sequence of spaces is developed for the fastest travellers, then successively finer layers of detail can be added subsequently for slower ones.

As well as making the best of the landscape, it is also important to try to avoid or reduce the impact of intrusive features such as pylons, derelict buildings, transmitters and quarries. These can be screened if they cannot be redesigned, removed or otherwise blended into the landscape.

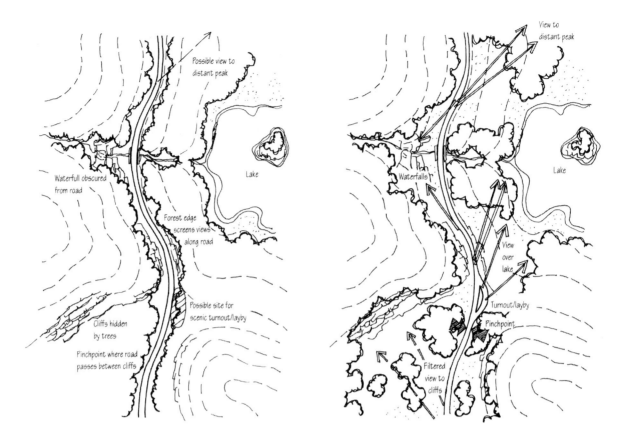

This diagram shows how the speed of traffic along a road can be used to determine the scale of variation along the edge, the duration of views and the size of openings.

The entrance

The point where the visitor turns off the public highway, or emerges from a coach, railway station or other form of transport, into the specific area where the visit takes place is important for several reasons:

- The visitor is likely to be on land under your management from now on. He or she is your guest and deserves the right treatment.
- Because the visitor is on your land there are factors of liability for damage or injury to consider. Safety issues need to be included in the design and management of the area.
- The visitors have chosen your area to visit. The facilities that help them to have an enjoyable experience that matches their expectations, and the setting in which it will take place, are all bound up together.
- The entrance may mark the point where payment has to be made by visitors and collected by site staff.

The design of the entrance itself needs some thought. If the entrance is from a public highway on to an access road there are several factors that must be considered:

- highway safety, such as sightlines for vehicles turning out of the entrance onto the highway;
- signs warning approaching drivers of the entrance, giving them adequate time to slow down and make the turn;
- correct surfacing at the entrance to ensure safe braking and to prevent loose material spilling on to the highway.

Additionally, some succinct information indicating what visitors can do at the area, using symbols as far as possible, is helpful. Some important safety or regulating information such as fire risk warnings, which people need to be aware of as soon as they enter the area, should also be plain to see, although most of the information should be left until deeper into the site.

A good example of an entrance to a forest recreation area at Glenmore Forest Park, Scotland. The layout is clear and simple. The sign is of subdued colour, relying on symbols to convey much of the information. The foreground landscape is uncluttered and well maintained. The only feature to spoil the scene is a pothole in the road surface, probably caused by cars stopping and starting as they leave. Such wear and tear should be repaired as quickly as possible.

An entrance at Tervete Nature Park in Latvia, where a more dramatic structure has been used, based on early wooden castles built in the area in the ninth century AD. This employs a lot of skill in traditional construction techniques.

Security requirements in the form of gates, barriers or cattle grids (guards), which are needed to help manage people and animals at particular periods, may also have to be accommodated. Their design will have to balance robustness with simplicity, the use of appropriate materials and ease of operation. Heavy metal barriers may be effective, but will look ugly and out of place in a wild setting, as well as being awkward for some people to use. Less intrusive methods, using reinforced lighter materials, may be possible.

The design and management of the landscape at the entrance should seek to unify the various signs and structures that may be needed; it should form an attractive threshold and set the standard for the setting of the main visitor facilities. Pruning of trees or shrubs and mowing of ground vegetation may be necessary to maintain visibility of signs and sightlines needed for access.

The capacity of the entrance should be based on expected visitor levels, length of stay and distribution over time as well as the type of vehicles likely to be using it. A significant length of the access road in the vicinity of the highway may need to be double lane to facilitate passing and queuing, depending on the traffic on the highway at peak time. Large vehicles, such as camper vans, trailer caravans and recreation vehicles

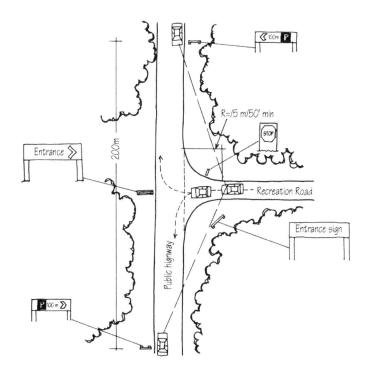

The layout of an entrance to a facility from a highway should combine an attractive landscape with the safe movement of vehicles. Signs, sightlines and road geometry must conform with safety requirements to reduce the risks of accidents in often unfamiliar landscapes and foreign countries.

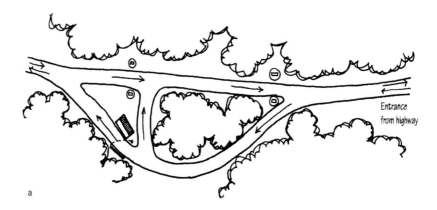

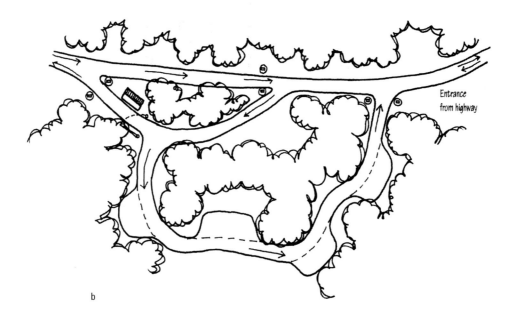

Two options for lay-outs for entrances with pay stations. These show arrangements for the British, Australian or New Zealand driving side: reverse them for North America, Continental Europe, etc. (a) In this example, a loop allows people to leave before they pass the pay station if they decide that fees are unacceptable. The entrance can be closed while one-way flow control allows people to leave after the entrance has closed. (b) Some parking for limited use is worth providing for local, frequent users or during the low season, when the main site is closed: shown here as a short loop off the entrance area.

(RVs), take up more road width and length and so may need greater queuing space.

If payment has to be made at the entrance, as is frequently the case in national parks and similar places, two-way traffic segregation, temporary parking ahead of the pay station and an exit loop for those visitors who change their minds at the last minute, may be needed. This should prevent congestion at the entrance during peak periods or complicated reversing to turn around across the flow of traffic. The location of pay stations should be far enough down the entrance road to prevent queuing back onto the public highway (see Chapter 5).

Pedestrian entrances should contain broadly the same elements: a gateway with signs and information, perhaps a barrier for closing the site, or special gates to keep animals out or in. If the entrance also acts as an exit to a highway, then some sort of deflector device to prevent people, especially children, from inadvertently

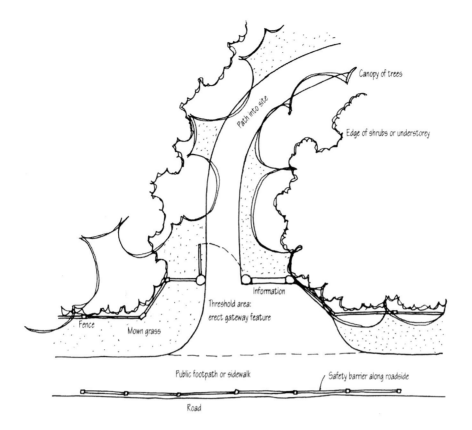

A pedestrian entrance from a public road should present an attractive, unthreatening appearance. Information and safety near the road should be considered, while the visibility and attractiveness of the area should be maintained. Litter and vandalism may discourage some visitors who are anxious for their safety in wilder places.

walking or running out into the traffic will be advisable. Management of vegetation and structures, and good visibility into the area, will maintain the sense of welcome and help to allay fears in those areas where some people are worried about being attacked or mugged. Signs to the entrance from the main directions of approach will usually be helpful to the visitor, as will reassurance at the entrance with a sign or name board welcoming them.

All entrances of this sort should be barrier free to people of all abilities. Any gates or other structures required to prevent animal access or unwanted use by vehicles such as motorcycles should be designed to be accessible by wheelchairs, strollers/pushchairs, small children, etc. This also means providing good surfacing, avoiding kerbs from highways and overly steep gradients (see Chapter 9).

The main entrance sign may be part of a sign system that includes the threshold signs described previously. The same design principles apply, although the sign may convey more information about the area. If the information is necessarily more than can be taken in at a glance while driving past, the sign should be beside the road in a lay-by or turnout, allowing first-time visitors to pull in for a few moments without holding up others who want to drive on. Ideally, the information should be designed so that drivers and passengers can read it without leaving the car. The height at which the sign is erected, the amount of information, the size of the typeface and clarity of maps need to be suitable for reading over 2 or 3 yards/metres from inside a car.

The wind-down

After having driven, often for long distances and perhaps in heavy traffic and stressful conditions, it takes a little time to adjust to the ambience of the outdoors. The adjustment can be aided by a stretch of road between the entrance and the first stopping point, such as a car park or scenic turnout, which helps the car occupants

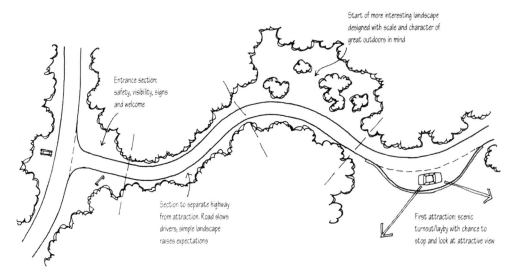

Start of more interesting landscape designed with scale and character of great outdoors in mind

Entrance section: safety, visibility, signs and welcome

Section to separate highway from attraction. Road slows drivers, simple landscape raises expectations

First attraction: scenic turnout/layby with chance to stop and look at attractive view

The wind-down stretch of road helps the visitors to develop a more relaxed frame of mind, ready to make the most of their experience.

to relax a little, absorb the scenery and become used to the possible presence of wildlife near or on the road, walkers crossing or small children playing. The length need not be very long if space does not allow it, but even a short wind-down can be very useful.

As well as benefiting the car occupants, the wind-down also helps to ensure that there is adequate physical separation between the main car parking area and the public highway. In Europe or Japan and in urban situations everywhere, where traffic is heavy, getting away from noise, pollution and physical danger to children and pets is an important issue. Noise may be difficult to avoid unless landform can be used to absorb it, but physical separation should be as great as is feasible. Even in remoter, quieter landscapes the drive down a winding lane from the highway can increase anticipation and the sense of mystery, as well as helping to slow vehicles down.

The slower travelling speed can be achieved with a narrower road width, rougher surface and tighter curves, as well as speed limit signs. Glimpses of scenery along the road (see 'Roadside landscape design' above) can also be used to increase anticipation and reduce speed.

The arrival

The culmination of the journey – the arrival at the main destination – is now to hand. After all the careful development of the landscape and provision of information along the way, the first experience on arrival must live up to its promise. How this is handled depends on what is there. If it is a natural wonder, such as a mountain range, the visitor should be rewarded with a stunning view to a dramatic peak, not obscured by parked cars or other clutter. This technique can be used widely: for example, for a lake, canyon, grove of giant trees or sand dunes and cliffs. Alternatively, the drama might be saved and revealed only later, so that the trappings of the visitor facilities are left behind when the main feature is finally revealed (see the discussion on the Franz Josef Glacier in Chapter 2). A glimpse or hint of this might be needed in order to whet the appetite of the visitor and to raise expectations.

A less dramatic destination should make the most of the features it possesses, perhaps even a building containing a visitor centre if one is present. The management of the setting can help, creating or enhancing a sense of *genius loci*, by reducing the impact of car parking, reflecting the qualities of the place in the use of materials, and so on. It is at the point of arrival that the *genius loci* is at most risk, especially in places with subtle qualities. For this reason it is important to the subsequent design to consider the factors that contribute to *genius loci*, and to develop a concept for the site development around them.

The visitors should also obtain some impression of the organization of the site on arrival. Not everything there will be visible, but a reasonable degree of orientation is advisable. This can be achieved by, for

At this recreation area at the Pacific Rim National Park, Vancouver Island, Canada, the sense of arrival is given by the view of the shore, the waves of the Pacific Ocean and the backdrop of forest. Unfortunately, the impression is spoilt by the cars parked along the edge, which screen much of the view.

example, a glimpse of the main attraction, the visitor centre or a picnic area, before the last stretch of access road turns into the car park. This is an old but effective device, which subtly reinforces the expectation just before arrival.

The general layout of the site should then be organized around the axes between the point of arrival and the main attraction, if there is one. The movement of people and their associated activities, from car parking and toilet facilities to picnicking, playing, hiking or whatever, needs to flow in an easy and obvious fashion. This is particularly important in heavily used sites with a large throughput of people. Congestion caused by confusion slows down the movement of people and reduces the carrying capacity of busy sites. Wayfinding principles, using the landmarks of the site as well as signs can help to ensure that everything flows in a logical fashion.

Four

Providing visitor information

At the point of arrival, some information is normally needed so that visitors can make the most of opportunities to enjoy their visit. This may be in the form of a leaflet picked up from a dispenser at or near the entrance or pay station, or in the form of boards or panels in a strategic location on the site, or both.

Information requirements

This information is part of the range of signs that are needed for visitor management. It is useful to develop a hierarchy of signs, starting with the threshold or entrance sign described in Chapter 3, and including orientation signs placed at the point of arrival at each facility, vehicle management signs and way markers. All these signs need to be properly planned during the comprehensive site design phase or at the time of major refurbishment. Each category of sign planning and design will be covered in subsequent chapters. An example of different sign functions is given here, developed by Scottish Natural Heritage (Table 4.1). Any of the functions can be combined in a single sign. While the information board may not be visited and read until after parking the car, its location and use as a key orientation and visitor management feature can be so important that it is worth considering first.

From the point of view of the visitor, the information needs to convey the essentials about the site, such as the layout of different areas, the routes of paths and trails, special activity areas, toilets and camping grounds, hours of opening, codes of behaviour and any special dangers or safety information. This is the basic information to enable visitors to find their way around the site and into the landscape beyond without getting lost, straying into danger, trespassing or missing the best features. Additional information such as site or landscape history, interpretation of special scenic attractions or wildlife and natural history are secondary at this point.

The manager may also be interested in conveying certain information to visitors, such as rules and regulations, safety information, advice on footwear or clothing suitable to the site and climate, equipment, registration before proceeding on trails into back country, any permits required for certain activities such as fishing, or warnings about locking cars and leaving valuables out of sight. There may be legal requirements to display by-laws or regulations, but all such information should be conveyed in as positive and user-friendly a way as possible.

When the information is about protecting the environment from damage by trampling, fire, allowing stock to stray, feeding wild animals, and so on, then a code of conduct is useful, such as the Country or Forest Codes used in Britain. This invites the responsible cooperation of visitors, and offers them a 'partnership' with managers in looking after the environment. In remote locations this information may be vital to prevent inexperienced visitors from coming to harm, while in the urban fringe it might concentrate on avoiding damage to the landscape.

When providing information structures, there are three components to the design: the message, the medium used to convey it, and the structure used for displaying it. Table 4.1 presents the function of signage.

(From top – a) An example of a sign from Slovakia where the managers are concerned to warn visitors about what they cannot do. This gives a poor sense of welcome. (b) An example from Japan where prohibited activities are shown in red and permitted activities in green, using little drawings. This is more balanced than (a). (c) A heavy- handed and somewhat crude set of signs from Samarskaya Luka National Park in Russia which include warnings against forest fire.

Table 4.1: The function of signage

Description	Function
Pre-arrival	Advance roadside information
Threshold	Marking the main entrance to the area of management or ownership.
Orientation	Helping people to locate themselves, perhaps before deciding where to go and what to do.
Direction	Guiding traffic and pedestrian navigation.
Identification	Labelling a feature or object.
Information	Displaying details of opening hours, events, facilities etc.
Interpretation	Revealing the significance of the landscape or an aspect of it.
Regulation	Displaying rules and warnings.

The message

There are some basic features of any message: it should be short, to the point, and should use as many symbols, pictures, maps and diagrams as possible instead of words.

A map or maps showing the area being visited, the immediate site and any other smaller areas within the main area, such as a trail or special feature, are vital. Scales should be chosen to show sufficient detail and context without taking up too much room. A main map at 1:50000, 1:25000, 1:20000 or 1:10000 for larger areas, or 1:5000, 1:2500 or 1:1250 for smaller ones, may be presented, with inset details at larger scales. The cartography should be to the highest standard, with a linear scale, a north point, and an indicator of where the information panel is. Contours, roads and paths, forest and open areas, cliffs, viewpoints, rivers and lakes, buildings, boundaries and special features such as archaeological sites should be shown. There is wide evidence to suggest that many people have difficulty in reading maps, even those of a high standard. The three-dimensional 'landscape view' map is often easier to interpret for many, and should be considered as an option. For visitors with visual impairments, a tactile or three-dimensional map may also be considered.

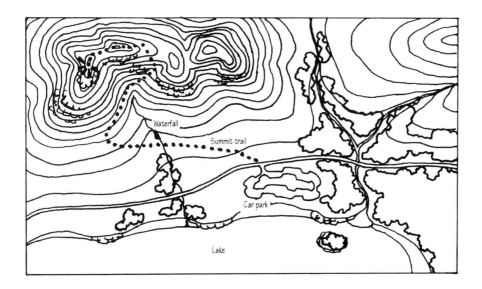

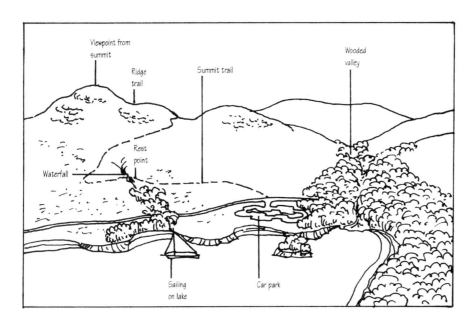

(From top – a) A generalized layout of an information panel using a map. Some people find such maps difficult to understand. (b) The same layout using pictorial information is more accessible to many people, who can gauge the scale of the landscape and a sense of its three-dimensional form. (c) An example of a very effective pictorial sign from the High Tatras in Slovakia.

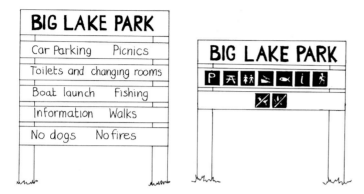

(Left) Information about facilities conveyed in text occupies a lot of space. (Right) The same information presented using symbols takes up less space, is quicker and easier to read, and needs no translation into foreign languages.

The detailed site area should show the layout of car parks, toilets, picnic areas, the start of trails, play areas, water, boat launches, etc. This might be diagrammatic or pictorial rather than cartographic in style.

In all cases, landscape features should be named, but most other features shown should use standard symbols as far as possible. The library of international symbols for different places, activities, safety instructions, and so on is now extensive and well used. Its use reduces the space required, and minimizes the need for translation into foreign languages.

Other information might concern the various activities possible in the area. This can combine pictures depicting these with short descriptions. Path or trail conditions, suitability for disabled people, recommended footwear, or anticipated duration would be the kind of information to give about a hiking trail, for example.

Information of a temporary nature might also be provided, such as fire danger rating, expected weather or water conditions, recently seen wildlife, warning of theft, lost property, work in the woods, and so on. These can be posted daily in a special area.

Finally, the chance to welcome visitors and to ask for their comments is always useful. A phone number, a contact person or an address to write or email to can be provided for this purpose. This gives unmanned sites a human touch, and offers some reassurance to those visitors apprehensive of wild places that they are looked after.

The medium

To convey the message, a medium is required. There are two main possibilities: leaflets or signboards. Leaflets are an important alternative or supplement to fixed signs. They can be reprinted annually with up-to-date information. As they are carried around by the visitors, they can easily be referred to at any time. Their preparation requires skill in graphic design and printing techniques, for which expert advice should normally be sought. It might also be useful to consider leaflets in Braille for blind people and in large print for others with visual impairment. In any case good practice with regard to accessible leaflet design as explained in Chapter 3 should be followed.

A fixed signboard, if chosen as the medium, needs to withstand a wide range of changing weather conditions, such as heat and cold or rain and sun. Accidental damage or vandalism may also take place. Hence materials need to be either robust, long-lasting and durable, or cheap, easily replaced and short-lived. Early techniques used to convey information were either some form of printed material such as paper protected by either glass or Perspex (Plexiglas), painted wooden panels normally routed (often freehand) with the information, or (later) the use of screen-printed panels. All these media are limited in their durability when placed in the open air. Paper gets damp, printing fades, paint cracks and peels, and all may be damaged by accident or vandalism and need frequent maintenance. In addition, some of these techniques limited the quality of graphic design that could be achieved.

The following paragraphs describe materials that can be considered.

Solid wood panels

Wood used outdoors always tends to move or distort through shrinkage, swelling or warping as temperatures and moisture conditions vary. This poses problems for many types of printing, painting or graphic design. The choice of wood is important. Close-grained, slow-grown varieties of hardwood or softwood are preferred, as these are less likely to split and can be smooth finished for the application techniques described below. Durability is also important. Some species are naturally more durable than others although some, like western red cedar, are highly durable but not good for the application of printing, routing or sandblasting. Fir, pine, larch, oak or chestnut are among the better woods to use, although resinous conifers can cause problems for paint application.

The message can be applied using the following techniques:

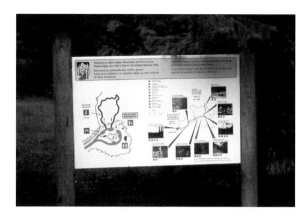

An example of an information sign provided at the Thingvellir National Park in Iceland. It is a simple structure with maps and other information at a major entrance location. The information is provided in several languages. The material is printed and mounted on a panel. It has to be very durable in the Icelandic climate.

A sign from Mount Revelstoke National Park in British Columbia, Canada, made of fibreglass and with both regional and local information clearly presented in two languages.

- **Routing**. Text, diagrams and maps can be engraved into the surface using hand-held or computer-guided routers. These produce very fine lines and accurate reproductions of text types and symbols. The routed information can be left natural, or can be in-filled with paint of different colours. However, routing is best used for simple graphic designs. Complex maps, for example, are beyond the scope of the technique.
- **Screen printing**. Smooth-surfaced panels can be screen printed in one or several colours. Quite fine detail is possible depending on the original surface quality. However, such printing weathers poorly unless protected by a varnish of some sort.
- **Sandblasting**. This method uses sandblasting to erode and cut away areas of wood between the letters or symbols, which then stand out in relief. The grain of the wood also becomes more obvious, often making attractive textures. The information is made into a mask, which is overlaid onto the panel surface before sandblasting. As with routing, the technique has limitations, and should be used for what it is best at: simple bold type, symbols or diagrams. The finished panel can be painted or left natural. A more recent development has been to use sandblasting to create an overall form with flat areas left behind onto which transfers of pictures and other techniques of image presentation are used. Sand blasting also produces quite tactile surfaces and is one way of creating signs suitable for people with visual impairments.

Composite wood panels

Plywood is the usual type of composite wood panel that is used. Marine-quality ply is durable, less prone to warping than ordinary plywood, and does not shrink or split. It can be used as a base for laminate application (see below). Marine ply is often made from tropical hardwood, which might be an unsustainable source and therefore unacceptable under certain circumstances.

Enamelled steel

This is long-lasting when undamaged, and can be produced to a very high standard. Good reproduction, a wide range of colours and fine detail are possible. This is an expensive medium, and when chipped it is difficult to repair properly. Stones or metal implements can easily chip it, and the steel base will rust quite quickly in the open air. It is not possible to produce tactile surfaces using this method.

Glass-reinforced plastic (fibreglass)

This can be used to produce extremely durable panels in a variety of colours and finishes. It can be used as a base for printing or painting, or can be constructed with printed materials laminated into it (see below). It is also possible to produce three-dimensional maps or other tactile surfaces suitable for people with visual impairments using fibreglass. A mould can be created to provide a 3-D model of the landscape, for example.

An interesting sign structure using an upturned boat to make a shelter. Kolka, Latvia. The use of timber, the colours and the siting relate well to this coastal location.

A stone structure used as the base for an information sign. Although used in a forest, this might be more suitable in an open rocky landscape where stone is a dominant material. The workmanship of this example is good, but there is wear and tear around the unpaved sides of the structure. Glen Affric, Scotland.

Perspex (Plexiglas)

Transparent unbreakable materials like Perspex can be screen printed in reverse so that the message is visible through the material. High-quality printing is possible, but the surface of the Perspex is easily damaged by scratching or gouging. This material has largely gone out of fashion.

Laminated paper

Printed paper can be encapsulated in a hard-wearing resin to produce a durable and high-quality result. The printing can include photographs, and if an ultraviolet filter is inserted the problems of colour fading in sunlight can be reduced. These resin laminates, when bonded onto a plywood or fibreglass base, are resistant to scratches or chips and can be repaired relatively easily. They are expensive but very durable.

All the sign types described so far can be quite expensive to produce, and many are designed for a long life. If the information is unlikely to change or go out of date, they may be the most cost-effective solutions. If the information needs to be changed within two to three years of production, it might be sensible to opt for cheaper sign materials of a temporary nature. One version is to laminate paper between two sheets of thick, clear PVC film, heat-sealing the edges. This can be damaged but it is very cheap to replace the whole thing, attaching it to a baseboard in such a way that it can be easily removed.

Sign structures

Early information boards erected by the US National Park Service or Forest Service have provided models that have been frequently copied elsewhere. They were substantial structures with a heavy framework set in stone-built bases, topped by a shingle roof to protect the information panels located beneath. Some shelter or shade was also given by the roof to those reading the information.

Nowadays, while shade or shelter may be necessary in some locations, it is often better to keep the structure as simple and unobtrusive as possible, thus concentrating on the message and reducing the number of artefacts that the site has to manage and maintain.

Natural materials usually fit best into the wilder landscapes, although metal structures can have a purpose. These structures need to be sturdy, easily maintained and positioned so that the message can be read by all, including children and people in wheelchairs as well as standing adults of varying sizes. This means keeping the structure fairly low while maintaining its visibility on a crowded site.

The following materials can be used.

Stone

A substantial and robust structure can be erected using locally occurring stone such as boulders or quarried rock. A low wall upon which the signboard is fixed, or a plinth, can be built either dry or mortared. Mortar will make the structure stronger, but pointing should be recessed out of sight, so good workmanship is

Round timber can be used to build a sturdy yet simple frame upon which to mount an information panel. Here two deep slots in the horizontal members hold the panel in place, the top section being removed to extract the panel.

A structure using sawn timber, where the panel slides into place through slots in the uprights. Hidden bolts secure it into place. This design was developed by Forest Enterprise in Britain, and is used widely with laminated panels.

essential. Boards can be secured by bolts set into the rock or mortar, and the whole structure is very robust. It is best used in mountainous areas where rock is the main material, where digging post holes is difficult or where strong winds may shift lighter structures.

Alternatively, a flat surface can be cut onto a large boulder or rock face, the panel being anchored directly onto this; or the message could be sandblasted directly onto an appropriate rock surface, this latter technique being very effective but rather permanent, so if messages need to be changed it can be a problem.

Wood

This is frequently the most common material, used either in the round or as sawn components. Round timber should be straight, cylindrical, of low taper and debarked. Large dimensions work best, especially in forests of big conifer trees. Upright poles with horizontal cross-members provide a simple framework. Panels are fixed onto this by recessed bolts, whose holes can be plugged to hide the nuts and tidy the end result.

In most other circumstances sawn wood, either hard or soft, is used. Once again, sturdy, well-proportioned members jointed simply with good workmanship are better than fussy composite units. Some successful types used by the British Forestry Commission include pairs of upright flat slabs between which panels are fixed using diagonal slots and hidden threaded rods with nuts at both ends. The fewer components there are, the better. This example has only three.

Tubular steel, either galvanized or of the 'Cor-ten' rusting type, can make a strong frame. A panel can be bolted to flanges fixed to the tubing.

Instead of one all-purpose structure, it is possible to use several, each providing a different element of the message, grouped together. A system used by Scottish Natural Heritage uses slabs of timber, singly or in groups, carrying routed or sandblasted messages. These look simple and unfussy in a wide range of settings, and require much less maintenance.

The choice of timber to be used will partly depend on what is available, perhaps from sources nearby, and on its durability. Many species of tree are not durable in contact with the ground. Spruce, some pine, hemlock, birch, poplar, beech and ash are not durable, whereas cedar, oak, larch heartwood and chestnut are naturally durable. Many other species, especially pine and fir, are ideal when pressure treated. The chemicals used in pressure treatment – copper, chrome and arsenic – might not be appropriate, or might be considered unsustainable in some environments. A compromise might be to treat only those parts in contact with the ground. The rest of the wood can be left to weather and blend into the surroundings, or can be stained. There are a wide range of coloured wood stains on the market, many of which are of suitable colours to blend with different landscapes.

Metal

Galvanized steel tubing, enamelled or plastic-coated steel or aluminium structures can be used. The galvanized option will weather to a dull grey matt finish, which suits rocky landscapes. Enamelled or plastic finishes are acceptable as long as they are undamaged, but work better in more urban areas. Where vandalism is common, the galvanized tubing is a deterrent, as is the use of 'Cor-ten' steel, which weathers to a rust patina.

Composite materials

Laminate materials can also be used, for example, resin-bonded plastic-wood, or recycled plastic made into a material that can be worked like wood. These are also extremely durable and can be very cheap while actually looking better than initially might be expected.

Vandalism

There are many situations where vandalism might be a problem. Not all are in urban or urban fringe settings. Many of the materials described above are sturdy and durable, and can be used with confidence in such places. Others can easily be repaired or repainted if vandalism is sporadic or rare. Materials such as Perspex, plastic-coated steel, enamel and screen-printed wood should be avoided in high vandal-risk situations. The alternative of low-cost, temporary installations is well worth considering if information must be provided in high-risk areas.

Five

Parking the car

Having arrived at the destination, the visitor needs to park the car. The design of car parking has to take several factors into account:

- Cars may be left on the site for some time if visitors go off to hike a trail or do some other activity. Security of the car and its contents from theft, shade in hot weather, and the prevention of accidental damage from other car park users, ensure that the car will be protected until the occupants return. If people feel that their car is safe, they will enjoy their experience more.
- Once the more relaxed landscape of the site has been reached, and the attractions of the facility start to divert attention, then car speed and disorientation should be reduced by laying out the car park with simple, easy-to-follow routes.
- Disabled visitors need dedicated spaces which are located closest to the routes to toilets and other attractions and with extra space and good level surfaces.
- Equipment such as bikes, boats, sailboards or other large objects often have to be unloaded. Space is needed around the car in order to get things out of the back or side doors, or off roof-racks, and put onto the ground nearby out of the way of other cars.
- People on the site are likely to be more relaxed, wander around more and be less vigilant, so that there may be some risk of accidents: from reversing vehicles, for example. Small children and pets may be particularly at risk.
- The character of the landscape and the concept of contrast with the urban scene will determine how far the layout of the car parking will blend into its surroundings and reinforce the sense of difference. The Recreation Opportunity Spectrum or other planning tool should already have determined this.
- Sites may be used all the year round. Snow and ice, hot dry summers, rainy periods or other extreme climatic conditions may have to be accommodated in the use of materials, their durability and maintenance and the layout of the area with respect to drainage, snow clearance operations, dust and glare.

How many spaces?

The first design consideration concerns the number of spaces and the types of vehicle required to be accommodated, as this may dictate to a large extent the type of layout to be adopted in the space available.

Accurate calculation of the number of car spaces required for a new facility is not possible, as the pattern and level of use will vary from one site to another. However, it is worth comparing figures for other similar sites and locations to obtain an idea of the right order of provision. Seasonal and weekly fluctuations in use also need to be assessed and some judgement made as to whether to cater for the busiest periods or average demand. On many sites there may be peak usage on certain public holidays that is significantly higher than the rest of the year. It is unlikely to be economic to cater for this demand, and so the provision of overflow parking may be a better option.

A formula has also been used to calculate the expected number of car spaces. It provides a rough guide in the absence of other information, but depends

An informally laid out car park in a woodland setting, where the cars are parked in bays separated by clumps of trees and shrubs. The natural crushed stone surfacing completes the contrast between this and a typical urban layout. Glen Affric, Scotland.

A larger car park in loops with bays of each, beneath a canopy of large trees. Forest of Dean, England. Both these are typical layouts used by the British Forestry Commission.

on the assumptions used to provide the initial figures:

$$N = \frac{v \times s}{p \times h}$$

where N = number of spaces required, v = number of day visits, p = average number of people per car, s = average length of stay, and h = average daily period for which the site will be in use.

The parking requirement may be complicated by other factors. In many areas coaches may be used to bring visitors to a particular beauty spot. In others, trailers for boats, kayaks, horses or trailer caravans may need to be accommodated. Such large or unwieldy vehicles have less flexible requirements for turning or manoeuvring, and take up more space per unit.

Types of layout

The type of layout will also depend on the space, the terrain limitations and the budget available. Generally, the layout should respond to the terrain and the shape of the landform. This will help to ensure that the least impact is caused by cut and fill; that the landform can be used to create irregular, naturalistic layout shapes and to help screen vehicles from external views; and to ensure that easy grades and good drainage can be achieved. To make the best use of awkward terrain, more travelling surface may be needed per parking bay. This may increase the overall cost but may make maintenance easier.

A linear layout type to avoid is one where the road is positioned on the main attraction or view with an avenue of cars on either side. This puts the cars before the view and is very intrusive.

In forested areas it is frequently ideal to disperse the parking among the trees. In this way the ambience and character can be maintained, shade can be provided during hot weather, snow can be intercepted during the winter, and the impact of the whole can 'lie lightly on the land'. Damage to tree rooting can be avoided by careful construction and the use of porous surfacing materials.

Vehicular circulation can be one-way or two-way. One-way traffic is generally easier to control and safer for all concerned. The following examples of different layout plans are suitable for a variety of circumstances. The precise setting out needs to be adjusted on the ground to accommodate local landform variation or the precise position of trees, as detailed site surveys may not be carried out in many circumstances.

Loop layout

This is usually a one-way system, but may be two-way if need be. The simplest layout consists of a loop road along which are spaced bays capable of holding between three and seven cars. These may be all on the one side of the circuit (either exterior or interior) or on both the exterior and the interior sides. In the latter case they should normally be staggered. Multiple loops may be used in various combinations, depending on the site and the capacity. Such car parks tend to fill up from those areas nearest the main focus of the site, so the layout should allow for short alternative loops so that cars do not have to go right round again if part of the

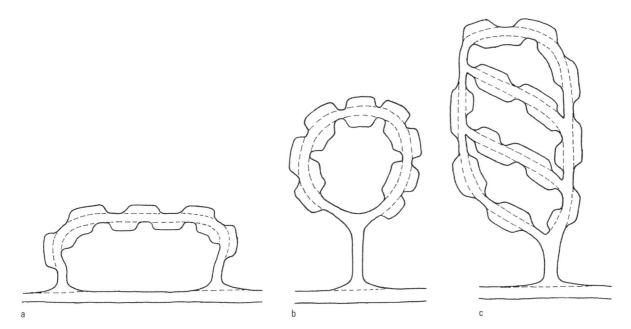

a   b   c

(a) A simple layout where a side loop is made from the access road. Bays to accommodate varying numbers of cars are made along either side of the loop. (b) A loop that can operate on a one-way system from a main access or public road. The circular shape would be varied in practice to take account of local terrain, trees, rocks, etc. (c) This version contains several sub-loops accommodating many more cars, and is suitable for busier sites. It should operate on a one-way system, and can be laid out for either left-hand or right-hand driving sides.

parking area is full. The advantages of this type of layout include the ease with which it can be extended, either by enlarging parking bays or adding extra loops. It is often a good idea to plan for additional parking from the outset, so that if demand increases quickly, enlargements can be made quite easily without a major redesign.

The loop layout is especially suited to fairly flat forested landscapes, where the road can wind its way among the trees and bays can be tucked in between them. It does require a significant amount of room, although quite dense layouts are possible in more open landscapes.

Loop layouts are also good when passengers need to be dropped off from coaches. A drop-off zone can be provided near the focus of the site, and the coach can then be driven to a special parking area away from most of the cars. This prevents coaches from dominating the site or becoming a safety hazard. Equally, where boats or other large equipment need to be delivered, they too can be located in a special storage area on the access section before the empty vehicle moves on into the car park. One requirement is that longer vehicles or those with trailers need larger bays, which must be clearly identified: pull-through parking is not so easy to accommodate with this layout.

Linear car park

Linear car parks are often better suited for restricted terrain, for example, along a river bank terrace, on a ridge top or along a lake shore. A two-way access road has parking bays along it on one or both sides, with a turning area at the far end. This layout is suited to places where good views can be had from each parking bay, where a long frontage is attractive and helps to spread people out for activities such as fishing or boating. Landform, such as a natural terrace, can help to fit the car park into the landscape and reduce its impact. A second variation of this type is to provide small side-loops off the main spine road. This makes turning easier, particularly for trailer-towing vehicles. One-way linear layouts can be designed with a separate exit road back to the entrance, in effect using the public highway to close the circuit.

Area car park

This is the more common urban type of layout, where an area is surfaced and divided into sections for parking or manoeuvring, perhaps subdivided with patches of trees or shrubs or surface markings. This type is the most compact, and uses least ground. It is suitable for

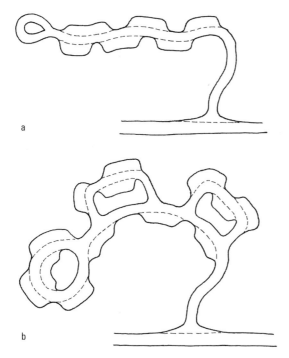

a

b

(a) This linear layout is suited to terraces or side slopes, where it is aligned along the contour. A turning loop is provided. The layout must operate a two-way traffic system. (b) This version has greater capacity, with small loops giving greater bay numbers and the use of the turning loop for parking.

smaller sites or where intensive developments such as a visitor centre have a high turnover of large numbers of visitors. It is also easily maintained when, for example, snow has to be cleared, except that large amounts of snow have to be disposed of somewhere. Security is easier with this type, as more cars are visible and more people are generally around. Hence it might be very appropriate in some urban fringe situations. This layout also enables pull-through spaces to be incorporated more easily for vehicles towing trailers. This avoids reversing, with its attendant problems and danger to pedestrians. The shape of this type of car park can be made less geometric and urban by creating irregular, more naturalistic outlines, and the impact of its size can be reduced by breaking it up into smaller subsections, with vegetation and/or earth mounds.

These basic car park layouts can all be multiplied, extended and modified to suit the design requirements. When planning the layout it is a good idea to think of how the car driver will use it, what circulation problems may arise, and how the layout relates to the siting of all the other requirements such as toilet blocks or trail entrances, as well as respecting the character of the site.

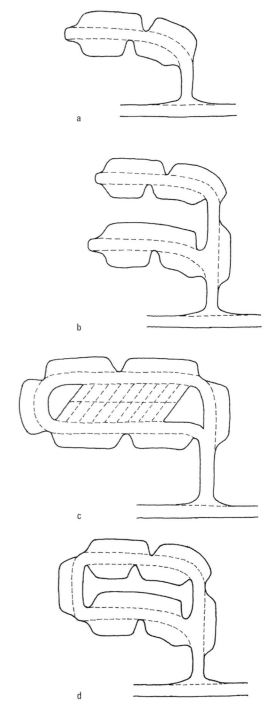

a

b

c

d

(a) An area car park where the scale of parking is partly broken up by small indentations, perhaps of trees. It is a very cost-effective and denser parking layout. (b) The basic layout can be extended. (c) Instead of two separate arms, the two are linked with a space divider to break up the mass of cars and allow for level changes. (d) This layout allows a number of pull-through spaces, which permit trailer-towing vehicles to park without reversing. This version is set out for left-hand drive countries. The reverse would be used in Britain or Australia.

Table 5.1: Dimensions of visitor vehicles

	Space					
	Length		Width		Road width	
Vehicle	m	ft	m	ft	m	ft
Car	6	18	3	9	4.6	14
Mini-coach	6	18	4	12	6	18
Coach	12	36	4.5	14	7	21
Disabled car	6	18	3.6	12	5	15

Parking design

Once the planning aspects relating to site layout, vehicular circulation and management of the expected vehicle types have been dealt with, then the car park designer will fit the layout to the landscape and decide on the appropriate use of materials, vehicle barriers and direction signs.

Parking spaces

In the loop and linear layouts, where parking bays adjoin the sides of the road, the best arrangement is to make bays that can accommodate anything from three to seven vehicles parked at right angles. Because of the importance of the setting in the more natural landscapes, and the need for more space around each vehicle, it is better to give a generous space allowance per car. Table 5.1 sets out the dimensions of visitor vehicles.

The following design assumptions should be made for each car parking space. Parking spaces at right angles to the road are more economical of area, although spaces set parallel may be used in certain circumstances. Either type is acceptable for one-way or two-way traffic. In one-way circulation patterns, parking in echelon to the road is also possible. This is also economical of area, and prevents cars from inadvertently driving the wrong way around a one-way loop.

The parking spaces are set within bays whose outline needs to be designed to blend into the road shape and features of the landscape. A curving design works well with flared outer edges running smoothly into the road edge. This reduces the regularity of the geometry, creating instead a series of flowing lines and shapes, which can be fitted into those of local landform and among trees. This shape is also useful for construction

and maintenance purposes, especially where unpaved or gravel surfacing is used, which needs occasional re-grading or rolling.

If the bay is slightly bigger all round, the notional spaces within it do not need to be marked, and if the parking is looser than in urban areas, this does not normally matter.

Designing the parking area into the setting is usually best done on the ground. The general alignment of the access road should be laid out to minimize cut and fill and to wind gently among the landform and/or trees. Parking bays should, as far as possible, be located in hollows or other places where only minor excavation is needed, such as on the slopes above the road. This ensures that the cars are always nestled in among the landscape, thus reducing their visibility and impact. Using the cut material to build up bays on the slope below the road should be avoided unless mounds can also be created to give some screening. The cut material should be taken off site, or used to make mounds that reduce the visibility of vehicles further and prevent them from driving onto other parts of the site (see below).

One circumstance where parking in prominent areas is acceptable is to give a view to people who cannot reach a proper viewpoint, perhaps through age or disability. In this case, earth mounding or planting can be used to reduce the intrusion of the vehicle. When designing the car park among trees it will be necessary to remove some trees and keep others. Any disturbance to the site and creation of gaps in the canopy may cause problems of wind damage later on. Thus the trees to be kept should be of stable, well-rooted species, and should be in locations where root damage or alteration of the water-table will be at a minimum. A good tree canopy over the parking area is ideal in many situations, as it keeps the cars screened from views into the site and gives shade in hot weather. The choice of trees to be kept and the location of bays in relation to those trees should aim to maximize shade at all times of the day but especially at or shortly after noon in summer when the sun is usually at its hottest. Shady trees also reduce glare or reflection from cars, which might otherwise increase their impact and intrusiveness. Any dead, decayed or diseased trees should also be removed before construction so as to reduce the risks of falling timber or branches during construction and subsequent use.

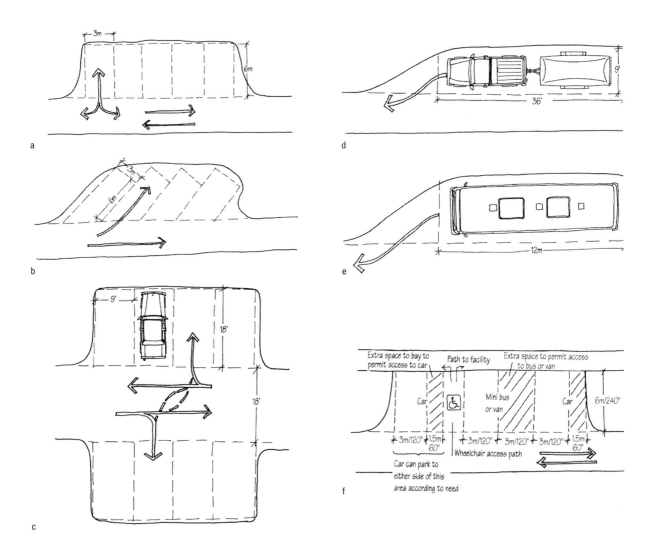

(a) British and European parking dimensions for the more generous scale needed in the countryside, for right-angled parking and two-way traffic. (b) The same dimension takes up more space with echelon parking for one-way traffic. (c) American dimensions are actually smaller than British ones, despite the generally larger car size. It would be sensible to adopt the British/European variety, with its roomier sizes and less formal result. (d) A parallel parking bay with dimensions for American long vehicles such as trailer-towing cars. (e) European dimensions for coach parking and other long vehicles. Once again these are more generous than the American sizes. (f) Dimensions for parking for people with disabilities.

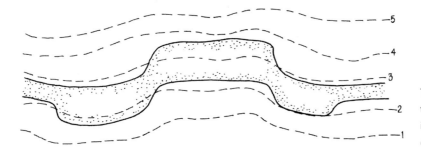

This diagram shows how to use the contours to minimize cut and fill. The bays either push up into hollows and concavities or extend down onto spurs or convexities.

This urban car park example in Berlin shows how a complete canopy of plane trees creates a very shaded micro-climate in the hot summer.

Forested car parks like this one help to provide shade for most of the day. This is important in sunny and hot summers, when cars can heat up severely if parked in the sun. The shade also reduces glare from surfacing. 'Head of the Metolius', Deschutes National Forest, Oregon, USA.

Parking for visitors with disabilities

The layout of the parking area, bay markings and location of facilities should take account of the needs of visitors with disabilities. Usually a number of bays should be reserved for their use, located as near as possible to the main features, the toilets, access to other areas and so on. People with disabilities need more space around their vehicle for moving equipment like wheelchairs in and out, for transferring themselves to wheelchairs from car seats, and for slower movement generally. Kerbs should be flat, surfaces firm, smooth and level and gaps in barriers sufficiently wide to allow wheelchairs through them comfortably. Signs showing the standard disabled symbol should be placed at the centre point of each bay to signal to other users that the parking is reserved for users with disabilities only, and to show drivers of cars permitted to use this parking where the bays are, if no surface marking has been provided.

Surfacing materials

There are two main options available: sealed (paved) or unsealed (unpaved) surfaces. The choice depends on the following factors:

- **The expected wear and tear and thus the maintenance cost**. Unsealed surfaces are cheap to install and maintain if this needs to be done only infrequently. Sealed surfaces are expensive to lay but need less maintenance. Unsealed surfaces can be made with locally won material, which is frequently cheaper.
- **Appearance**. Natural materials, especially those from the site or nearby, can reduce impact and blend into the landscape. Used for unsealed surfaces, they also present a coarser texture than sealed surfaces and so tend to fit better into the wider landscape. Sealed surfaces such as bituminous macadam or asphalt are darker in colour, usually black, and very fine in texture. However, this can be ameliorated by using a spray-and-chip top layer (tar spray with spread and rolled chippings) of local material. The same technique can also be used on an unsealed surface in order to improve wear and tear. This is the kind of surface finish commonly used on rural roads in many places. The spray-and-chip finish can be added to the access road but may not be needed on the parking bays, where wear is less. The slight difference in texture and colour then helps to delineate the two areas.
- **Climate**. In hotter, dry areas, dust from unsealed surfaces can be a serious problem all through the summer. Any vehicle travelling even at slow speeds tends to throw up dust, which is very uncomfortable when breathed in or deposited on skin or clothing. In other places a very wet climate may result in frequent potholing on unsealed areas with much reduced surface quality. Snow clearance in winter may be necessary, and unsealed surfaces are more easily damaged by snow ploughs than smoother, sealed ones.
- **Distance from sources of material**. Stone, tarmac and asphalt are expensive to transport over long distances. When budgets for recreation provision are limited, it makes sense to use locally won materials where these are cheaper and suitable for the degree of wear and tear expected.

Urban materials and finishes used in a wild setting: sealed surface, white lines and light-coloured concrete barriers. 'Big Four', Mount Baker-Snoqualmie National Forest, Washington, USA.

Unsealed surfaces can be subject to heavy wear and tear, erosion, potholing and puddles unless regularly maintained. 'Sheepwash', North York Moors National Park, England.

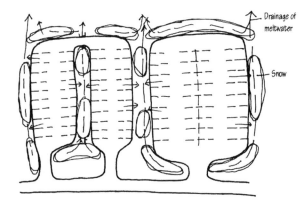

(Top) Diagram showing how snow storage can be designed into the car park layout together with the meltwater drainage. (Bottom) A large car park in Finnish Lapland where snow clearance and storage are needed.

- **Expected degree of use**. In remote, lightly used locations, the lower wear and tear expected will favour unsealed surfaces; the converse will apply at popular, heavily used areas. This also applies at short-stay facilities, where the turnover of visitors means that the surfaces are likely to be heavily used by vehicles.
- **Location**. If the ROS is being followed, then the remoter, wilder areas will favour unsealed surfaces, whereas in the more urban settings sealed finishes will be more acceptable. It may also be appropriate to use unsealed surfaces near urban areas to emphasize the more relaxed, rural or wild setting and atmosphere being created.
- **Drainage**. Surfacing must include proper attention to drainage. Sealed surfaces produce more runoff, which has to be channelled away. Expensive pipe drains can be entertained only on large developments. Laying the surface to gradients allowing run-off into French drains (rubble-filled ditches), into open ditches or over the surface of nearby areas may be acceptable instead. Care must be taken to avoid drainage water flowing directly into streams, as the silt and pollutants (oil, fuel, and exhaust particles) could be harmful to aquatic life. The use of SUDS systems (sustainable urban drainage) may also be considered. In this system a pond is excavated into which surface run-off flows. Reed beds filter out sediment and absorb any pollutants before the water is discharged into streams.

Unsealed surfaces also need to be kept drained, although water may percolate through them to a

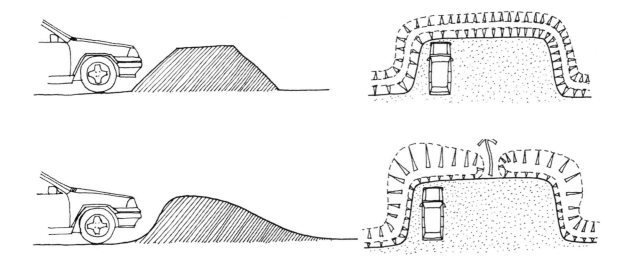

(Top) A plan and section of a poorly designed earth barrier. It is too symmetrical and angular in form. (Bottom) A better-designed barrier, asymmetric, rounded and blended into the local contours. It also allows a way through into a picnic area beyond.

greater degree. Good gradients across the area are needed, but areas to be drained should be broken into sections to avoid the danger of erosion, particularly during heavy rainstorms. Unsealed surfaces can be prone to washout. Excess water in the structure of the road weakens it and can make it more prone to structural failure under heavy loads such as fully laden coaches.

Construction

The car park construction will normally include a certain amount of excavation, which should be done in stages. For example, turf should be stripped and stored, followed by topsoil removal and storage, and then subsoil should be excavated to a depth to create the road and parking bays with the appropriate gradients for drainage. Roots, wood and other organic material must be removed. The rocky base material for the car park can then be laid out and rolled to a sufficient depth for the strength required. Hard rock, crushed and angular in form to include all sizes down from 50 mm (2 in.) to dust should be used. Then the surfacing is added, either the sealed paving or unsealed material, which will be similar to the base. Finally, the preserved topsoil and turf can be used to cover excavated surfaces and to tidy up the road and bay edges. Zones where no traffic or materials storage is permitted should be fenced off. Care will be necessary in the vicinity of trees to be retained on site. Soil should not be built up around the bases of trees. The drainage should not seriously affect

A well-designed earth barrier prevents cars from straying off the car park, and partly screens them in the open setting. Beechenhurst, Forest of Dean, Gloucestershire, England.

the degree of water received by the trees or alter the water table.

Excess excavated material can be used to make mounds (see 'Vehicle control' below), spread over areas to be grass seeded, or taken off site to be disposed of in an approved way.

Vehicle control

In many areas the landform and open nature of the site are such that there is nothing to stop vehicles from being driven off the road or parking areas and into other areas.

(Top) Poor design of rock barriers: too even in size and spacing, parallel with the bay edge and sitting on the ground.

(Bottom) Here the rocks vary in size, spacing and alignment and are partly sunk into the ground.

This is usually undesirable because it poses dangers to pedestrians, and causes damage to soil and vegetation. Access into the hinterland may cause all manner of problems. Visitors with four-wheel drive vehicles and motorcycles are often tempted to go beyond the car park, while ordinary cars may well be parked off the surfaced areas during busy periods. Where the natural terrain does not prevent such access, control devices are needed. All need openings sufficient to allow wheelchairs, prams and baby buggies through. Few will restrict motorcycles, but all will restrict cars and most all-terrain vehicles.

The following types are most commonly used:

- **Earth mounds**. These can be constructed from spare excavated material. They need to be steeply graded on the side facing the parking spaces, and should be graded into the landform on the other side unless they are intended to resemble hedgebanks or similar rural features. The steepness and height are essential to prevent four-wheel drive vehicles from climbing over them. In confined areas the face nearest the parking can be constructed of timber or stone revetment. Trapezoidal-section mounds should be avoided as these look too engineered. The mounds can be sown, planted or turfed with appropriate vegetation. If they are of a height similar to that of the bonnet/hood of the cars, the mounds will help to screen them from views back to the car park. Trees can also be planted, which will hide the cars further and provide some shade and shelter. The gentler slope of the mound can also be used as informal seating.

An example of large stones used to control cars in Baxter State Park in Maine, USA.

- **Rocks**. In areas where rocks are commonly found, either as individual elements or as outcropping, they can be used to make very suitable barriers. Large rocks can be dug into the ground so that they look fixed and are difficult to shift. They need to be big enough so that high-chassis vehicles cannot attempt to drive over them and so that any cars that accidentally bump into them do so with their bumper and not their sump! Rocks look better placed at irregular distances apart rather than in equally spaced rows. If some of the rocks have flatter tops, they can make informal seats.
- **Log barriers**. Simple, stout barriers constructed from thick, straight logs placed on two short, upright posts of similar dimensions and set fairly deeply into the ground are quite effective. Varying the length

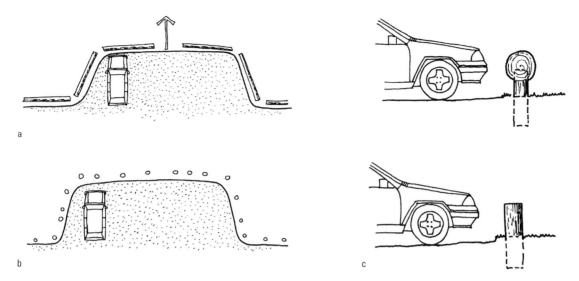

a

b

c

These diagrams shows how to lay out and construct log barriers, both horizontal logs and large timber posts (a) and (b).
Their height should match that of most car bumpers (c).

A mixture of log posts set into the ground work well, especially in wooded settings. Near Cap Ferret, Aquitaine, France.

and direction of barrier sections enables them to be aligned in different ways to follow the outside edges of the parking areas. Solid debarked logs should be used, sufficiently thick to be both physically and visually strong. The wood can be left to weather or can be stained to blend into the landscape, although the logs do need to remain visible. They should be set at car bumper height, which also makes it difficult to lift a motorcycle over them. If vandalism is a problem, the logs can be protected against chainsaws with a wire inlaid along their length on at least two sides.

- **Log posts**. Stout wooden posts can be set into the ground at suitable intervals following the edge of the

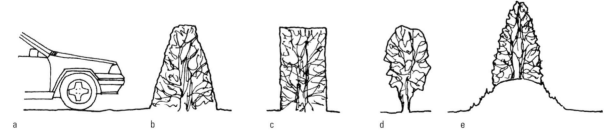

a   b   c   d   e

Hedges used as a barrier. Their structure is important: (a) A tapered section is easier to maintain and keep dense at the bottom.
(b) Square shapes are difficult to trim properly at the top. (c) Poorly trimmed hedges lose their lower branches to become thin
and transparent. (d) A hedge on an earth mound is both physically and visually more effective.

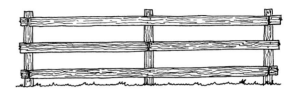

A dry stone wall makes an effective barrier in areas where they are traditional. They are easily repaired, and will last a long time if left undisturbed.

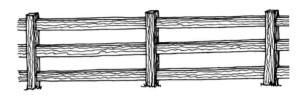

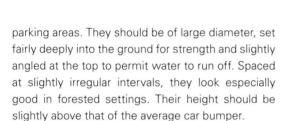

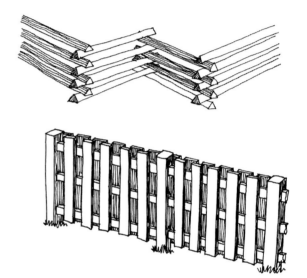

Wooden fences can be used as barriers: (From top – a) A simple post-and-rail construction works well. (b) This version is mortised for a stronger finish. This is a traditional form of construction in some places. (c) The zigzag fence is a traditional type in North America. (d) A vertical board-on-board fence makes a visual screen, perhaps more appropriate in urban fringe areas.

parking areas. They should be of large diameter, set fairly deeply into the ground for strength and slightly angled at the top to permit water to run off. Spaced at slightly irregular intervals, they look especially good in forested settings. Their height should be slightly above that of the average car bumper.

- **Hedges**. A hedge planted on a low mound is not so physically strong but is an attractive and effective screen, which can save space. A wire or post-and-rail fence can be used while the hedge is becoming established. Once the hedge is established, it should be a suitable barrier in more rural settings.
- **Walls**. These can be very effective as screens and physical barriers. Drystone construction is traditional in many rural landscapes, while mortared stone is appropriate in more urban settings or near buildings or other structures. Local stone which weathers usually fits the setting admirably.
- **Fences**. Post-and-rail or other traditional constructions can also be used. They may not prevent determined people from breaking through them, nor are they so visually useful. They are best in rural settings where such forms are appropriate and robustness is not required.

Vertical board-on-board fencing provides a visual screen where this is needed. It will usually be appropriate to use a range of these barrier types on many sites. The sight of one type of barrier used extensively can be overpowering. Rocks in mounds, mounds with posts in between, barriers alternating with posts and so on all give variety. Also, the choice should reflect the setting. Mounds and rocks are more appropriate to wilder, more open settings; posts to forests; and log barriers, walls or fences to rural or urban situations.

Vehicle management

Most car parks require some form of vehicle management signing, particularly the larger ones. Drivers need to be informed if one-way systems operate, when rights of way vary, and where special areas for coaches, trailer-towing vehicles and people with disabilities are designated. As the general rule is to keep signs to an absolute minimum, the site layout should be analysed at the design stage in terms of the driver's requirements,

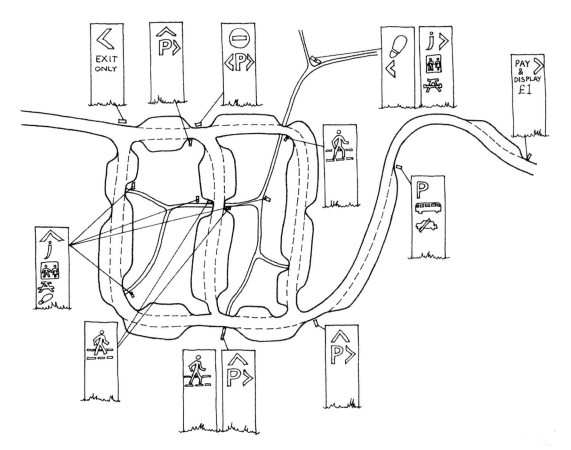

A diagram to show how a vehicle-signing layout should be prepared. At each place where a sign is needed, the exact information is worked out in the correct orientation. This plan is given to sign makers and to those responsible for installing and maintaining the signs.

and a schedule of signs should be proposed showing their positions and messages. Siting of signs should ensure that they will not be obscured by other vehicles.

The signs should use standard symbols in standard colours so far as possible. Where text is necessary, it should be expressed in positive terms ('Please do not park along the road edges'). As the scale of the landscape and road areas is usually smaller and the speed of vehicles slower, the signs can be smaller than those needed on public highways. Sign structures should be as unobtrusive as possible, being of a simple yet robust construction and materials. Slabs of wood or stone set vertically into the ground and routed or sandblasted with the symbol, which is painted in the appropriate colour, are one type. Plastic, wood or metal symbols fixed to wood or stone are another.

Low-level signs will work in car-only areas, but signs may need to be taller where higher vehicles such as coaches use the site. Vegetation should be kept trimmed around signs, and damaged signs should be quickly repaired or replaced.

Marking of parking spaces should not be necessary unless long ones are needed, or pull-through spaces in an area car park are provided. Surface markings are not easy to provide in car parks with unsealed surfaces, but stone setts, can be used if required. Horizontal barriers can also be used as indicators. In some area layouts, marking may be unnecessary if people follow the habit of parking around the edges first and then using the middle area. Car parks with sealed surfaces can be marked with white or yellow lines, but these appear urban and should be avoided if possible, especially if continuous lines are used. Pull-through spaces can be signalled by island beds of trees or shrubs, which help to direct traffic flows.

Payment for parking

If the site operator intends to collect money from visitors as a means of payment for parking or for general use of the area, the method and arrangement of payment collection has to be fitted into the design. There are several basic methods.

Payment at the entrance to the site

This can be by means of a manned kiosk, such as are commonly found in US national and state parks. The entrance layout is split into two lanes – an entrance and an exit – so that all visitors pass the payment window on their way in. In large sites where there is a steady use all year round it may be worth manning the kiosk all the time. In other instances manning it at busy times only, and using a machine for all other occasions, ensures economical collection.

A ticket-vending machine can supplement the entrance kiosk in low-use periods or be the sole means of payment collection. The level of honesty may vary between 20 and 70 per cent, depending on the location. Local, frequent visitors may object to paying every time they visit 'their' site. Honesty can be increased if there is a 'pay and display' policy on car windows, with some attempt to control it by issuing reminders to those who do not comply. Too heavy-handed an approach may be counter-productive and reduce the loyalty of visitors, who may feel victimized. It all depends on the circumstances and the way the whole site is managed.

Any signs at the entrance must make it clear whether payment is expected, how much it is and whether there is a limitation on coins accepted by machines. The use of entrance payment can be coupled with the management of visitor numbers. In many sites the capacity of parking, picnicking, the risk of wear and tear or of overloading toilet facilities at busy periods might suggest that the entrance should be controlled to prevent site degradation and overcrowding to the detriment of the visitors' experience. Numbers of vehicles entering or exiting can be monitored visually or automatically and notices saying 'Site full' posted as required. This prevents frustration; people refused access can try elsewhere without the annoyance of driving fruitlessly looking for parking or waiting for someone else to leave, with all the stress and site circulation problems that this can cause.

Payment within the site

This is common in many places where a pay-and-display machine is located in a central place, or in large sites where several machines can be distributed. Honesty ratings may be low unless they are controlled, but the operating costs of such machines can also be low.

While payment might seem desirable in order to help pay for the maintenance of the site, there are several issues that need to be addressed. First, ticket machines have to be emptied regularly, especially in locations where theft is known to occur. This requires staff to carry out collection and ticket replenishment. Second, there is the cost of checking on levels of payment compliance, and the difficulty that most operators might have in enforcing a fine or seeking payment of the parking fee. Even where rangers are law enforcement officers, as they are in some national parks, the adverse reaction from visitors caused by attempts to extract payment can outweigh the benefits. Third, the machines have to be maintained and kept in working order. The extent of this depends on the choice of machine.

Electrically operated ticket machines need power on site, from mains, battery or solar power (increasingly the case). If this is possible, they could be the better choice as they can print out a ticket with time and date recorded on it, which may be useful for management purposes. They also take a range of coin sizes, and can be calibrated for different lengths of period per payment level.

Mechanically operated machines will work on sites without electricity, relying on the action of the coins falling and the push of a button to activate the dispenser. One rate of payment based on a single coin or combination of coins gives out a set ticket. This means that one payment is made whatever the duration of the visit, thus deterring short-term visitors from paying. The machine is easier to maintain, as it is robust and has no complicated timers to adjust.

Safety and security at the car park

In many areas people using car parks in quiet, wild places are anxious about leaving their cars. This is paradoxical, because it might be expected that getting away to the outdoors would involve fewer concerns about risks of theft or vandalism to property than in the city. Sadly, places where a number of cars are parked with owners absent can be a lure to thieves in many areas, especially in Britain and Europe. Even with modern electronic security systems and car alarms it takes only a few seconds for an experienced thief to break into a car and steal the radio or any property lying on seats. In such car parks, people come and go at different times and are normally strangers to one another; someone casually opening a door and entering a car or taking something from it would hardly attract attention even if there were other people on the site. It might be thought that cars spread around in well-screened countryside car parks might increase the risk, as fewer people would be able to see the cars or the presence of thieves. Therefore it could be prudent to incorporate the following precautions into designs of those areas where the risk of car theft is considered to be significant:

• Cluster more cars into bays and keep the bays closer to one another. This increases the turnover of parking in any one place and therefore the numbers of people visiting the parking area.
• Keep the parking visible from picnic areas. Many people prefer to move only a short distance from their cars so that they can keep them in sight. Often this is partly anxiety about security as well as about getting lost; the car becomes a landmark for them.

• Place warning signs to remind people to lock their cars and to put their property in the boot/trunk or to carry it with them.
• Management of the area can also reduce the risk, perhaps through the use of rangers to maintain a presence, which reassures visitors and deters would-be thieves. It is also important to liaise with the police for warnings, for advice, and to ensure that the thefts that do occur are reported.

Six

Toilet facilities

Once the visitors have parked their car, it is frequently a call to the toilets that is next on the list of priorities. If it has been a long journey to the site, the urge to respond to the call will probably be acute for any children present. The presence of a clean and well-ventilated toilet block in such circumstances is very welcome. Whether to provide toilet facilities, the capacity and the type of sewage disposal required as well as the design of the building are all important decisions to be made. On the one hand, the comfort and hygiene of visitors are important; on the other, the cost of construction and maintenance of toilet blocks can be high compared with other costs associated with running the site.

Should a toilet be provided?

The decision on whether to provide a toilet depends on several factors, as follows.

- **Location and character of the area**. Remote locations of wild character suggest that the impact of human activities should be kept to a minimum. Toilet buildings, however well designed, may spoil the atmosphere of remoteness attached to such places. However, if there are large numbers of visitors, the risk to health and the problem of pollution caused by too many people resorting to 'going behind the bushes' may be worse evils. Urban, rural or other locations containing more buildings do not present such a dilemma.
- **Numbers of visitors, especially at weekends**. In places where there are fewer visitors it may be

difficult to justify the capital outlay of a building, especially if there are no apparent problems on the site or its surroundings. In areas of limited size, the smell and sight of previous visitors' use of the bushes may be excessive, especially in hot weather, requiring either some small-scale facility or a regime of burying, covering or removal. On larger sites with more visitors, the need for facilities becomes self-evident.

- **Duration of the visit**. If the majority of users come for only a short time, such as an hour's stroll with the dog in a country park near a town, then facilities should be unnecessary. If visitors spend most of a day at the site, they will need toilet facilities, especially if refreshments are consumed.
- **Distance travelled to the site**. A short journey to the area reduces the need to use a toilet, while a long one usually makes use unavoidable. This is especially true if there are no obvious alternative facilities elsewhere on the route.
- **Presence of water-based recreation at the area**. The risks to health from polluted water are an ever-present concern. If the water is to be used for bathing, swimming, boating of similar activities, then toilets are essential for hygiene purposes, and probably for changing too, although separate buildings are often appropriate (see Chapter 10).
- **Presence of food outlets at the site**. Some sites have food vendors who come during high-use periods. This will attract more people, and could emphasize the need for toilets, although not necessarily more than if people brought their own refreshments.

A toilet building at a highway rest stop in the north of Norway. The wooden building positioned by some trees and a rock is stained dull grey in colour and blends in well with the wild, remote landscape.

A view of the interior of a toilet for disabled people, with space, rails, an alarm, bins, a washbasin with special taps and an electric dryer placed at a suitable height.

- **Winter use of a site**. If site has regular use throughout the year, this may tip the balance towards providing toilets for the comfort of visitors in very cold conditions.

Scale of provision

Having made the decision to provide toilets, the extent to which they are provided is in part determined by the factors described above. A remote location where small to medium numbers of visitors spend some time might justify a single, unisex all-purpose facility also suitable for disabled visitors, whereas a large site with many visitors staying for long periods would need multiple facilities divided into male, female and disabled. The actual scale of provision may in part depend on:

- the local and national public health or similar regulations;
- the social acceptance of, for example, unisex facilities;
- the correct balance between male and female provision;
- the need for disabled use;
- use by coach parties, including school groups.

National and local public health, employment and other regulations may help to set the minimum provision. As these regulations vary in different countries, provinces or states it is not worth dwelling on them here, but they must be investigated. If employees work on the site,

for example, as rangers, there may be other regulations that also apply. The social acceptance of using unisex facilities may vary. In many instances it is assumed that male and female facilities should be separate, yet frequently unisex ones are used. Aircraft, the home, small offices or restaurants generally have only unisex toilets. If a feeling of safety and privacy is ensured and numbers of users are low, then this approach can be perfectly acceptable. It saves duplicating facilities and the significant extra costs of buildings.

The balance between provision for men and women is difficult to estimate correctly, as their requirements differ. Generally men spend less time using lavatory facilities than women do. If a urinal is provided for men, then the numbers of WC pans supplied can be half those needed for the women's side in small facilities and a third of those in larger ones. However, sometimes other factors may alter these calculations. For example, some sites are more commonly used by men because of the activities available, such as snow-mobiling.

People with disabilities need their own facilities in most instances, laid out with extra space for wheelchair access, special rails, taps (faucets) and other features. The question of whether or not to keep disabled facilities unisex depends on how they are incorporated into the site. In a large building with a foyer at the entrance to male and female areas, a door leading to segregated disabled toilets is possible, but in a smaller block a single unisex toilet is probably preferable. Another reason for favouring unisex is that a person with a disability may have to be accompanied by a person of the opposite

Table 6.1: Car numbers and provision of toilet facilities

Number of cars	Number and type of toilets
15–35 cars	1 M/F and 1 D or 1 unisex
35–50 cars	1 M*, and 2 F + 1 D or 3 unisex
50–100 cars	2 M + 4 F + 1 D
including coach drop-off:	2 M + 6 F + 1 D
100+ cars	3 M + 3 x 3 F + 2 D†

M = male, F = female and D = disabled. All assume an average length of stay and distance travelled to the site.

*M assumes one urinal and one pan when segregated toilets are provided, no urinals in unisex toilets.

†Increase ratio to 1 M = 3 F, increasing total numbers at 1 M per 20 spaces greater than 120.

sex. A unisex toilet prevents any embarrassment for companions if segregated toilets contrast with their gender. Of course, in many circumstances, there is nothing to prevent able-bodied people from using the special toilet, thus allowing a single, all-purpose facility on the smallest sites.

If the site is used by coach parties, including school groups, an increase in toilet provision is likely to be needed because of the large number of people who wish to use the toilet at the same time. If the school use is generally from co-educational schools, roughly equal numbers of boys and girls can be expected. Coach parties of elderly people might include more women than men, as women tend to live longer. The period of use by children or older people also tends to be longer than average. On the basis of the factors described above provision can be provided on the basis of the calculations shown in Table 6.1.

Types of provision

The type of toilet described is based on the method of disposing of the sewage, and related requirements for the structure and other aspects of construction such as ventilation, washing facilities, and so on. There are five possible options for sewage disposal, as follows.

Composting toilets

In these, the toilet seat is set above a box or hole into which all waste accumulates. If the moisture content can be kept reasonably low, for example, by the addition of soil, ashes or bark, then the waste material breaks down into a relatively odour-free compost, which can be emptied from the receptacles at the back of the toilet building and safely disposed of in a suitable location.

There are various proprietary makes that have developed this type for relatively low-use sites. Plastic containers prevent contamination of groundwater. Special bark is put into the toilet after use by the user, which reduces the odour and helps the process of composting. No water is required, and the unit can be constructed above ground. This is important in areas

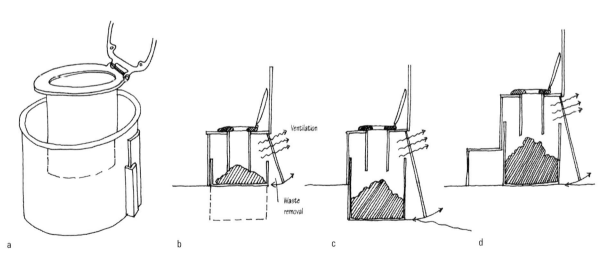

a   b   c   d

Composting toilets: (a) A unit available as a proprietary set and used in cabins and small toilets in Scandinavia. (b) Arrangement of the unit on level ground. Access for waste removal is via a flap at the rear of the building. (c) A unit with greater capacity dug into a side slope. (d) A unit with larger capacity inside the building with a step up to the seat.

A well-designed and built composting toilet at Abriachan Community Forest in Scotland. The floor is raised above the composting unit, so the ramp allows disabled people to access it. The final waste liquid is treated in a reed bed behind the building. The building materials and construction are also very good for a forest landscape.

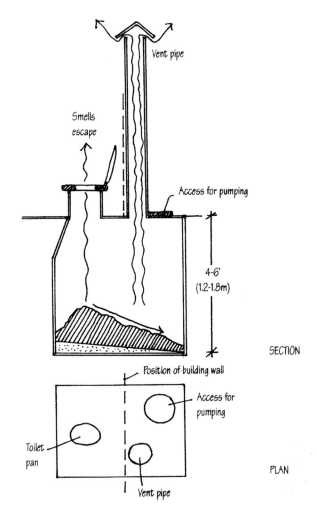

The vault, pit or 'big drop' toilet unit commonly used in North America. It has to be pumped out. The build-up of liquid in the vault can cause powerful smells, which the ventilation system cannot always remove.

where groundwater is sensitive to pollution, where the ground is rocky, or where it becomes frozen in winter, so making holes difficult to dig.

These toilets are common in Scandinavia and Eastern Europe, where, instead of seats, 'hole in the floor' systems are still common – difficult to use by older people and impossible for those with disabilities. They are increasingly available in North America, where proprietary systems have been recently perfected. In Britain their use has been limited except by groups such as the Scouts, for whom pit latrines are traditional. Interest in this low-cost sustainable technique is increasing. The use of proprietary systems creates a small amount of relatively odourless fluid which can be drained away quite safely, although in some cases the use of a reed bed to filter any remaining pollutants can be used before any effluent finally reaches a stream.

Vault (pit or big drop toilets)

These are similar to the dry composting toilets except that they have a larger capacity and tend to stay much wetter. Their main drawbacks are the odours that are common in hot weather and, for some people, a fear of falling into them. Adequate ventilation is difficult in many versions unless assisted by fans. These types are widely used on recreation sites in North America. They have to be pumped out at intervals so that access by special truck is needed. These types can also be provided with chemicals that help to break down the excreta and mask the smells. Various proprietary versions claim to

have solved the odour problem with better ventilation systems. Some can be ventilated by fans powered by solar energy or heavy-duty rechargeable batteries.

Both the types described above are suitable in locations where there is no water or power supply available. The composting type is acceptable for low usage, but only the vault will cope with a high use. The next categories depend on either a water or a power supply in order to operate.

Flush toilets with septic tank or cesspool

This type requires a consistent water supply to flush the system. This might be obtained from piped water services or by abstraction from a nearby stream, spring or lake. In many places, the water can be collected and stored in a tank or cistern to cover drought periods. The reliability of local water supplies needs careful assessment before deciding whether or not to use it.

Where piped water is available, there is no such problem. Flush toilets and a water supply to basins all help hygiene and enable the toilets to be cleaned more regularly and easily. Sewage is then disposed of in a septic tank, which is either connected to a soakaway field or which yields an effluent clean enough to be discharged into a stream (as long as the relevant pollution control standards can be met). A soakaway allows the effluent to soak into the subsoil if it has good porosity (sands and gravel rather than clay) and the groundwater table is at a reasonable depth. Periodic de-sludging of the septic tank is required, but otherwise it operates to produce clean and non-polluting materials by bacterial breakdown.

Cesspools are merely a means of storage in large tanks without treatment, so pumping out and transport for treatment are necessary. They can smell foul, and may pollute surrounding areas if tank maintenance is not carried out properly. They are not recommended.

Chemical toilets

These use a special sterilizing chemical, which flushes through the lavatory pan and kills the odours of the sewage. Such toilets work without water, but generally need some power if the chemical is to be re-circulated to act as a flushing agent. The systems work well, and are used most on temporary sites where self-contained trailer units are provided, but can also be used on permanent sites. The chemical renders the sewage sterile, so it can be stored for long periods if need be. It must be pumped out periodically and disposed of in a suitable location; exceptionally it can be discharged into a soakaway if permission or licence to do so can be obtained.

In terms of sustainable development, there is a question mark over the appropriateness of using and disposing of large quantities of sterilizing chemicals anywhere in the environment. For this reason, this type may not be widely favoured.

Flush toilets with access to piped water, drainage and electricity

In urban and many rural situations, especially in the more heavily populated rural areas of Europe and parts of North America, full services are often available within a reasonable distance of the toilet site. Usually they will run along the public highway, and can be connected to the site with a relatively short run of pipes of cables. These allow the highest standard of facility,

A proprietary chemical toilet unit set into a wooden outer building. This is a very practical solution given the coloured plastic structure of the unit. Irving Nature Park, Saint John, New Brunswick, Canada.

with fully flushing units, hot and cold running water for hand washing, lighting, heat to reduce the risk of frost damage if the toilets are open all year, electric hand dryers, and so on.

As long as a gravity connection with the foul sewer main can be obtained, then low maintenance can be virtually guaranteed, which will offset the increased cost of construction and the expense of connection. If the site does not permit a gravity connection, for example when the main is higher than the toilet, a pump is needed. This will not be a problem, but it will require some maintenance.

Flush toilets with mains services are almost standard in most areas of Britain, and are the most expensive of the types described. Visitors may come to expect such a standard everywhere, and there could be some concern over non-flushing types if these are used. However, if any unit is well equipped, clean and well maintained, there should be few causes for complaint.

This toilet block is a very simple design and construction for a remote area in Australia. The form and construction use the vault system. Abercromby River National Park, New South Wales, Australia.

A neat solution to the problem of small buildings is to combine two single units into one. Here two vault toilets have been arranged side by side. The overhanging roof provides shelter and a lobby before the doors with a washbasin. South Island, New Zealand.

Toilet block design

There is a very wide range of building types in use for toilet blocks around the world. It might be expected that some standard layouts and forms might have evolved based on best practice, but expensive mistakes continue to be made. Fundamental to the design is how to combine the internal layout of different combinations and sizes of toilet provision within a building form that fits into the landscape without intrusion. This has to be balanced with a toilet block that is welcoming, and not hidden away in a dark corner or camouflaged out of sight.

Many of the building forms in use are visually badly proportioned, look domestic or resemble weather-houses or cuckoo clocks. They have small floor plans that need to accommodate an upright adult, and this emphasizes the vertical proportion, which stands out in open landscapes. Where two buildings occur together, the result is exacerbated. The scale of such buildings also tends to be too small for the size of standard materials such as shakes (shingles), board-on-board cladding, or pitched roofs.

Each site should be considered separately, and the type of building form should be developed to fit its essential character. Forests, for example, have many vertical forms and lines. The scale of spaces is determined by the degree of enclosure of the trees, while subdued, earthy colours and coarse textures are unique to the forest. These characteristics can be expressed in a timber building with forms reminiscent of the tree-trunks and branches that form the canopy. Coarse textures of overlapping vertical board, shakes

A toilet building designed for a forest landscape. Coarse textures of cladding and roof, exposed beam ends and the use of large dimension timbers work rather well.

(shingles) and protruding beam ends further enhance the sense of a forest 'style'.

A more open site may require a stronger horizontal emphasis, with wide overhangs to a low-pitched, monopitched or hipped roof, in order to make the building hug the ground more. Local stone, a turf roof, a location tucked into a hollow or against a bank would add to the effect of a building 'growing out of the landscape'.

A rural setting may suggest forms based on vernacular buildings, perhaps connected with local farmsteads or small industrial buildings. These links could be reinforced with fences, walls or other structures to tie them into the landscape. Traditional colours of doors or window frames might also be appropriate.

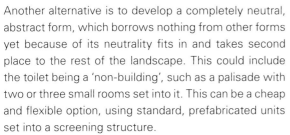

This design borrows from more domestic forms and materials: a tile roof, stucco, a dormer window/vent and steep roof pitch. It would be suitable where other vernacular buildings are already present.

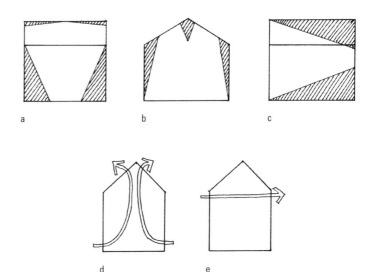

Light and ventilation are important factors in design: (a) Light from windows set high in gable ends works quite well but can leave corners rather dark. (b) Skylights are very effective and maintain privacy. (c) Side windows leave much shadow and need to be of clouded glass, which reduces their effectiveness. (d) Ventilation needs to be at both ground and roof levels to allow proper air circulation. (e) High-level ventilation clears only the upper area, not the floor.

Another alternative is to develop a completely neutral, abstract form, which borrows nothing from other forms yet because of its neutrality fits in and takes second place to the rest of the landscape. This could include the toilet being a 'non-building', such as a palisade with two or three small rooms set into it. This can be a cheap and flexible option, using standard, prefabricated units set into a screening structure.

Initially the form of the building has to be developed from the functional requirement of the facilities. These depend on the resolution of several different issues, as follows.

Is there to be a lobby area?

It is normal for simple types such as the single unit with no hand washing facilities to open directly into the surroundings. In larger facilities with separate toilets and hand washing for male and female, there is usually a lobby-cum-circulation area inside the building, from which each lavatory unit is accessed. One reason for including a lobby is to provide shelter when queues are likely to occur. Separate lobbies for separate male and female lavatories are more acceptable than shared lobby areas next to unisex units. Other solutions include setting the doors to the respective units at opposite ends of the building so that they are out of sight of each other. A deep roof overhang for a lobby can give sufficient shelter without the lobby being part of the internal layout.

How is the space to be lit?

Low-level windows are not usually practical, nor do they ensure privacy. High-level windows (above eye level) or skylights are usually preferable. Light spaces always have a better atmosphere than dark ones. High-level windows can be set in the gable ends of pitched roofs or along the higher wall of a monopitch structure. Skylights work with any roof style. The interior can be open up to the rafters or can have a slatted ceiling, allowing natural light to reach the space below. Artificial lighting may be necessary in some seasons, but it should not be relied upon as the main form of lighting.

Will there be hand washing?

If so, extra space will be needed in the toilet unit to accommodate a washbasin. When there is more than one lavatory per side in each unit, a lobby space can be used for hand washing. Only one or two washbasins should be needed, even in larger blocks. Together with towel dispensers or electric dryers and mirrors, a space is therefore needed to accommodate two or three people at a time.

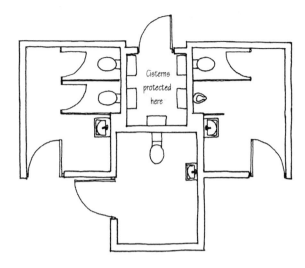

This layout places all the cisterns in a separate space with secure access, which can be frost-proofed or heated, allowing year-round use of the toilet building.

Will the toilet block be open all year round?

There are implications for maintenance, heating and frost protection if a toilet block with a flushing system is to be kept open during the winter months. Problems of frozen plumbing can be solved by arranging all the pipework or cisterns within a compartment that is insulated and possibly heated (at a low level to maintain temperatures just above freezing). Only the pans and handles for flushing are situated in the unheated, ventilated area. The pans can be protected from frost damage by the use of stainless steel or heavy-duty porcelain. This arrangement also has the advantage that all the vulnerable fittings are locked away, and the service room can be used to store refills and cleaning equipment and to house meters for water and electricity.

Is there a risk of vandalism at the site?

In urban fringe areas, or places where anti-social groups might be expected to congregate, some degree of vandalism might be expected. This will affect the use of materials. Wood might be deemed a fire risk; lobby areas or shelters might encourage loitering and graffiti; porcelain fittings are easily smashed. It is tempting to choose materials to withstand a bomb attack, but this can create an uncomfortable and unwelcoming design; it is better to accept some risk of damage that can be repaired easily. Nevertheless, it is prudent to consider a range of design techniques to reduce the opportunity for vandalism, such as robust fittings, high windows, stainless steel, good-sized timber sections, and finishes that make graffiti removal easy, such as smooth wood which can be sanded or re-stained or melamine-coated panels.

There is no reason why a fairly standard internal layout should not be adopted once the best arrangement has been found to suit a particular organization. There are several advantages to this, including the ability to bulk purchase fittings and replacement fixtures, and to specify standard maintenance contracts. Visitors to the site will know that a high standard has been provided and will be well maintained.

The incorporation of a few extras into toilet block layout will also help. Baby-changing shelves can be provided in the disabled toilet so that either parent can use it. (The disabled unit usually has more space and less use, and so a fold-down shelf is easy to fit.) A large sink suitable for washing pots (subject to health regulations), boots and clothes might be provided at larger sites.

Building construction

As previously suggested in terms of building form and function, there are also certain materials and finishes that are more appropriate to the outdoors so as to reinforce the contrast with urban places. Therefore, while the layout should be to a high standard, materials should, wherever possible, be ones that are the least urban or domestic. A variety of construction methods can be used, but the choice depends on the location.

Timber

This can be traditional log-cabin construction using round logs of substantial but not over-large dimensions. This works for bigger structures but not smaller ones, as the horizontal emphasis given by the logs conflicts with square or more vertically proportioned buildings. A good overhang to the roof with protruding beams and rafters, shake (shingle), turf or split-log roof looks good. However, this technique is generally not suited to Britain, as it is not traditional, but in central and northern Europe and North America, in forests of big trees, it is a good method. This type of construction is naturally well insulated. Interior partitions of boards, open roof spaces with roof lights or high-level windows in the gables work effectively. Materials can be used on site unless special construction techniques are used.

Sawn timber can be used in all manner of ways. In Scandinavia, construction methods traditional to the

A toilet building made of logs at Akasamylly in Finnish Lapland. The result is a little 'rustic' because the logs are small. However, the main problem is the sole use of window holes cut into the doors to give light. This is inadequate, and may cause privacy problems.

This Swedish example is an excellent composting toilet. The sawn log construction is sturdy. It uses traditional overlapping boards for the roof. Windows in the gable give adequate light and privacy.

A large toilet building with over-hanging pyramidal roof of sawn timber construction. The large skylights give good illumination to the interior. Cannop Ponds, Forest of Dean, England.

A toilet building made of non-natural, though traditional materials – corrugated iron – in this Australian example from the Snowy Mountains. This approach is an alternative to more vernacular or 'folksy' styles.

landscape have been adapted for use in recreation buildings. Timber frames clad in overlapping vertical boarding and roofed with specially milled boards for waterproofing work very well in a drier continental climate. In wetter conditions such as Britain or the Pacific Northwest of the USA, where timber warps, this method is not suitable unless waterproof material can be used beneath the roofing timber. Shakes (shingles) can be used for roofing, as can other materials such as profile steel, which can be obtained with integral insulation, or old-fashioned 'corrugated iron', still a vernacular material in Australia and New Zealand. The coarser textures of wide roughly sawn boards and board-on-board or overlapping clapboarding blend with those found in wilder settings. Vertical boarding looks good in forests with plenty of vertical shapes. Horizontal boarding can look better in open landscapes with more horizontal lines.

Timber can be left to weather to a dull silvery grey, which fits into most landscapes. Stains can also be used to give colour and to help preserve and fireproof the wood. Bright colours should be avoided in favour of the more subdued tones found in the landscape – rusty red, ochre, mossy green, greys, sandy browns and black – which relate to the rock, soil and natural vegetation of the locality.

Buildings often need to be made to hug the ground to reduce their visual impact, and so darker colours should be used on the roofs than on the walls. Emphasis can be given to the doors and certain parts of the framing, perhaps with a brighter colour used sparingly.

Two examples of toilet buildings using traditional materials for a desert setting: (left) is made of stone and (right) adobe for the landscape of Arizona, USA.

Other materials

Stone can be a good material where it is plentiful in the locality. The same basic forms and layouts can be constructed, with stone used in the supporting walls or as cladding around a timber frame or cinderblock (breeze block). Stone construction needs careful craftsmanship. Different stone types are built using different methods. Drystone walling techniques can be used, with hidden mortar to secure the stones. Natural or rough-quarried rock is usually better than cut and dressed stone except in specific circumstances, such as using a vernacular building form. Artificial or reconstructed stone can have an unfortunate suburban appearance and is usually unsuitable. Brick is an inappropriate material in most circumstances unless reflecting a local style or if rendered with wet or dry dash roughcast (a mixture of wet cement and stone chips spread on the wall surface or dry stone chips applied to damp cement on walls respectively). The same applies to cinderblock, which can be a cheap material for construction, and can be clad with roughcast or stone. Roofs for stone buildings can be tile, slate or flags, occasionally profile steel or corrugated iron. Wooden roofs do not look appropriate with stonework.

In hot, dry climates other materials such as adobe have been used, for example by the US National Park Service in Arizona and New Mexico. This uses traditional materials and construction which fits very well. Flat roofs are acceptable in low-rainfall areas and are often traditional.

Transparent materials such as toughened glass or polycarbonate can be used for windows or rooflights, occasionally occupying quite a large proportion of the roof area. Coloured varieties such as smoky grey or brown look better than clear.

Details

Details such as door fastenings, hinges and rainwater goods (gutters and downpipes) all need to be considered. Craftsman-type products with chunky, thick dimensions work well. Those produced by the Civilian Conservation Corps for the US National Park and Forest services in the 1930s have a 'folksy' character produced by local blacksmiths, although fussy details should be avoided. Consideration should be given to omitting rainwater goods unless wooden ones can be used on wooden buildings. Plastic gutters and drainpipes look out of place on sturdily constructed buildings in wild settings. Rainwater deflectors above doorways, if needed, can be adequate. Gravel around the building base can collect water without splashing the walls and staining them.

Interior materials and finishes

- **Floor**. Smooth concrete, quarry tiles or wooden boards are all suitable materials for flooring. Whatever the material, it should be easy to keep clean by hosing and sweeping. Tiles are the best because of their durability and appearance, although they are probably the most expensive. They should rise up the walls slightly as a skirting, and end flush with the paving or path material outside, with no step.
- **Walls**. Boarding should be left bare, stained or sealed but not painted, unless the building is of a traditional or vernacular form. Melamine-faced board in earthy colours can also work, especially behind urinals. Cinderblock walls, emulsion painted in matt, pale earth colours, are a fireproof alternative.
- **Ceilings or roof linings**. These should be timber boarding or spaced wooden slats to let light in. Light-coloured stains or natural finishes look good.
- **Doors**. Traditional close-boarded, framed timber construction looks better and is stronger than panel doors or flat plywood finishes. Brighter colours such as reds or oranges frequently help to signal where the entrances are, and give variety and accent points to the design. Handles of wood, zinc-coated steel or chunky plastic look better than some aluminium ones. Self-closing mechanisms are usually essential.

Seven

Picnicking

Having completed the preliminary requirements on arrival, visitors are now ready to enjoy themselves. While they are free to hike, fish, sail or whatever, many people will wish to have something to eat. This usually means a picnic of some sort, perhaps with a fire or stove to boil water for coffee or tea, to cook freshly caught fish or to grill some steak. To many people, it also means finding a picnic table and establishing a base from which other activities may begin.

Behaviour of people in an open space

As well as providing a location in which to eat, with an attractive view and a convenient table and/or fireplace, the picnic spot has to fulfil some territorial requirements. For many people it has to become 'defensible space' for the duration of the visit. Some people establish their space by going some distance along a trail, or to the extremities of the site, where the presence of near neighbours is least likely. Others do not mind the proximity of other people as long as there is some way of creating a physical or psychological distance between them. This is borne out by observation that when people arrive at an area for a picnic or to sunbathe, most try to find an edge – against some bushes, a large tree or the shore of a lake. The next visitor will look for a good spot a suitable distance apart from the first, and so on, until all the first choices are exhausted. Later visitors may choose the widest space between established groups and take up a position halfway between. Others may be forced to use some open ground. What this pattern indicates is that for many people to feel comfortable and relaxed, their personal space is important. There will

always be a range of people with different tolerances of human proximity – some who want to be completely alone, others who always want to be near other people, and a range in between. The layout of a site with picnic tables, fireplaces and benches should reflect this, giving the widest possible choice and making best use of the ground.

There are some interesting regional differences in the way people use picnic sites. For example, in northern European countries such as Finland or Sweden where visiting the outdoors, especially forests, has a major cultural aspect, picnicking is unlikely to take place in a site along with other people and organized facilities such as picnic tables are less likely to be found. In southern

A picnic site in the Troodos Mountains of Cyprus, where very large numbers of people sit crowded together – a type of experience that would not be desirable in many other countries.

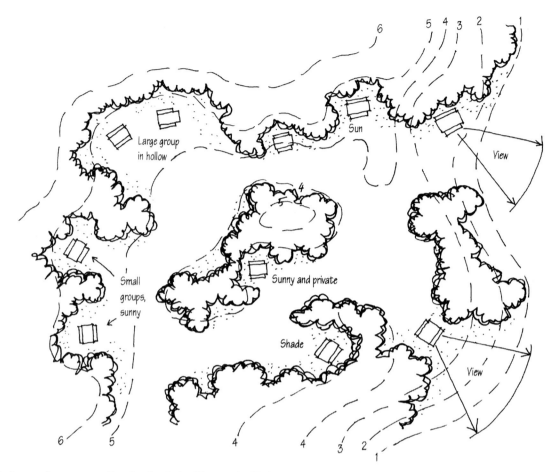

This diagram shows a range of locations for picnic tables on a site. Maximum use is made of edges; some locations are in shade or sun, some are for large or small groups, and others give views.

European countries such as Cyprus, visiting a forest in the mountains is a good way to escape the summer heat of the lowlands and to have a big family party. Because of the risk of forest fires, which are a major problem in southern European countries, picnic sites with communal cooking facilities capable of hosting several hundred people at a time are provided and used quite happily. Most Finns would not feel comfortable in such a place! This difference in the way people have a picnic can also reflect the ethnic background of minority groups in other countries such as the UK or Germany.

Depending on the character of different sites it may be more or less desirable to restrict the presence of furniture, or put more out. A wild (primitive ROS) area may forgo such things as tables, fireplaces or any structures. Lunch is packed in and refuse packed out. In urban settings with higher numbers of people, especially in the vicinity of cafés or visitor centres, more densely arranged sites with picnic furniture may be perfectly acceptable.

Layout of picnic areas

Any site that contains a picnicking area, whether tables, benches or fireplaces are installed or not, should be laid out to give a variety of spaces by using the structure of landform, vegetation or whatever is available. In forests or at the forest edge spaces can be created that offer a range of shelter, open views, sunshine, shade, large spaces for big families, small spaces for couples, and so on. The landform can be used to identify the potential for making spaces and clearings that take advantage of the variety of the sites.

The area should be developed with a hierarchy of spaces of different scales. The first task is to consider the overall extent of the picnic area and the main pedestrian circulation likely to be developed from the car park, toilets and other features such as water edges, viewpoints and trail starts within the immediate vicinity. There will be obvious entry and exit points, which will become important lines of access (desire lines) into the

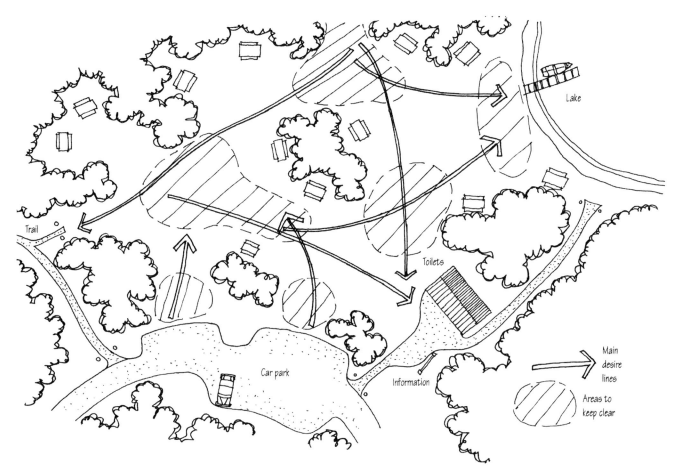

As people walk around sites taking the shortest, most direct routes, it makes sense to predict where these are likely to be, and to ensure that picnic areas avoid them.

area. Spaces within which picnicking can be set should be developed in relation to these circulation routes and the landform, vegetation and site variety described above. Some locations should maintain views of the car park for those who feel safest keeping their car in view, or who cannot or do not wish to carry a great deal of equipment for any distance.

This large layout can be subdivided into different-sized smaller spaces for one or more picnic units. The orientation of spaces should reflect the micro-site features, giving warm, sunny aspects to some and greater shade to others. This will depend on the climate. In Britain, or other cool, moist climates, sunshine in summer is at a premium, and so suntrap sites are much appreciated. However, in the Arizona desert, shade is essential, and this will be a deciding factor.

In enclosed landscapes such as forest glades, the spaces can be subdivided with other trees and shrubs in clumps, groups or promontories from the edge. In open landscapes the landform, if there is any, can be reinforced with shrubs, if trees are not appropriate. Where a particular feature such as a water's edge occurs, then this provides a lure. Picnic spaces should be spread along the edge at wide intervals.

The number of picnic places required will depend on the amount of parking to be provided and the way in which the site serves the main functions for the area. If the main purpose of the site is to stop and picnic, the number of places should be roughly the same as the number of car spaces, although not all need be equipped with furniture. At other sites many people might hike or sail and not wish to picnic, thus considerably reducing the number of places needed.

As well as creating a variety of spaces for picnicking, there will be a need to maintain and manage them over time. There are many examples where an attractive sunny space was created among trees that subsequently grew and shaded the space. Hence trees and shrubs

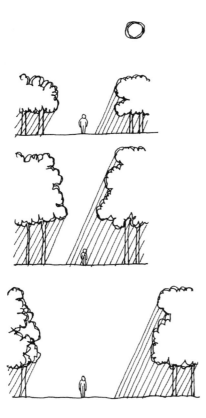

These picnic tables are fixed to the ground. They cannot be stolen, but wear and tear of the ground around them can make a mess.

These picnic tables are moveable. They may be stolen unless very heavy or anchored down in some way but they allow worn areas to be repaired and can be put into storage over the winter.

In wooded areas, tree growth affects the scale of spaces and the degree to which the sun reaches the ground. Management over time might include gradually enlarging open glades so as to maintain their sunny nature.

may have to be cut to maintain the size of the space and its microclimate as well as the access routes or paths among the area. Grass cutting may also be required several times a year during the growing season.

Picnic furniture

Once the area has been laid out to present spaces that are attractive and feel comfortable, any furniture to be provided should be considered. There is a wide variety of picnic furniture of different design and construction to choose from. Many of these are functionally inefficient, ugly and look out of place in the outdoors.

Any furniture should be welcoming and comfortable to use, easy to maintain and able to withstand ill-treatment or theft. There are two basic kinds of table: those fixed to the site and dug into the ground, and those that are movable and placed on top of the ground. The former type is not so easily stolen, and can be of simpler construction, such as separate bench and

table pieces placed together. The latter can be stolen, unless anchored in some way or extremely heavy, and they are generally made in one piece. This means that strength and bracing are needed, which can often present problems to the user.

Sets of fixed tables and benches can be positioned around the site, but any maintenance of the area such as grass cutting has to be carried out around them. Wear and tear of the surface, leading to erosion, puddles and mud, can also occur on busy sites unless the furniture is laid on hard surfacing. It is important to adjust the site to enable the tables and benches to be laid level.

Movable tables and benches allow worn areas to be repaired by shifting the furniture to another place. Their positions can be changed to allow mowers onto the site, or to take advantage of locations of better sunshine, and they can be taken off site into storage during the winter. They often need to be anchored by chain to a buried anchoring device, and sometimes it is difficult to level them.

A good example of a picnic table made suitable for use by people in a wheelchair. Abriachan Community Forest, Scotland.

These examples are of poor general design: (From top – a) Here unevenly split logs have been used, and no attempt has been made to align the table surface and benches, or to place them horizontally. (b) The concrete ends of the table are hard on the knees, the whole effect being crude and brutal. (c) This very common design is difficult for many people to sit at. The cross-supports for the seats mean that the legs have to be swung over the seat in order to be placed under the table – quite a feat for those who are not so young or fit.

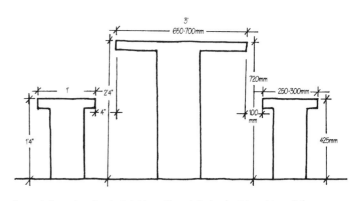

General dimensions for picnic table and bench design (metric and imperial).

Table and bench sets should be designed so that anyone and everyone can use them. Benches that require agility to swing legs over cross-members or beams in order to sit at the table, or which do not permit wheelchair use, are badly designed. Also, the surfaces should be smooth and flat. Rough-cut warped boards or round timber are not acceptable. Adequate room to move about on benches is needed without the risk of banging knees on protruding bits of wood or bolt ends. Table tops should extend lengthways, have gaps left in the benches or be designed with shorter benches placed at one side to allow wheelchairs to fit beneath or at them. A flat and firm route should be provided to tables equipped for wheelchairs.

The dimensions of tables and benches are fairly straightforward (see image above), based on normal dining table and chair sizes, but the depth to which a bench or table is to be set into the ground must be allowed for. Benches that are too low or too high are uncomfortable to use.

Tables and benches should usually be fabricated in sections so that they can be assembled on site, and so that damaged or worn sections can easily be replaced. Maintenance should include tightening of bolts if the structure loosens in very dry weather. Protruding bolts and nuts should be countersunk and trimmed off to prevent snags to clothing or knees.

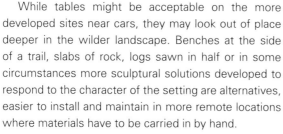

Some furniture made from more natural materials: (a) Rocks placed in such a way as to offer themselves as a picnic table and seats. (b) A log sliced across to give a level surface becomes a bench.

An example of steel tubing for the frame and sawn wood planks for table and bench tops. This offers good leg-room for getting in and out. It fits surprisingly well into this wooded landscape, where the curve of the frame seems to echo the tree-trunks and branches. Acadia National Park, Maine, USA.

While tables might be acceptable on the more developed sites near cars, they may look out of place deeper in the wilder landscape. Benches at the side of a trail, slabs of rock, logs sawn in half or in some circumstances more sculptural solutions developed to respond to the character of the setting are alternatives, easier to install and maintain in more remote locations where materials have to be carried in by hand.

Materials that have been used for tables and benches include concrete, steel, plastic and wood. Concrete frames with wooden bench and table tops are sturdy and durable but unyielding on contact, frequently ugly and look urban. Different types of concrete – varied aggregate colour and rough-textured finishes – have been used, but they rarely fit into the landscape. Only when rock is a significant feature of the site and the table supports are simple and of the same colour does concrete fit in at all.

Metal
Metal, usually steel, is used as a frame and occasionally for the table and bench tops. Painted steel looks urban, while plastic-coated or enamel-coated steel is similarly too highly finished. Galvanized steel can work in the more urban settings and is vandal resistant. With a simple form, and by using wooden table and bench tops, it can be acceptable.

Plastic
Plastic is being used as a wood substitute in some places. This sounds strange, but a material made from recycled plastic looks like some timbers, is hard-wearing, can be worked like wood, and is durable. It might be a substitute for durable tropical hardwoods or chemically preserved softwood on some sites where applying principles of sustainability is important.

Wood
Wood is the all-round favourite, but it can be used well or badly depending on the site and its construction. The usual problems include the use of round timber to give a 'rustic' effect. This tends to look very suburban if the scale is not large enough or the timber cylindrical. The bench and table top must be level, and can be made from half-round sections of logs properly sawn and finished. Sawn wood is better but needs large sizes to be robust, durable, heavy and to blend with the scale of the landscape. Simply cut sections can be bolted together to form strong structures without the need for diagonal bracing, which gets in the way of people's knees. All surfaces should be planed smooth to prevent splinters. Narrow gaps between planks on the table and bench tops should be left to allow drainage of rainwater. Domestic designs that resemble schoolroom desks should be avoided.

This is a better effort at a table from Norway; it is made from round and half-round timber, peeled and without taper, although it remains quite clumsy and looks potentially unstable.

This is a well-designed example from Britain's Forest Enterprise. It has the right proportions, and is placed level. The unit has been set into the ground so that there are no obstructions to visitors' legs or feet. An area around the unit has been laid with gravel to prevent wear and tear of the surface. Where there is easy access for people with disabilities, the table-top can be extended so that a wheelchair can be set at it. Beechenhurst, Forest of Dean, Gloucestershire, England.

Good durable timber can be left untreated to weather, and will last for years if water is drained off and air circulates around the wood. Cedar, oak heartwood, larch heartwood and chestnut can be suitable timbers for this, and to a lesser extent Douglas fir and Scots pine. Some eucalyptus species are also highly durable. Others need preservative before being left to weather. Stains can also be used to tie the furniture into the landscape or to other artifacts.

Paints can be a problem if they crack or split with the swelling or shrinkage of timber. 'Corporate' or house colours should be used sparingly, as they can frequently look out of place for the local setting. Varnish and paint finishes seal the surface so that in wet weather water tends to stand in globules on the surface, taking longer to dry than on stains, which allow water to run off or soak in a little.

Although the designs of many tables and benches in the outdoors originate from the home, other constructions can be considered. If sitting on the ground in traditional picnic fashion is not ideal because of damp grass or an uncomfortable surface, low pallets can be provided. Wide benches or structures that can double as benches or tables might also allow a more free-and-easy way of having a picnic. All these can be experimented with. Some might be more flexible for parties of different sizes or ages.

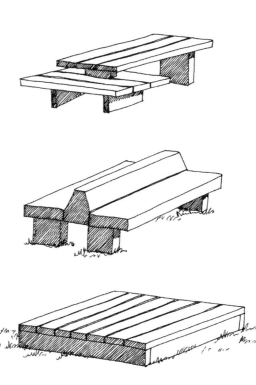

These designs try to vary the traditional picnic table theme: (a) An interlocking bench and table can be used in a variety of ways. (b) Back-to-back benches can double as informal tables. (c) A pallet can be used to sit, sprawl or lie on, and avoids the perils of sitting on damp grass.

This family has taken the opportunity to light a fire and cook some food by the side of a river in northern Sweden. This increases the sense of being away from civilization, and can raise the quality of the experience.

Fireplaces

Although many people bring food and eat a picnic without the need for cooking at the site, the idea of cooking outdoors, or at least of boiling a kettle for tea or coffee, can add much to the experience. In North America or Australia, making a fire outdoors is part of a long tradition connected with frontier life and the quality of self-reliance in wild places. In Europe this is not as pronounced; in fact, lighting fires except at specially permitted places such as picnic sites or campsites is generally discouraged or even illegal, especially in southern European countries. To many people the flavour of food cooked outdoors is quite special, although there can be hygiene risks if grills are not clean or food is not thoroughly cooked. Portable stoves may be safer, and may be preferred by some authorities instead of open fires.

Facilities for cooking outdoors are ubiquitous in North America and quite common in Europe, but relatively rare in Britain. Many picnic places in America have a fireplace of some sort with them as a standard fixture. Perhaps the better climates of continental countries make outdoor cooking a more reliable activity than in rainy Britain.

Fire risks to the landscape are so high in many areas that the choice of suitable sites for outdoor fires and their safe use is fairly important. Fireplaces give a clear signal that lighting a fire is welcomed in that spot and nowhere else. The type of fireplace can vary, and can be related once again to the degree of wildness or civilization offered by the site. In the most primitive areas, if lighting fires is permitted on environmental safety grounds, then the visitor would be expected to cut out a sod, build a fire, make sure it is extinguished after use, and replace the sod to leave few traces. Alternatively, a portable safety stove can be used. Elsewhere some form of hearth can be constructed, with varying degrees of sophistication. There are two basic varieties: low-level campfires and waist-level or altar fires.

Low-level campfires

This type generally consists of a circular hole surrounded by stones, or a steel hoop or drum in which the fire is lit. Food is cooked on a metal grating, plate or from a hook on a pole which may be provided. The grill/hotplate/ kettle hook can be an integral part of the construction, arranged to be adjustable for position and height. Ugly varieties to avoid include those where the stones are cemented together (the cement will crack in the heat), and ones made crudely from old truck wheels. Some excellent proprietary makes are simple to use, with attention to detail such as stay-cool handles and the correct spacing of the grill bars. If wear and tear to the immediate surroundings is a problem, crushed stone or gravel may be laid around the fireplace.

A second version of these campfire types is constructed from larger pieces of rock laid in a U shape, with fold-over grill plates and rudimentary chimneys to help the fire draw. These can be lined with firebrick to prevent the stone from cracking. The large stones can be used as seats or for warming plates, and they look very rugged in rocky terrain. They may not work too well if the wind is in the wrong direction.

The choice of stones or rock is important. Larger rocks usually look better than smaller ones in the large scale of the outdoors. Flatter or more regularly shaped pieces are more stable, and better for warming surfaces or places to keep the coffee pot than round ones, unless these are typical of the area, say, a river bed. Hard stones that are less likely to crack in heat should also be chosen if possible, such as igneous or metamorphic rock types.

Waist-high or altar fireplaces

These have greater similarity to the suburban barbecue than the campfire type, and so provide a utility for cooking rather than a social event. They are more convenient, as the food can be prepared on a table and

(Left) This low-level campfire has a stone surround and an ingenious grill/hot plate, which can swing over the fire once it is hot enough. Mount Orford Provincial Park, Quebec, Canada. (Right) This example is constructed of steel plate and set in a concrete base. Abercromby River National Park, New South Wales, Australia.

This is a range of excellent campfire designs to suit many places: (a) A simple circle of large stones to contain the fire. This is the most primitive, least developed variety, and is suitable for the wildest areas. (b) This example from a 1930s US Forest Service design is made of several rocks placed together. Steel rods set into the side sections form a grill, which cannot be moved or stolen. (c) This version, also from the 1930s, has a firebrick lining to prevent weaker rocks from cracking. A grill secured by a chain can be placed across the firebricks. (d) This 1930s design has a special chimney notch to help the fire draw. A specially shaped hotplate can be laid across, fixed to a chain to prevent theft. (e) More recent examples include the use of cast steel rings or drums to contain the fire. This one has a grill welded part-way over the ring.

An excellent steel altar fire with adjustable direction to catch the draught or shelter the fire, and adjustable grill/hotplate with stay-cool handles. Targhee National Forest, Idaho, USA.

A stone-built altar fire with a hinged steel grill, which can be lifted out of the way. This is quite well built, but the surroundings are rather muddy. Westskoven (West Forest), Copenhagen, Denmark.

moved back and forth without bending down. It is less at risk from dogs, from being kicked over or stood on. There are two basic varieties of this type.

The first is the steel pedestal fire. A steel box with an open side and a grill and hotplate is mounted on a steel pole set into the ground. These can be made by a blacksmith or purchased from proprietary makers. The best can be turned to take advantage of the wind direction, have adjustable grills and stay-cool handles. They can be set in a concrete base hidden below ground to deter theft and vandalism. The tops can be detached using special keys, and stored over winter. Treatment with matt-black stove paint helps to prevent them from rusting.

The second type can be constructed from stonework, with a slab of stone as the floor and, if need be, firebricks to make the three sides of the fireplace. A grill can be set into the stonework or laid over the top. This is a substantial structure, which has to be properly constructed to look right. It can be built with an extension for working and storage purposes, possibly surfaced with wood similar to the top of a picnic table. Such structures should be built facing the prevailing wind direction, otherwise getting the fire to draw can be a problem. A variety is also possible built more as a shelf enabling a person in a wheelchair to use them.

Fuel for fireplaces can be wood collected or provided at the site. If wood is not available in some areas such as moors or coasts, or if it is not sufficiently abundant or if it is ecologically undesirable to be collected from the area, then it must be provided by the site operator or brought by the users. If wood is provided, a storage

An altar barbecue system designed to be accessible by someone in a wheelchair. Abriachan Community Forest, Scotland.

bin should be located to service a number of sites. This might even be a shed, as is found in Scandinavia, in order to keep the wood snow-free as well as dry. Wood, cut and split into suitable lengths, can then be provided and, if need be, paid for in some way. This requires maintenance and management, so it may only be appropriate on large sites where the costs can be lower or where unregulated collection of firewood causes problems.

Charcoal can be used, especially in the altar types. Users can bring their own; it provides more heat, is easier to carry and produces less ash.

The campfire circle: a large fire area surrounded at a safe distance by log seats. Ideal for summer evening singsongs!

This site at Listvyanka on Lake Baikal in Siberia suffers very badly from litter. The bins are large capacity but they attract so much it spills out and creates a terrible mess. There is as yet no tradition of taking litter home in Russia.

The area around the fireplace is likely to become trampled and have food remains, spilt fat or ashes and cinders around it. This can be unsightly, and so periodic moving of the fireplace might be considered on heavily used sites. Simple rings and steel altar fires can be moved quite easily. Otherwise, harder surfaces can be provided around picnic tables and fireplaces, which are easier to keep clean and tidy.

Low benches or logs around the campfire types can encourage their use for social purposes. Occasionally, less responsible people are tempted to use the bench tops as fuel, unless they are secured, perhaps by joining them together and anchoring them to chains set into the ground.

Litter

On picnic sites and around fireplaces litter of various kinds is generated all the time. If food sales, such as ice cream on hot days, also take place, then the volume of litter is multiplied many times. There is nothing as unsightly as a site where litter is left lying around.

Thus, litter management at picnic sites is crucial, and there are two approaches. One is to encourage people to take their litter away with them, and not to supply bins anywhere on the site. This is usually successful in the remoter sites, but is less so in the busy ones where litter left by the small percentage of people who are careless or less responsible will still need to be picked up. Signs suggesting that people should take their litter home should then be posted around the site in key locations to and from the car park.

The second approach is to accept that people will want to or are culturally conditioned to leave litter and to provide bins for it. These have to be of sufficient numbers and be located in suitable places, such as next to the exits from the car park to the picnic area and toilets, at the toilets and in key locations in the picnic area. Places to avoid are next to tables (attracts wasps, nasty smells, hygiene risks), attractive views or hidden corners where people have to go out of their way to deposit litter.

Bins have to be convenient for anyone to put litter in and for workers to empty out, and must be secure from vermin, ranging from bears, ponies and sheep to chipmunks, squirrels and seagulls. Depending on the circumstances the bins might require heavy lids of fireproof materials that are chained to frames or posts. While wire baskets made to fit custom designs might be attractive, it is best to use polythene or paper rubbish (trash) sacks placed inside wooden, metal or plastic containers. Many designs for bins exist, most of which suit urban areas but are of inappropriate materials for the outdoors, such as plastic-covered metal, brightly coloured plastic or combinations of them.

Bins should be fixed to a solid base or dug into the ground to prevent them from being knocked over by people or animals. Lids are often needed to prevent the litter from blowing away or animals entering, but sometimes they can be too heavy for small children to use. Smaller, self-closing flaps in larger lids can be used instead. The size of bins should reflect the level of use of the site and the frequency of emptying. Overflowing bins surrounded by rubbish are worse than having no bins at all, and reflect badly on the management of the site.

This is a good design for a large-capacity bin. The wooden slats help it to fit into the forest landscape. The lid, made from black plastic, is unobtrusive. It would probably not be bear-proof. Akasamylly, Finnish Lapland.

Some litter bin designs: (From top – a) A single wooden slat design to hold a wire basket or polythene sack. Unfortunately, the lack of a lid can mean that litter blows away or is attractive to birds and animals. (b) A well-designed bin. The frame and lid are made from galvanized steel clad in timber slats. Litter is collected in a paper sack. The bin is fixed to a firm base such as a concrete slab. Aarhus City Forest, Denmark. (c) An unusual bin made of concrete and fibreglass and painted to fit into the character of its surroundings – ancient cave dwellings at Walnut Canyon National Monument, Arizona, USA. (d) A bear-proof steel bin with special lid, unable to be opened by bears, and weighted with a concrete slab so as to make it impossible to push over. The hard metal character is relieved by the wooden slat cladding, but it should be possible to cover or bury the concrete base. (e) Another bear-proof bin swinging by chains from a stout frame. Made of an oil drum with a special top, this is ungainly and not very attractive.

The best materials for litter containers in the outdoors are slatted timber, half round or sawn and left to weather, or stained to fit into the surroundings, and sometimes zinc-coated steel. Plastic lids of earth tones with animal-proof devices can also be acceptable. The enclosing structure can be emptied by opening the top or a side panel to release the internal sack, which can then be tied up and carried to a truck for disposal. Stone-built devices sometimes fit, but they are not movable, and they have to be emptied by lifting sacks out of the top. Metal frames with lids to hang black plastic sacks have also been used, but they look unsightly, and the bags risk being damaged by people or animals, allowing the rubbish to escape.

In environmentally aware places such as Scandinavia and Germany, recycling of rubbish is practised in the outdoors. Several bins might be located by the car park and people are encouraged to separate glass, aluminium cans and other litter, placing the refuse in the appropriate container to be sent for recycling. While involving more work for the operator, this vastly reduces the overall requirement to dump rubbish elsewhere and, as good sustainability practice, it should be considered in every circumstance.

Some site operators may be tempted to install big skips or dumpsters on the site so that low-cost collection can take place. These are industrial, unsightly, may not be collected for weeks and develop nasty smells. They also need to be sited for easy access which usually means near the entrance to the car park. They often attract unauthorized tippers, and are examples of cost factors outweighing the needs of the visitor and the environment.

Drinking water

In many outdoor areas the climate and the activities taking place demand that plenty of drinking water is available. Hot, dry weather and any form of exercise can result in dehydration; food utensils might need washing, as might hands or fruit. Water on the site, such as a stream or lake, might not be safe to drink, either from pollution or from bacterial infection such as beaver fever in North America. While visitors should be encouraged to bring their own water, they may not be aware of how much they need. Therefore taps or drinking fountains may be supplied, particularly in rural or urban fringe sites where visitors may be less aware of the need to bring their own supplies. Drinking fountains can be mounted on simple but elegant wooden posts around the car park or at toilet blocks. Fountains are hygienic to use, waste little water as they are self-closing, and prevent people from using water for other purposes to which they might be tempted by ordinary taps (faucets). If water is provided, a mains supply can often be brought in relatively easily if no on-site sources exist, or water can be filtered from a stream and treated on site. Water fountains should be placed at a height suitable for small children and people in wheelchairs to use.

Picnic shelters

In some places the climate and the landscape may suggest that picnic shelters could be useful. Examples are: rainy climates, where the benches, tables and grass are frequently wet; hot climates, where shade is important but cannot be provided by trees; windy cold climates, where a warming shelter with a fireplace inside is very welcome; or insect-prevalent locations, where a shelter or hut can reduce their annoyance.

In hot climates, a roofed shelter with no walls is adequate. Sturdy timber uprights and a simple pitched roof built in similar designs to the toilet blocks described earlier will suffice. Versions that resemble large umbrellas can be effective and decorative, using a single upright around which a table is constructed. Fireplaces can also be included.

Where strong winds occur, then some walls may be needed to keep out the rain. These can be devised so that at least one half of the shelter will be out of the wind whatever its direction. Slatted sides may

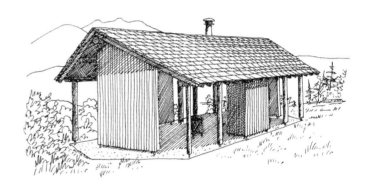

Two examples of picnic shelters: (Top) This old shelter at a state park in Maine, USA, still exists from the 1930s Civilian Conservation Corps (CCC) design. It has stood the test of time well. Sturdy uprights support a shingle roof. Picnic tables are set out beneath. (Bottom) This shelter also has a shingle roof and some side windbreaks. Inside is a stove as well as tables (not shown in the drawing). Glacier National Park, British Columbia, Canada.

prevent wind eddies back into the sheltered space. Benches can be set against the walls and a fireplace provided, with a chimney and movable sides to help it draw.

In cold climates, particularly when winter sports such as cross-country skiing are taking place, completely enclosed shelters with fireplaces could be appreciated by visitors. In Finnish Lapland the traditional Lapp shelters, which look like wooden teepees or wigwams, are used at recreation sites. These have self-closing

This shelter is an enclosed fireplace where cooking can also take place. It is well supplied with firewood. Such a shelter is ideal during the cold, dark winters of northern Sweden, where this example was found.

An example of a log shelter with a fire and benches. This has to be rented and is very cosy in winter. Evo, Finland.

doors and a fireplace in the middle. The smoke may be left to find its way to a hole in the roof, or may be given a chimney.

Shelters near the car park should be better finished than more rudimentary structures located in wilder settings. If there are toilets on the site, the shelter should relate to them architecturally, in form and materials. Some of the old Civilian Conservation Corps designs for the US National Park Service in the 1930s are excellent examples designed to fit into different landscapes.

Eight

Children's play

Our visitors are now fed and watered. They should have plenty of things to choose to do. For families, one of the options is for the children to play for a while, either with or without their parents' participation. Play provides an important opportunity for children to learn about themselves, their limitations and the world around them. This may be more beneficial than taking children, particularly small ones, along with parents on a hike, where they might become bored, overtired or frustrated. In urban edge situations children may also have the opportunity to go and play in the nearby woods or other natural area, not only as part of a day out. This is to be encouraged.

In the past few years it has become obvious in many countries that children are not being allowed out to play freely as they once did. Competing attractions such as computers and video games are causing generations of children who not only lack physical fitness and are suffering from obesity but who are also losing out on many benefits that play provides. Research from Scotland suggests that adults who visit natural areas, woodlands and the like also did so freely as children and that, conversely, those who do not visit as adults did not do so as children and are less likely to feel comfortable doing so. This means that unless children develop a level of confidence about being in the outdoors at quite a young age, they are more likely to grow up with no motivation and a fear of such places, potentially leading to whole generations failing to benefit from physical exercise and the positive effects of being close to nature. The reasons children are not allowed out by themselves in countries such as Britain include traffic danger, fear of children being abducted by strangers, fear of the children hurting themselves and a generally increased sense of risk. While such child protection concerns are clearly important to some extent, they should be placed in context and the damage done to children by not being able to gain fitness, confidence and self-reliance may well outweigh any benefits that such over-protection might be thought to have. Managers should recognize that parents need to feel that they can let their children out to play in a safe but not over-protective environment where some risk-taking in a controlled way is desirable, and endeavour to provide such opportunities. An understanding of play theory and the benefits of play is essential for this.

Play theory

Quite a lot of research into children's play and its place in the outdoors was conducted in Britain in the mid-1980s by the Forestry Commission and the Countryside Commission for Scotland. This has since been developed and more experience of its provision gained by providers of outdoor recreation, particularly in Britain.

Many people think of play as a physical activity, letting off steam and getting rid of surplus energy. This concept gave rise to many municipal play areas that used to be, and many still are, just collections of equipment for swinging, sliding and climbing. Most recent research suggests that this is too simple a view, and that play fulfils more important aspects of a child's development. The natural environment presents an ideal setting for play, which should not be overlooked.

In observing children's play – and they do this either as a natural response or by learning from each other – three broad types emerge:

- **Motor play** is physical activity, such as running, jumping, swinging and climbing. The activities help to develop robust hearts and lungs, and strong, flexible muscles. They encourage children to be fit and healthy.
- **Social play** occurs as children learn to interact with one another in social situations. There are four levels at which social play occurs. The first is **solitary play,** in which the child plays on his or her own and with their own materials. The second is **parallel play,** where the child is with other children and playing alongside them. They may share materials but they do not influence what each other does. The third level is **associated play**. Here all the children are engaged in a similar activity, communicating about it and sharing materials. However, there is no sense of organization amongst the children or a goal to what they are doing. Fourth, **co-operative play** can develop, in which the children organize themselves as a group to participate in a particular activity. Some will emerge as leaders, others will be more or less content to follow that lead.
- **Cognitive play** occurs when the child begins to learn about his or her relationship with the environment and various cause and effect relationships. This may involve physical effects that can be repeated, or ones where there is some uncertainty and unpredictability involved. Children use this play to develop and perfect aspects of their behaviour.

It is rare for play solely to encompass one of these types: usually they are blended together to a greater or lesser degree. Team games like football consist of lots of physical activity, the social interaction involved with co-operative play, and the development and practice of skills with a cause and effect nature. An activity such as constructing a tree house has a similar mixture. The activity requires the social organization of a task between several children, physical activity in fetching materials and climbing about in the tree, and the development of an understanding about materials, how they fit together, the use of tools, and so on. In the right circumstances, when provided with the right stimuli, the play can be constructive as described above.

Children play in different ways at different ages. This needs to be taken into account when considering how to provide play opportunities, as otherwise some age

This play area, in a forest, is much more interesting than the average urban example It uses the forest for inspiration although it still misses opportunities to use the forest more widely. Abriachan Community Forest, Scotland.

groups may be frustrated. The different stages of play can be described as follows:

- **Functional play** dominates play from 0 to 2 years, and generally starts with simple, repeated actions. Children learn what a different action does, and they repeat it until it is perfected. Later they are pleased with the results of their action. Simple activities of a motor variety and objects to be carried, dropped or thrown should satisfy the early stages. Later such play remains important, but it is subsumed into more complex play. The levels of skill required to become adept at new functions are higher.
- **Constructive play** develops from functional play. Instead of merely repeating actions, the child begins to use materials in a more creative way: for example, building rudimentary sandcastles rather than just filling and emptying buckets of sand. The constructive aspect can be nurtured by providing materials that allow children to build, demolish, alter and rebuild. There should be sufficient materials and equipment for use by a number of children at a time. The natural environment is full of potential materials for constructive play.
- **Symbolic play**. Once children begin to talk they can use words and images in play. The world of make-believe and imaginary situations develops, through which they can explore conflicts and needs. This helps to develop an understanding of the environment and how it can be managed. Without this experience, their ability to anticipate and adapt to changing circumstances is reduced.

- **Role play**. This is believed to contribute to social, creative and cognitive skills. The child pretends to be different people in different situations together with others. The situations might be ones already experienced by the children, or entirely make-believe.
- **Rule games**. Children eventually become able to organize their experiences into logical concepts, and they become interested in games with rules. These range from board games to team games out on the sports field. Children can make up their own rules, but unless they are supervised or have some way of keeping the rules, disputes can occur and frustration develop. Rule games become popular from around the age of 6 years.
- **Co-operative play** is the most fully developed type of play (see above). This play needs opportunities and facilities such as open areas or structures that will accommodate several children at a time. Solitude remains a valuable asset, and children may want to go off to a quiet place on their own to reflect on things or to pursue a solitary activity.

From this it is clear that most of the basic requirements and skills of adulthood are to be found in children's play. Hence providing for play can be an important part of a recreation experience.

Whether children play as part of their evenings, weekends or school holidays in nearby nature or as part of a family day out (where there is more likelihood of parental participation), it is worth understanding that they go through phases of interest in the outdoors. These phases are different for boys and girls and they relate to the stages of development that children go through. It must also be noted that older children may participate in activities that adults may not consider 'play' in the strictest sense and which are seen as anti-social.

Young children, pre-school age, should play under parental supervision but be allowed to experience all sorts of environments and also be allowed to get wet and dirty. Primary age children when they reach 7 or 8 should be capable of crossing roads unaccompanied, of riding a bike and (nowadays) of using a mobile phone. They should be allowed to play by themselves in well-managed but still 'wild' areas close to home or as part of a recreation site. They will enjoy constructing things and are keen on exploring, on wildlife, especially 'mini-beasts' and on getting wet and muddy. Later primary school or early secondary school age children will become more adventurous as their confidence increases and be keen to range further afield. These groups may also be wary of meeting older children or late teenagers and they may feel threatened by them to some extent.

At about the age of 14–15 in girls and 16–17 in boys there is likely to be a sudden loss of interest in the outdoors (except for a minority of boys who develop and maintain an interest in activities such as fishing or bird watching and for girls who remain keen on horses). This loss of interest is connected with the onset of puberty and the development of adolescence when social concerns become more important, especially among girls. Later teenage boys may then return to the woods or other places for their own social activities away from the gaze of adults, perhaps to try what are normally deemed to be anti-social activities such as beer drinking, smoking, drugs or sexual activity. This is not play but is part of a necessary stage of development that needs to be accommodated somewhere and somehow. It may cause damage to the site or play equipment, it may frighten older people and women and younger children. These boys should grow out of this phase and then, hopefully, return to become active users of the outdoors in their adult years. If the boys are also active in youth organizations, their difficult phase might be better managed. All too frequently it is boys from deprived backgrounds who may indulge in this less welcome behaviour in urban fringe situations. More work is needed to understand how to engage with them rather than treating them as proto-delinquents.

This pattern of engagement with the outdoors provides a context within which the provision of play needs to be set, provided for and managed sensitively. The outdoors supplies some wonderful opportunities for play. There is a great range of new environments, features, materials and wildlife to see and explore. This exploration can help children to relate to nature and to learn and understand about food, shelter, reproduction and death, as well as how to respect and care for nature. There are several major advantages that the outdoors can offer to the principles of children's play.

Most children experience primitive fears, such as being alone, being in the dark, falling, monsters or wild animals, loud noises, or getting lost. In a natural area that parents know is safe, the child can explore these natural fears and experiment with the feelings they produce. In this way children can be more easily prepared to face life's dangers. An outdoor recreation area is a good substitute for the home neighbourhood, which may be physically dangerous, for example, because of heavy traffic, so that children may not be allowed out to explore their local area. A safe way of reaching places where such play can take place is needed, especially if busy roads have to be crossed close to home.

Getting to know your way around, finding the way between places and the mental mapping needed for this can be developed by experiencing different parts of the landscape, such as landforms, vegetation, rocks or water. Places with winding paths, no street names and different components from the urban setting can help with this.

Children can be as prone as adults to the over-stimulation given by urban settings. The wilder places can help them to wind down and increase their awareness of other things, where to get wet or dirty is expected rather than deplored. Children with ADHD (attention deficit hyperactivity disorder) may benefit enormously from this type of exposure.

The play that children enjoy in the outdoors as part of a visit is much more likely to be with other members of the family, especially parents who wish to relax and enjoy themselves. This helps in a number of ways.

Parents are likely to spend more fun time with their children, and the supervision they provide helps to give the child confidence to test themselves more: climbing higher, jumping further or exploring more scary places. It also means that the play area has to have more challenges for children who still have short attention spans by stimulating their imagination and communication skills. Parents can help children with disabilities to obtain the same thrills as they would normally only watch able children experiencing.

The outdoors as a playground

Compared with most urban environments the outdoors already has many key ingredients in a natural or semi-natural state. These ingredients present no dangers to children if used correctly and managed properly, while at the same time avoiding the reduction of excitement found in urban play areas. A balance must be struck between the need for children to express themselves and unacceptable risks of injury.

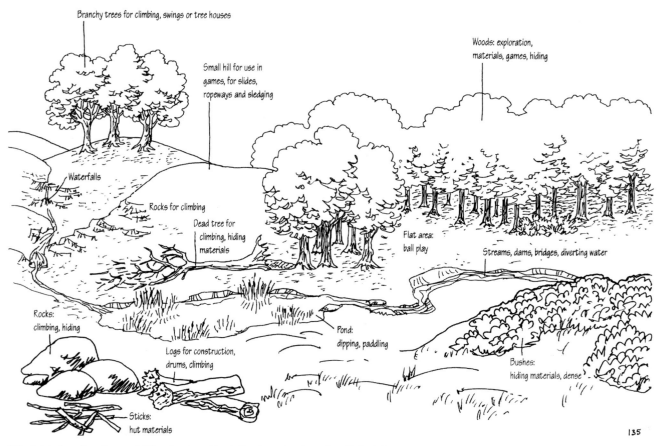

Branchy trees for climbing, swings or tree houses

Small hill for use in games, for slides, ropeways and sledging

Woods: exploration, materials, games, hiding

Waterfalls

Rocks for climbing

Dead tree for climbing, hiding materials

Flat area: ball play

Streams, dams, bridges, diverting water

Rocks: climbing, hiding

Pond: dipping, paddling

Logs for construction, drums, climbing

Bushes: hiding materials, dense

Sticks: hut materials

135

This sketch shows how the possibilities of a piece of land offer themselves for various kinds of play.
Even the most ordinary places have something to offer.

Rocks used for climbing, jumping or hiding – either natural or specially put in place.

Climbing trees or playing on a platform in a tree are opportunities that everyone should be able to experience.

- **Space** is usually greater, so that exploring the area takes much longer. Games can take up more space, and it will be easier to find somewhere quiet. There is plenty of room for places for small children to be separated from those for older ones.
- **Landforms** can be a great asset. High points, steep slopes, valleys, dark hollows, ledges and natural amphitheatres all provide excellent starting points for role-playing games, as places to explore and conquer and locate challenging equipment. Swings are always more exciting where they fly out over a hollow. Ropeways can run across valleys or down slopes. High points make 'castles', or give views to the wider world. Rolling down slopes, climbing steep banks and hiding in hollows or small caves are further ideas.
- **Water** is a magnet to everyone, especially children. Running water can be dammed or channelled, squirted, splashed, bridged, fished and used in many other ways. Ponds or shallow lakes can be paddled in, sailed on, made to splash when stones are thrown in, fished in and so on. They may also present dangers unless children are well supervised. Pumps, taps, grooved and hollow logs, stones and planks all help the imaginative use of running water.
- **Rocks and stones** can be used *in situ* if they are too big to move for climbing, although they must not be too high or rough. They can supply hiding holes, shelter, imaginary defences, castles or dens. Smaller stones can be moved to build with, to dam a stream, to make stepping stones, or to be used as seats. Gravel and sand can be dug, shovelled, drawn in, made into hills and used for all sorts of games.

- **Grassy swards** permit all manner of impromptu or organized ball games, as well as running around, lying on and rolling down a hill or slope. Ball games in natural open areas can be more stimulating than on an urban playing field, especially when a ball shoots off into nearby undergrowth.
- **Trees and shrubs** also give plenty of opportunities for play. Climbing trees is a rare pleasure to most urban children, and is usually far less dangerous in a forest with soft earth and dead leaves beneath it. Broad-leaved trees with spreading branches are safer than conifers. Getting used to heights, developing climbing skills and seeing the world from a new perspective are all values associated with tree climbing. Swings may be attached to sturdy branches and tree houses constructed, which children can relate to fairy tales, folk legends or other stories.
- **Shrubs** are often as tall as or taller than children, and so they give a greater sense of enclosure. Adults are tall enough to be able to look into areas where children are exploring and so oversee them. Shrubby areas are also ideal for making 'dens', and they provide other materials such as twigs, leaves or edible fruit. In the right circumstances dead wood can be used to light a fire and experiment with camp cooking (see Chapter 7).
- **Vegetation** can also be used to separate the overall area into different spaces for different uses. It can give shelter, shade, a physical barrier, for example, against dogs, and show seasonal changes to help children become aware of the cycles of the natural world.

- The outdoors offers a chance to observe **wildlife** at relatively close quarters. Shy mammals will mostly move away while birds, butterflies, beetles, frogs and toads may all be more easily seen. Chapter 11 expands on ways to incorporate wildlife watching into outdoor recreation.

Provision for play

Although most urban play areas are equipped with elaborate and colourful structures, it does not follow that these need be used in the outdoors; indeed many may offer only a low play value. We should instead start by making the most of what the site has to offer, and add artificial components selectively to enhance and dramatize rather than to substitute for natural objects. In this way the unique quality of play in the outdoors can be highlighted.

The selection of the area in which to develop play is an important decision. Finding a place that is near to the picnic area and car park and yet has many of the resources listed in the previous section would be ideal. Some areas will be well endowed with landform. Others are going to be good for water, while some may have few features unless these are introduced. Mounds can be created in flatter areas; quick growing shrubs can be used to provide enclosure and mystery if the site is too open. Natural materials such as rock, sand, logs and branches can be brought onto the site.

Site design will be needed to develop some of the features, and to divide the area into zones suitable for different age groups. Such zones can be signalled with certain key structures to show the size of child expected, by placing more seats for parents near areas for small children and also by signs.

More compact sites may have sections with closely spaced play structures, while larger ones can be more dispersed. A play trail can be developed, where paths lead from one area to another through woodland or

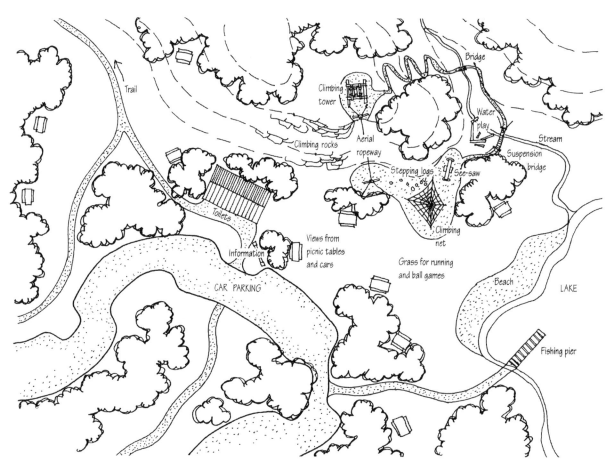

The layout of a play area has to be incorporated with the layout of the other components of a site so that it all works functionally in terms of people's circulation, safety, supervision and freedom.

among shrubby areas. This can heighten the sense of exploration and discovery, and also challenge some of those fears described above, yet reduce the risk of actually getting lost by providing markers or a path.

A few structures of a more dramatic sort can enliven most sites, but opportunities to explore and develop the social and cognitive aspects of play are important. Collecting and using materials found on the site to construct features is usually more interesting and creative than using those that are provided. A 'den' or hut built from branches and other vegetation can provide far higher play value than a readymade hut, however artistic or cunning it might be.

Safety of play areas

Safety aspects must be considered at all times during design, especially when new structures are being provided and children being invited to use them. When moving structures are included, whether they be rope swings from branches or something more sophisticated, such as an aerial runway (zipline), safety margins around them are vitally important. The circulation for children moving from one place to another around the site needs to avoid crossing beneath such structures in order to prevent injury (see image below).

Any structures likely to be moving, or of any height above ground, must be properly constructed in order to take the weight of children and to be durable. Soft materials such as bark should be laid beneath high features, and moving parts should be designed for strength and to prevent trapping fingers. Good design can increase the apparent risk while ensuring safety. Beams can be wobbly to walk on yet safely fixed; swings can seem to go higher than they actually do; scramble slopes can appear tall yet comprise several levels with safe ledges in between to reduce possible drops.

(Opposite) Safety and the proximity of different pieces of equipment must be considered: (Top) This layout allows safety or minimum-use zones around different play structures. These must not overlap. (Bottom) An example of recommended minimum-use zones around moving equipment such as a swing.

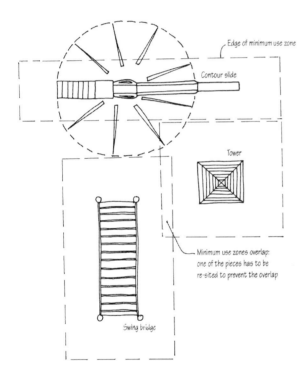

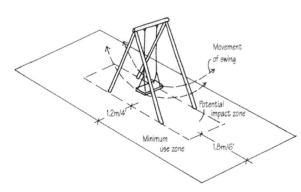

An example of a play area at Tervete Nature Park in Latvia. There is no safety surface, something that would be necessary in other countries. It uses a lot of wooden structures made from local materials.

A sketch of a play trail where children can move from one interesting piece of equipment, structure or experience to another.

Themed play areas

As well as making use of the natural attributes and materials of the site it is possible to develop aspects of play around a specific theme. This can be used to impart a special quality to reflect those of the place and thus enhance its cognitive play value. Often the recreation area will have particular geological, historical or natural history features that lend themselves to the development of play. Sculptors can help to create stimulating structures that relate to the special character and thereby add further interest.

In a forest, for example, the trees and the forest animals offer an abundance of ideas:

- Climbing structures, tree houses and ropeways can be developed to take children up into the tree canopy, using ropes and swings to descend.

- Hollow tree-trunks and holes under root plates can be used for crawling through, while spiders' webs, giant badgers' setts and other animal homes can be recreated.

- As fairy tales abound in forests, meeting gnomes, elves or goblins can also be built into the play area.

- A maze cut among small trees, bridges that tilt as you walk along them, structures that blow in the wind or are operated by ropes to make strange noises, all stimulate the imagination, spring surprises on the children and help them to overcome some of their latent fears.

- Hollow logs can make drums to send signals or to create strange music.

- Teams of children can play mystery games, or pretend they are the Swiss Family Robinson or Robinson Crusoe.

Children can use their own imagination and materials found in the landscape. Here a primitive hut has been made from branches. Dalby Woods, Sweden.

This interesting bridge has a drawbridge section on it. Walk on to it and it descends, allowing a person to cross. Haldon Forest, Devon, England.

Music in the outdoors: (Left) A series of hollow logs hanging from a frame and arranged to make different notes. Wooden mallets are used to play tunes. Helsinki City Forest, Finland. (Right) Large hollow logs make primitive drumbeats for sending messages.

In water areas, provided the water is not too deep or liable to flooding, there are many ideas to be developed:

- hollow logs, or ones with channels cut along them, which can be used to divert streams;
- suspension bridges and stepping stones;
- small dams with sluices;

- floating pontoons or shallow-draught boats;
- small waterfalls that shoot out over ledges, allowing children to crawl behind them without getting too wet;
- piers from which dipping with nets can take place;
- paddle wheels that can power pumps or lifting devices;

Water is always attractive. Here, hollowed split logs make conduits, which can be moved to channel the water in various ways.

The army-style assault course is always popular with older children. It offers a physical challenge, which fits in with other challenges of the outdoors.

This example of an imaginative play structure is highly popular with visiting children. Parents are involved too, so that the whole family gains from the experience. Ringwood Forest, Hampshire, England.

Part of a play area at Grizedale Forest, Cumbria, England. Here sculptors have created play equipment based on different kinds of wild animal. The pheasant is a slide. Note the extensive use of bark as a safety surface, retained by a log edge. This is an ideal surface to use in outdoor areas.

- shallow sandy-bottomed pools that permit bathing or paddling.

Fitness and strength can be developed using assault course-style equipment set out along a path. Scramble nets, climbing walls, balancing beams, stepping logs and an aerial ropeway can be exciting and competitive.

For smaller children, structures in the form of animals and their activities can be fun:

- slides made in the form of birds or animals;
- snakes made from logs to walk on;
- tunnels like rabbit holes;
- spiders' webs to climb on;
- a merry-go-round like a fox chasing a rabbit.

(Top) Some structures or equipment can be made accessible to children with disabilities so that they can join in as much as they are able to do so. (Above) A play area at Cary, North Carolina, designed to be accessible to children with a range of disabilities. The ramp allows access up to the structure and there are facilities set at a level suitable for wheelchair users.

Play for children with disabilities

The play area, structures and activities should be widely accessible to children with disabilities. With some help from their parents or friends they should be able to obtain as much of the play experience as possible. Slides, ropeways, swings, water diversions, pond dipping, mazes and drawbridges are all examples of features capable of being used by children with disabilities, under supervision and perhaps with some help. Such delights should be available to all and are worth the extra effort, especially for disadvantaged children, who may be experiencing them for the first time.

Materials and construction

Apart from the naturally occurring materials or earthworks, any structures constructed in the play area should be robust, free from safety hazards, and as far as possible should possess sustainable origins. Timber is likely to be a common material, and is best used in large dimensions because of the larger scale of the outdoors and to distinguish it from urban play areas. Other appropriate materials are sisal and polypropylene rope, galvanized chain and bolts. All of these are durable, require little maintenance, and can be constructed to meet the various safety and construction standards required by different countries or states. The following are some hints on construction and safety.

- Posts should be set well into the ground, and should normally be concreted in. Take care that the top of the concrete does not protrude above ground level. Even if it is set down low at construction, erosion during use might expose it.
- Ensure that bolts are countersunk, and that protruding ends are cut off cleanly and as flush with the nut as possible.
- Chains should have links that cannot trap small fingers.
- Timber should be peeled and rounded before use. Edges should be sanded and chamfered to reduce the risk of splinters.

Other materials that may be used are:

- old car tyres, which can be recycled as swing seats or shock absorbers on moving parts such as aerial ropeways;
- fibreglass (glass reinforced plastic – GRP) for tubes or special constructions;
- stainless steel for contour slides;
- galvanized steel tube for ladder rungs, strengthening of structures and for firemen's poles.

Not all of these are sustainable: wood laminate may substitute for fibreglass and stainless steel under some circumstances.

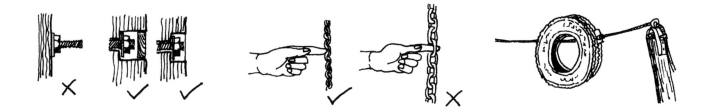

Structures must be safely constructed: (Left) No protruding bolts – trim, countersink or plug them. (Middle) No chains to trap fingers – check link sizes. (Right) Use tyres as shock absorbers on fast-moving equipment.

An example of play for adults as well as children – a system of ropes stretched between trees at different heights, with different challenging means of going along them, while wearing a safety harness and helmet. This one is near Bordeaux in France but it has been franchised in many places.

Materials to be avoided are: non-galvanized or non-stainless steel, as this has to be painted, and rusts too easily; and concrete, as this is too hard, urban, unforgiving and dangerous for children.

Surfacing beneath structures, particularly tall ones, should be soft and resilient so as to prevent injury if children fall. The following materials are well proven and sustainable:

- **Wood chips.** These work well in a forest or countryside setting. They absorb impacts well, are relatively hard-wearing and cheap. Once used or contaminated they can be removed and recycled as mulch.
- **Bark**. Pinebark has similar properties to wood chips. It is soft, has a pleasant 'forest' smell and an earthy colour that blends with the outdoors, and is cheap.
- **Sand.** This is better in seaside areas, deserts, heathland or other sites where bark or wood chips would not fit in or are not available. It is quite soft to land on if it is dry, but it tends to adhere to clothing, get inside shoes and blow into eyes. The abrasive quality of sand can increase wear and tear on moving parts.

Both wood chips and bark need periodic cleaning to remove litter, and must be laid on well-drained sub-bases, as they tend to soak up moisture. This can cause them to freeze in the winter, or ferment and release tannins from the material, which creates a strong-smelling effluent.

Safety surfaces should be retained within log kerbs, which should follow the outline of the safety zones, thus helping to demarcate them. It is essential that they are kept loose and clean. Pets must be kept clear of the area, and all glass objects should be banned. Surfaces to avoid are anything hard such as tarmac, and grass, which also wears too easily, especially under moving equipment.

Adult play

This chapter is entitled 'Children's Play' but it should be remembered that play does not and should not stop when children grow up. Playful activity is still necessary for adults. While the types of play advocated and described here are not especially suitable for scaling up for adult use, nevertheless, there are some activities that can be shared and undertaken by both children and adults. An example that has become very popular recently is a system of cables suspended at different levels in trees – some very high up. Moving from tree to tree – where there is a platform – by a range of devices while held safely in place by a harness clipped to the line can be very exciting. The system is used under supervision and it is only confidence that determines which level someone follows.

Paintball is another form of play suitable for both children and adults. Kicking a ball around, swinging off ropes or large-scale swings and assault courses are other examples. It is worth considering how such adult play can also be incorporated into the design of a visit.

Nine

Trails

Visitors may wish to explore the outdoors on foot, on horseback, on cross-country skis or by all-terrain bicycles. Some may wish to navigate by themselves using map and compass. Others, perhaps the majority, may need a path or trail to follow.

Before considering trail provision, it is worth deciding whether a trail is needed. Creating a surfaced path with its accompanying disturbance may have an adverse effect on the spirit of a place, removing the sense of wildness and introducing an atmosphere of tameness and obvious evidence of management. The trail might also disturb fragile habitats and increase pressure by concentrating visitors in one area. If no trails are provided, then erosion and unplanned path development may occur anyway, unless people are managed so as to disperse their approach and reduce pressure. Guidance to visitors on the fragility of areas and the need to take care might be needed.

Purpose of trails

In many cases, the effect of trail development on the special qualities of a place is outweighed by the need to prevent wear and tear and to control the access to an area by visitors. If a trail is needed, consideration should be given to the particular theme that it will be used to explore, and the objectives of its provision. Themes may be one of or a combination of the following:

- general exercise and relaxation by anyone, with an emphasis on multi-accessibility;
- scenic viewing leading to a viewpoint;
- wildlife viewing;

- visiting archaeological sites or other cultural features;
- educational visits to explore geology, geography, natural or cultural history;
- physically demanding routes for serious exercise.

The types of users of the trail will determine its physical characteristics, such as:

- surfacing, gradients and lengths;
- walking only, bicycle only or horse riding only;
- integrated routes, which may give rise to complications or conflicts;
- partially integrated routes involving loops for horse riding and cycling where conflicts are more likely;
- barrier-free routes to allow access by people with disabilities.

Trails can provide:

- a means of access into the outdoors and a route for people to follow with less chance of becoming lost, confronting physical dangers or damaging sensitive places – it signals that access is allowed and that the visitor is not trespassing;
- stimulating exercise in attractive surroundings – steep ascents and some rough scrambling can be incorporated in places;
- a variety of scenery, ranging from vista points to obtain panoramic views down to the small-scale details of plants seen along the side of the trail.

The design and layout of trail routes and surfaces depend on the degree of wildness desired and the wear and tear expected. In primitive settings, no surfacing should be provided except to restore erosion. Conversely, in less wild places used by many people, wide, well-surfaced paths on easy grades may be appropriate and necessary.

The needs of people with disabilities should not be overlooked. People with limited mobility, or wheelchair users, cannot always manage steep grades or rough surfaces, yet they should have a right to experience some of the dramatic views seen by everyone else.

Trail route design

Most landscapes have varying terrain, different vegetation and a variety of places within them. Some may have peaks to climb, others water of various sorts or stands of big trees to walk or ride through. Using maps and aerial photographs, a survey should be compiled of the landscape by walking or riding through it, to identify and record features of interest. These might include viewpoints of various kinds (see below), peaks, narrow valleys, waterfalls, ponds and lakes, cliffs and rock features, stands of special trees, areas of meadow, archaeological or heritage sites, shorelines, caves, dense vegetation, bogs, areas attractive to wild animals, sand dunes, islands, and sunny places at different times of day. All these are attractive features that people are likely to be drawn to, compared with the less obvious, hidden areas, which nevertheless contribute to the spirit of the place.

Hazardous areas and sensitive features where access is undesirable or dangerous must also be surveyed: examples are cliffs, steep loose slopes, easily eroded sand dunes, wetlands, deep water, areas where dangerous wild animals congregate, old mine shafts, dangerous currents, very cold water, vulnerable archaeological sites, areas where disturbance of wildlife and places for solitude may be a problem, and dangerous caves.

As with all recreation provision, the trails need to provide a reasonable match between the various visitor

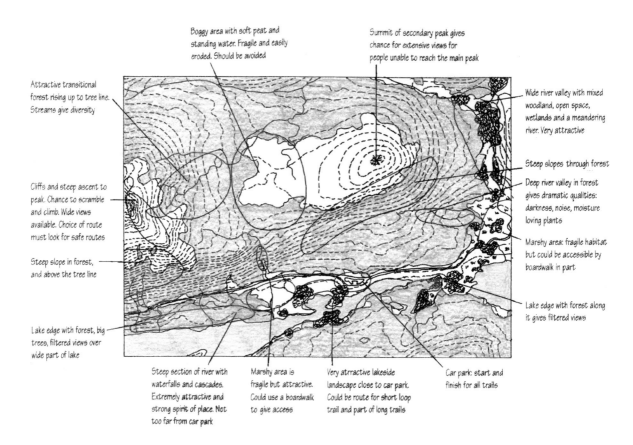

Trail planning: Before laying out a trail it is a good idea to carry out an extensive survey of all the features of interest that might be included on the route, and areas that pose problems for some people or which the trail must avoid because of the risk of damage or disturbance.

requirements and the features that the area has to offer. Large demand and a limited area might suggest wider, better-surfaced paths, as dispersal and lower use would not be feasible. The demand may already have been established at the planning stage or it may be obvious because of existing use gradually built up over some time.

Lengths of trail

Different people may be interested in different types and lengths of walk, depending on who they are, how fit they are and how much time they have. These needs can often be fitted into a range of circular loop walks. Walks of around one hour's duration are quite popular. A half-hour jaunt to a particular beauty spot or vista is also attractive for those with little time. Both of these types should have no barriers, in order to cater for people with disabilities and of all ages.

A two- or three-hour trail or a longer trail may be attractive to those who want to spend more time in the

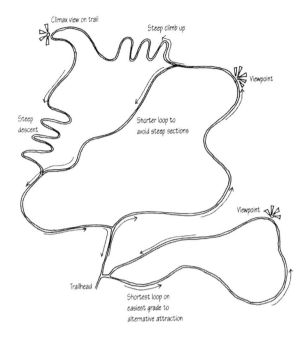

Trails laid out in loops of different lengths offer people a range of physical challenges, time scales or both.

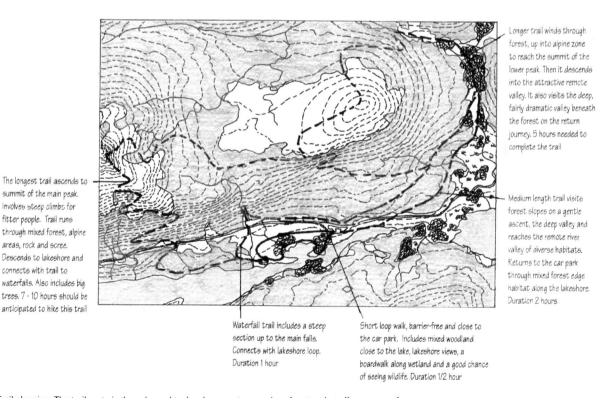

The longest trail ascends to summit of the main peak. Involves steep climbs for fitter people. Trail runs through mixed forest, alpine areas, rock and scree. Descends to lakeshore and connects with trail to waterfalls. Also includes big trees. 7 - 10 hours should be anticipated to hike this trail

Longer trail winds through forest, up into alpine zone to reach the summit of the lower peak. Then it descends into the attractive remote valley. It also visits the deep, fairly dramatic valley beneath the forest on the return journey. 5 hours needed to complete the trail

Medium length trail visits forest slopes on a gentle ascent, the deep valley and reaches the remote river valley of diverse habitats. Returns to the car park through mixed forest edge habitat along the lakeshore. Duration 2 hours

Waterfall trail includes a steep section up to the main falls. Connects with lakeshore loop. Duration 1 hour

Short loop walk, barrier-free and close to the car park. Includes mixed woodland close to the lake, lakeshore views, a boardwalk along wetland and a good chance of seeing wildlife. Duration 1/2 hour

Trail planning: The trail route is then planned to develop a route or series of routes that offer a range of interesting places, views and atmosphere. The best or most dramatic features should be planned as a climax, such as the view from a summit, a particularly beautiful hidden feature or archaeological site.

fresh air and go into wilder places. The length of time to walk such a trail by an averagely fit person should be increased to allow for stops to eat, look at views, swim in pools, and so on.

Even longer trails, taking several days to complete, might be part of a network connecting up with others and ending up at different locations. Walking these routes requires careful planning in terms of food, clothing, accommodation and transport. Examples of these long-distance trails are the Pennine Way in England, the Pacific Crest Trail in the USA and Tongariro Crossing in New Zealand.

The sequence of experiences along a trail route

Having established the qualities by survey and the types of trail required by visitors, the detailed route planning can commence. Much of this can be based on the survey/analysis map, but a more detailed survey will be needed on the ground, exploring the landscape and marking feasible routes ready for clearance or construction.

In most circumstances, the route design should start from the car park/picnic area at a logical and inviting place. Some kind of threshold is a good idea, such as a dramatic stand of trees, a large rock or a bridge over a stream. Beyond that, it is often helpful to design to enable the walker to set a pace and adjust to the type of landscape being entered before the first point of interest is encountered. Wild places may be unfamiliar, so an easy stretch will help to accustom the walker to this before anything too dramatic happens.

Narrow, dark or slightly stressful stretches can be introduced, which have the effect of raising expectations and increasing the sense of contrast between what has gone before and what is coming after. A slight degree of disorientation can give the impression that a small area seems larger than it really is.

The appreciation of scenery can be heightened by gradual disclosure through slot or filtered views before being revealed as a panorama. Where points of interest occur, seats can invite the walker to rest and absorb the surroundings or the view.

If the trail leads through a forest, emerging from beneath the dark canopy into an open sunny area can provide relief and a pleasant surprise. Larger open areas can be skirted by the path, keeping partly in and partly out of the forest edge.

Water is a great attraction to visitors, so trails leading to dramatic views of waterfalls, either to the top where the water disappears over the edge, or at the bottom, with the noise, spray and churning currents, can provide memorable experiences. Water crossings can also be exciting, whether stepping-stones over a smaller stream, a narrow bridge over a chasm, or a more dramatic structure such as a suspension bridge with its swinging movement.

Lakes and ponds also attract access, at least to some part of the shore. Views across the reflective surface of a still lake, the lapping noises of gently waving water, the chance to paddle or cool one's feet – all give a tremendous value, to say nothing of the wildlife that may be seen. When a small lake occupies a hollow, there is also a sense of space and enclosure, which enhances its quality and often gives an aura of mystery.

Curious and unique geological features also arouse interest: caves or overhangs beneath cliffs; strangely eroded rock formations that suggest weird life forms or fossilized trees; narrow canyons or gorges; lava formations; narrow knife-edged ridges or perched glacial erratic edges.

Seashore areas provide natural access routes; people enjoy following the edge of the sea and along such stretches there is rarely a need to go inland.

This set of sketches suggests how a sequence of features can be linked together to give an exciting experience when following a trail: (a) The threshold to the trail should be well marked and inviting, the path leading the walker and giving a sense of direction. (b) A slot view out of the foreground, here sited on a curve for maximum impact and effect. (c) The trail emerges from a dark, tunnel-like space, revealing a sunny open area beyond, increasing the feeling of movement through the landscape and of anticipation. (d) A water crossing will always be an attractive and significant feature where sound, light and movement occur together. (e) Access to a small lake is usually important and worth including. (f) Curious or unique geological features such as wind-sculpted rocks lend a sense of mystery and admiration at the forces of nature. (g) Archaeological or historical sites help to connect people with past human use or associations, and also demonstrate the capacity of nature to reabsorb our efforts. (h) A chance to see some wildlife can be a rare thrill for many people. The trail should maximize opportunities without causing alarm to the wildlife or risk to the viewers.

a

b

c

d

e

f

g

h

Sandy beaches are most attractive, but cliff tops or the edges of shingle beaches are also valuable. The sight of the sea, the noise and the movement of the waves at different seasons and in varying weather conditions and the special quality of light at the ocean – all provide variety, which keeps people returning.

Sites of archaeological or historical value should also be included in the trail route if they are robust. Stone circles, burial mounds or earthworks can be found in what are now wild landscapes in many parts of Britain and Europe. Remains of old settlements – even recent industrial relics or wartime defences – can be interesting. Far from detracting from the wild impact, they can serve to reinforce it, demonstrating how human endeavour can be reclaimed by time and nature. A poignant reminder can be given of the harshness of life and the vulnerability of earlier people trying to scrape a living in harsh circumstances.

Opportunities to see wildlife where they congregate should be identified: for example, salmon runs, bears fishing, deer lying up, beavers and their lodges, ospreys nesting or butterflies basking in the sun. The trail might need careful alignment to minimize the noise, sight and scent of people and hides can give a good view without disturbing the animals. Seeing wildlife can be a rare thrill for many people (see Chapter 11).

A trail should be designed to raise expectations continuously and fulfil those expectations in unexpected ways. The development of the route should pace this, with feature points along the trail interspersed with relatively simple sections, leaving the most dramatic climax until last, to be followed by a calming, more reflective wind-down back to the car park area.

Not every landscape will have all or even many of the features listed above. A trail can be made more interesting by winding the route among different vegetation types, creating spaces in a forest or planting trees in an open area. It should also be designed to respond to landform by rising in hollows and descending in convexities so that it blends in and reduces any feelings of intrusion to a minimum. Features can be created, such as ponds or small lakes; benches can be placed; vegetation can be managed to create a butterfly habitat; or sculpture can be introduced.

Trail construction principles

Once the route of the trail has been selected, it should be cleared, gradients found for barrier-free access (see below) where these are needed, and decisions made on appropriate surfacing.

There are some guidelines to follow when considering trail construction:

- Build as little surfaced trail as possible, if the ground is hard, naturally well drained and can withstand the expected traffic.
- Avoid steps and ramps if possible. This is obligatory on barrier-free trails, and is a general principle to follow elsewhere. Use short, steep pitches if needed in the more rugged places, but generally try to find suitable gradients for comfortable walking.
- Keep paths away from wet and soft ground, especially silt, clay or peat soils if possible. Erosion of exposed soil during rain and attempts by people to walk round muddy places exacerbate soil removal and create unsightly scars.
- Try to avoid routes crossing scree or talus slopes or heavy boulder fields. These can be loose, dangerous or difficult to stabilize.

In places where these guidelines cannot be followed, the construction of firm, dry, well-drained surfaces is necessary. The degree of finish that should be given will depend on the wildness of the landscape, the fragility of the surface to be crossed, the expected amount of use, the availability of materials and the resources available for construction and maintenance.

The standard of construction depends on the kind of trail required. If it is to be used by everyone, including people with disabilities, then a different specification will be appropriate from that expected to be used by fit, energetic people who are well equipped with hiking boots. It is possible to categorize trails as follows:

- **Barrier-free**: this should be easily accessible to wheelchairs, pushchairs (strollers), visually impaired visitors and those with walking difficulties. All weather surfacing, low gradients (not more than 1 in 12 for short stretches only) and no steps are required for such trails, which should be capable of being walked wearing light shoes. Edges should be easily seen or felt by people with visual impairments, for example, by providing a tapping rail.
- **Easy**: good conditions underfoot, gentle slopes, short steep sections or occasional flights of steps if absolutely necessary. Sensible footwear such as stout shoes would normally be needed.
- **Moderate**: some rough places, wet surfaces in parts, some longer sections of steep grades up and down. Wellington boots or hiking boots are desirable, especially in wetter climates and colder seasons.

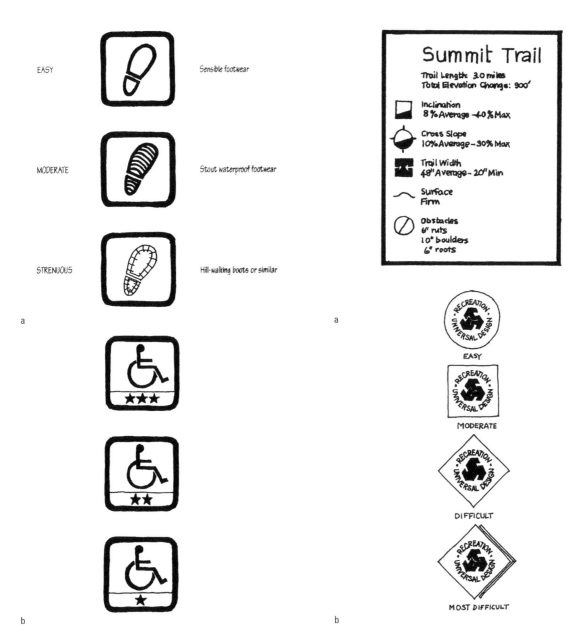

EASY — Sensible footwear

MODERATE — Stout waterproof footwear

STRENUOUS — Hill-walking boots or similar

a

b

Summit Trail

Trail Length: 3.0 miles
Total Elevation Change: 900'

Inclination
8% Average ~40% Max

Cross Slope
10% Average ~30% Max

Trail Width
48" Average ~20" Min

Surface
Firm

Obstacles
6" ruts
10" boulders
6" roots

a

EASY

MODERATE

DIFFICULT

MOST DIFFICULT

b

(a) The symbols make it clear what kind of trail conditions a walker can expect. (b) These symbols help people with disabilities to decide whether they want to attempt a particular trail. Both sets of symbols are used by Forest Enterprise in Britain.

(a) These symbols are used in the USA. A useful way of showing the actual trail conditions for anyone to decide if they want to follow it.
(b) Symbols showing the grading system – based on skiing grades – the graphics are clumsy compared with the British example earlier.

• **Strenuous**: rough conditions underfoot and steep slopes, making hiking boots essential. Where paths lead to higher altitudes there may be sudden changes in weather. Above the tree-line the path may be difficult to detect, and so map and compass skills are likely to be needed. These types of routes include mountain paths, long-distance trails, miners and stalkers paths.

Beyond these categories come routes that demand greater physical fitness, stamina and special equipment, and so are beyond the scope of this discussion.

Once the trail has been categorized, a specification can be developed for an appropriate type of surface. This is most important for trails intended for use by people with disabilities (barrier-free). To enable people to choose trails suited to their individual capabilities, a

This path in a Scottish forest has some problems for disabled users that need to be checked. The gradient may be marginally acceptable as long as the person pushing the chair is strong enough and the surfacing generally firm and smooth enough but the roots protruding from the surface may be enough to create a barrier. This is something that could easily be fixed by adding some surfacing.

star rating system was devised by the British Forestry Commission based on surface criteria set out by the Royal Association for Disability and Rehabilitation:

- **Three stars** indicates a walk with gradients no greater than 1 in 40 (up to 1 in 20 for lengths no longer than 10 m/11 yd) and with a smooth, hard surface without obstruction or potholes.
- **Two stars** indicates a walk with gradients up to 1 in 20 for stretches no longer than 100m/111 yd and with a smooth, hard surface with few obstructions or potholes.
- **One star** indicates a walk with gradients of up to 1 in 12 for stretches no longer than 20m/22yd and with sections of irregular surface no longer than 5m/5.3 yds.

It is a good idea to provide information about the conditions so that people with a disability can decide if it is likely to be accessible to them. A simple map showing the different stretches of different surface, gradient, side slope or obstacles can be very helpful.

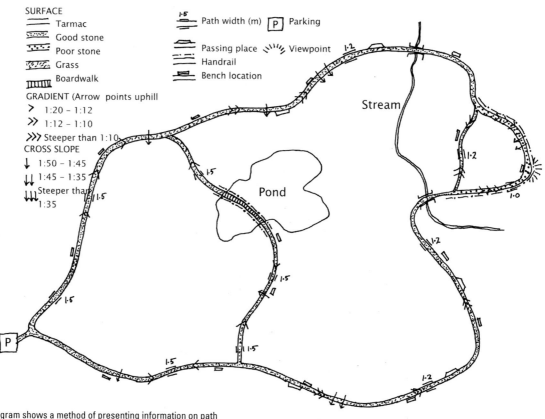

This diagram shows a method of presenting information on path conditions so that a potential visitor can decide beforehand if they are capable of following all or part of the route.

Although building as little trail as possible is preferable, when construction is necessary, it should be to the highest possible standard. This is because poorly constructed trails using inferior materials are unlikely to last long in the exposed, harsh conditions to be found in the outdoors. When they fail, such surfaces are difficult to repair adequately and become a drain on maintenance budgets.

Path drainage

In wetter climates, it is vital that the path is drained properly. As well as culverting small streams or drains that cross the path, its surface also needs to be drained. Water runs down the cut faces above the path, and if not collected and channelled away can cause serious erosion to the path surface and possibly to the foundations. Cut-off drains should be provided on the inside of the path along the bottom of the cut slope to collect water coming down it, and from the path itself. The path formation is best sloped inwards towards this drain. Culverts should be provided at intervals along the path to divert water collected in the side drains and reduce water flow. Silt traps, such as a basin below the entrance to the culvert, will prevent silt from finding its way into streams (see image below).

On steep sections where storms might wash away the surfacing, cut-off drains or water bars should be laid across the path at frequent intervals. These are normally open channels, which can interfere with wheelchairs or buggies. Some can be narrow to reduce this problem, but they are more prone to blockage and need more maintenance to keep them working.

The types of cut-off drain available are:

- a wooden board sunk into the surface across the path at a shallow gradient is functional, but it can trip people;
- a log can be laid across the path, sunk into the surface. A V-shaped groove cut along the length of the log channels the water. It is simple and effective and less likely to trip people;
- a box drain can be constructed out of durable or preserved timber and set flush into the path surface.

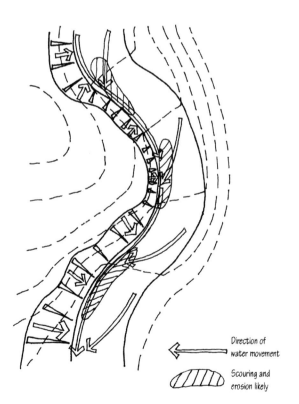
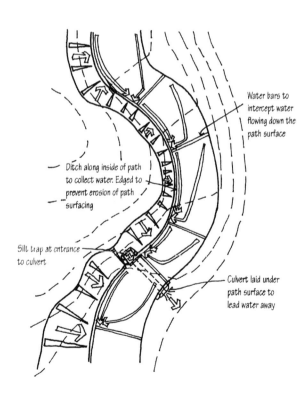

Water bars to intercept water flowing down the path surface

Ditch along inside of path to collect water. Edged to prevent erosion of path surfacing

Silt trap at entrance to culvert

Culvert laid under path surface to lead water away

Direction of water movement

Scouring and erosion likely

This diagram illustrates how to plan for path drainage: (Left) The movement of water and the identification of places where scouring and erosion during heavy rain are most likely. (Right) The positions of waterbars, the drainage ditch, culverts and silt traps are planned to intercept the water before it does any damage.

This wide, well-constructed path on a steep incline is well provided with cut-off drains or waterbars made from half-round logs with a channel cut into them. Krimml, Austria.

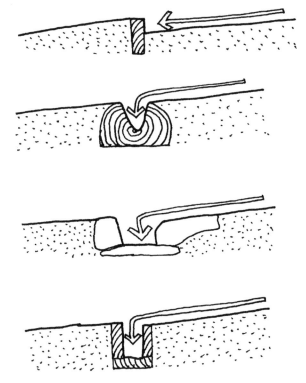

The design of cut-off drains or waterbars: (From top – a) The simplest is a plank set on edge in the path. This can trip people up and is no good where wheelchairs of buggies are used. (b) A half-round log with a channel cut into it is simple, robust and easy to lay. (c) A box drain made from stone is very effective. This also presents problems for wheels. (d) A wooden box is similar to the stone example, but can be prefabricated off-site.

It can be partially enclosed to leave a narrow slit so wheelchairs or buggies can cross, but it is prone to blockage by leaves or larger stones, so will need regular maintenance;

- a similar open cross-drain can be constructed from local stone. Flat stones are laid on the bottom between the sides to keep them apart.

Leading water under paths is best done using plastic culvert pipes. These are strong, light enough to carry into remote areas, and easily cut to lengths using a knife or saw. The pipe is laid in a trench dug across the path at a depth of 300 mm (1 ft) or more on a compacted base to prevent sharp stones from damaging it. The ends of the culvert pipe should be trimmed to match the sloping profile of the path.

If heavier loading is needed, concrete or galvanized pipes are stronger. These take more effort to lay,

are heavier to transport, and require special cutting tools.

Box culverts made from durable timber such as elm or from slabs of stone are a traditional type. These have a place where natural materials are the first choice, but they require more skill to construct than laying a pipe.

If the path edge or the fill material of the base is unstable, a protective surround to the culvert ends should be built of dry or mortared stonework or timber to prevent erosion during heavy storms.

Where the drains across the path may have to cope with sudden, large amounts of storm water, unless pipes are of large dimensions, they can be blocked with debris and cause flooding or wash-out of the path. In such cases, where early maintenance cannot be guaranteed, wider open culverts may be necessary, and walkers can be expected to step or jump across. If the path is in a remote location in rougher conditions,

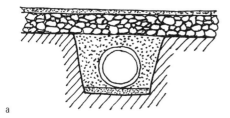

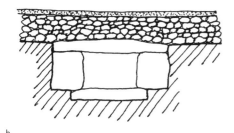

a

b

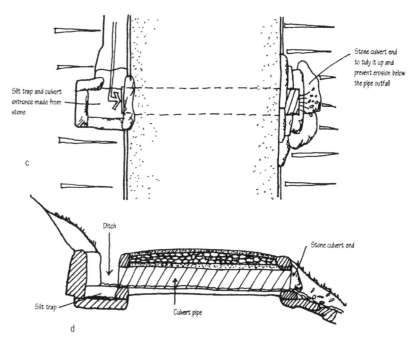

Silt trap and culvert entrance made from stone

Stone culvert end to tidy it up and prevent erosion below the pipe outfall

c

Ditch

Stone culvert end

Silt trap

Culvert pipe

d

Culvert construction: (a) Modern culverts are easily made from lightweight plastic tubing laid in a trench cut to fall across the path. (b) A stone culvert can be made from local materials. This is set beneath the path. (c) A plan view shows the layout of the culvert – its entrance contains a silt trap and its exit is dressed with stone. (d) A section through the culvert, showing the silt trap, the retained path edges and the culvert mouth set around with stone. (e) The culvert exit is tied to the path edge using stone to prevent erosion and to make a tidy result.

e

An example of a box culvert made from local stone and covered in large flat slabs. This is an attractive and durable solution. Glen Affric, Scotland.

wheelchair access may be less appropriate, but users could be advised to carry crossing planks.

Path excavation and surfacing

It is important to select the most appropriate methods of design and construction of the trail for different types of terrain.

Gentle terrain and freely drained mineral soils in areas with low or moderate rainfall

If trail use is light, no surfacing may be needed. The route is merely cleared of debris, trees and protruding branches are cut back to clear the way, drains or small streams are piped, and obvious rough places are smoothed or filled with local material. The path width will define itself by the feet of the users, and over time any wet patches or eroding sections can be repaired.

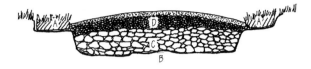

A typical section diagram to show path construction on firm, freely drained ground: (a) Turves are stripped and retained to be used to tidy the edge of the path after construction. (b) The path route is excavated down to firm subsoil, and large stones or roots are removed. (c) Around 150 mm (6 in.) of crushed stone is laid and rolled. (d) Smaller stone is laid and rolled for the surface, raised in the centre to help shed water and prevent potholes from developing.

Path construction in wetter soils: (Top) The worn, rutted and muddy result of wear and tear without a path surface or drainage. (Bottom) A path constructed by excavating the worn sections and laying the crushed stone on a layer of geotextiles. Drains alongside the path carry water away.

In conditions of greater use and wear and tear, trail construction is relatively easy. Turves are cut from the path route and stacked to one side. Large rocks and roots should be removed from the excavated route, and any drains crossing the route should be piped. Around 150 mm (6 in.) of graded crushed stone is then laid along the route and rolled. The turves are used to neaten the path edges, or to patch worn areas. The surface can be sealed to prevent dust or to improve it for wheelchair access using one of the proprietary glass fibre-reinforced surfaces, or by spreading tar and rolling on chips of local stone chosen to blend into the landscape. However, a good compacted surface is very suitable for wheelchairs, and smooth tarmac/ asphalt, which is in any case a very urban surface, is not preferred as it can be slippery when wet, causing a wheelchair user to lose control.

The surface of the path should be formed into a slight crown or double camber to shed water off each side. If needed, ditches can be provided alongside the path. This crowned surface is important for easy use by wheelchairs or buggies, as a side grade tends to pull them constantly to one side.

Construction can be by hand labour using hand-operated rollers and dumpers, or by machine, such as one of the mini-excavators now available. These are ideal for path widths of between 1.2 and 1.8 m (4–6 ft).

Gentle or flat terrain in wetter, less well-drained soils in wetter climates

Path construction is similar to that described above except for two factors: the need for more drainage, and the problems of the surface sinking into the wetter, weaker soils beneath. Drainage is provided by open ditches alongside each side of the path; these should lead water away without discharging directly into watercourses. The path can be prevented from collapsing into the ditches by placing stones or timber along its edges to retain the surface, or by setting the ditches a short distance away with side drains leading to them from the crowned surface of the path.

The problem of the surface material sinking into and mixing with softer ground beneath can be overcome by laying a geo-textile mat on the excavated surface before laying the surfacing. The turves replaced at the path edges help to keep the geo-textile buried, and tidy up the overall effect.

Peaty soils on flat or plateau areas

This is the weakest soil of all, but is so common in many places that paths on it may be unavoidable, while wooden boardwalks are too expensive for long

An example of an eroded path across peat. This is extremely difficult to restore or to lay a satisfactory path surface over.
Source: Courtesy Peter Ford.

Rafting construction using lengths of timber wired together into a continuous mat. This is laid straight onto the surface once any basic preparation has been carried out. Path surfacing is laid over this, covering the timber to keep out the air.

Path construction using fascines or faggots of brushwood pegged into place and covered with crushed stone. This is an old, well-tried method.

stretches. Experience with long-distance paths in Britain indicates that measures for crossing peat are needed at the outset for path use; otherwise, severely eroded surfaces will occur very quickly. There are several techniques for crossing peat:

- **Rafting**. Round timber of around 100 mm (4 in.) diameter, in lengths to suit the required path width, is wired and stapled together side by side to form a continuous roll. This is laid out along the path after minimal preparation such as levelling hummocks, filling hollows and piping drains across the route. Surfacing material is then laid over the raft, which floats on the peat.
- **Fascines or faggots**. This is a method that has been used for hundreds of years. Bundles of brushwood, slash from logging or similar materials are compressed tightly and bound using wire or nylon twine. The faggots are laid side by side lengthways across the path. They should be longer than the path width, because light wooden poles of around 75 mm (3 in.) diameter are used to hold them together and define the width. Wooden stakes are partly driven in at intervals next to the poles and nailed to them. They are then driven in further. This has the effect of compressing the faggots and clamping them in place. Crushed rock can then be laid over the faggots and turves laid over the exposed ends along the path edge. Deeper holes can be filled with piles of faggots.
- **Causeway construction**. As a last resort in the worst places, where peat cannot support a raft, causeways can be constructed. If there is a subsoil, the peat can be removed down to it and set on one side. Soil is then excavated along both sides of the

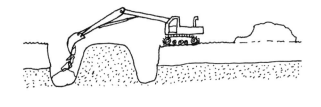

Causeway construction results in a permanent path, and may be the best solution in the most eroded deep peat areas: (From top – a) The peat is excavated and laid to one side. (b) Hard subsoil from beneath the peat is built up into a causeway to ground level. (c) The excavated peat is returned to the ditches cut by excavation of the subsoil. (d) The causeway is surfaced, and drains are left on either side. The result is a firm path that will not settle, sink or erode.

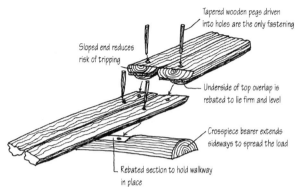

Tapered wooden pegs driven into holes are the only fastening

Sloped end reduces risk of tripping

Underside of top overlap is rebated to lie firm and level

Crosspiece bearer extends sideways to spread the load

Rebated section to hold walkway in place

The method of construction of a split log boardwalk.

A boardwalk constructed of split logs cut from the nearby forest, borne on wide cross-pieces to cross a mire in Ķemeri National Park, Latvia. All pieces are pegged together.

proposed path route and piled in the middle until it rises to the level of the desired path. It is firmed with the excavator (backhoe) bucket. The excavated peat is put into the holes along both sides and covered in turf. Side drains should be left unturfed. This method produces a very firm path. It may, however, disrupt the hydrology of the peat and so be unacceptable in some places.

- **Boardwalks**. If the ground is boggy with open pools of water, or too fragile to withstand foot pressure or a constructed path like those described above, then a timber boardwalk is a better option. These can be expensive to construct and maintain, but they might be the best option in terms of site protection. They are also exciting to walk along, and they have the added advantage of preventing people from straying from the trail. The following types are found.

The simplest walks are made from split logs. The two halves are laid flat face upwards, parallel to each other in the direction of the route. The ends and possibly the central point are fixed by nails or pegs to crosspieces, which extend outwards to spread the load and help the walkway to keep afloat. Sections can be joined by overlapping and pegging (see photograph

above). These can be made from sections of varying length, which allows the route direction to vary and wind across the area if need be.

Such narrow walkways allow single-file walkers only, and so it is useful if both ends are visible to enable walkers coming in opposite directions to avoid meeting in the middle. Signs might also be needed to advise single-file use, and the need for waterproof footwear where the boardwalk tends to sink into the surface of watery areas. Wider sections for passing can be constructed four planks wide, but these are less easy to keep level because of variable log widths. This method of construction is useful where timber is plentiful because the structures can be made on site from fresh-cut material that is easily replaced. Where rusting metal fixings might be a problem, simple wooden pegs driven through holes will fix the construction satisfactorily.

Wider and more sophisticated walkways are needed in other places with more visitors, and particularly for barrier-free access. Parallel beams set 600–900 mm (2–3 ft) apart are bolted to horizontal bearer sections laid on the surface. Planks are nailed to these to provide a walking surface (see figure on opposite page, right-hand column). The planks are set wide enough apart for drainage to help keep them dry and free from moss or

An excellent example of a floating boardwalk laid across bogland. The construction is of sawn timber resting on horizontal cross-bearers to spread the load. Pacific Rim National Park, British Columbia, Canada.

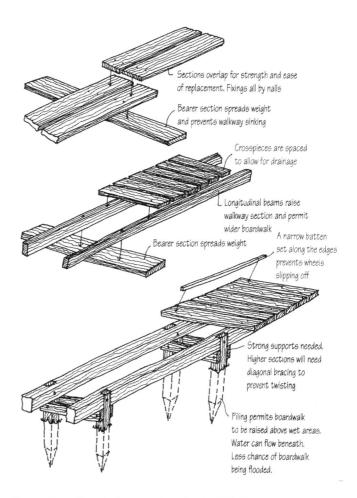

Sections overlap for strength and ease of replacement. Fixings all by nails

Bearer section spreads weight and prevents walkway sinking

Crosspieces are spaced to allow for drainage

Longitudinal beams raise walkway section and permit wider boardwalk

Bearer section spreads weight

A narrow batten set along the edges prevents wheels slipping off

Strong supports needed. Higher sections will need diagonal bracing to prevent twisting

Piling permits boardwalk to be raised above wet areas. Water can flow beneath. Less chance of boardwalk being flooded.

Three methods of boardwalk construction using sawn timber: (From top – a) Flat planks laid on bearers and fixed by nails. (b) A wider structure made by planking nailed to long beams, which in turn are laid on cross-bearers. (c) A structure built on piling to lift it above the water or to level out undulating or broken ground.

slime, which might make the surface slippery, but close enough together to prevent sticks or crutches becoming wedged. Extra grip can be provided by various means such as deck paint, proprietary paints which incorporate a grit, grit stuck to the surface with bitumen, or small-gauge wire netting stapled to the surface. However, this latter technique is not recommended because people using sticks or crutches may find the ends of the stick or crutch become stuck in the mesh. None of these techniques is particularly good either for looks, for convenience or for safety. It is possible to introduce more curves into this type of construction, where the surface pieces overhang the frames and can be cut into sinuous shapes after fabrication.

Where a floating construction is not needed and where the ground is firmer deeper down, posts can be driven in to raise the walkway well above the surface. Construction is similar to the example described above but the beams are fixed to cross-pieces bolted to the posts. This might be useful where water levels fluctuate seasonally, and to allow water to move more freely below the structure or to obtain a better view out over the landscape. Wider parts or viewing platforms can be added to the basic boardwalk for fishing or wildlife viewing. Smaller, wider areas can also be provided with benches.

Higher-built boardwalks may require handrails for reassurance and to help less able people to use them. This type is easier to build using shallow ramps to allow wheelchairs to use them comfortably. A narrow rail should be set in from and parallel to the outer edges of the boardwalk to prevent wheels from slipping off and to act as a tapping rail for blind people using white sticks to feel the edge. The gap between planks may present an obstruction for small, narrow wheels, especially where turns are needed or on sharp corners if the gap is too wide.

As with all timber used in contact with wet ground, rot will occur unless the timber is naturally durable, such as red cedar, elm or oak, or is treated with preservative. The chemicals used in preservation can be toxic to aquatic life and they should generally be avoided in favour of durable timber. Of the chemicals available, arsenates and creosote should not be used for timber in contact with water; Cuprinol is better, while boron

A large and ambitious boardwalk constructed in a meandering design which fits the landscape. La Dune de Bouctouche, New Brunswick, Canada.

A temporary boardwalk made in sections and laid across sand dunes during the summer season to protect the sand and make it easier to walk. Cap Ferret, Aquitaine, France.

A path cut into a steep side slope in easily excavated material and a firm base. This fits into the landscape quite well and there are no signs of erosion. Cassandra Peninsula, Halkidiki, Greece.

salts are the best, although expensive compared with the others. The subject of preservatives needs more research to look for sustainable solutions. Regular maintenance of timber structures is essential, with prompt repair of broken or weak sections to avoid the risk of injury.

Boardwalks have the added advantage of not disrupting the hydrology of wetland areas in the way that some of the causeway path constructions do.

Another type of boardwalk is used to cross sand dunes which would otherwise be loose and prone to erosion. These are laid temporarily in the summer and consist of sections of slatted timber laid end to end.

Sloping ground in mineral soil

In these circumstances, excavation to create the trail is necessary, and gradients need to be controlled. If possible, gradients should be found that preclude the need for steps. After initial clearance and pruning of vegetation, the route is set out with canes and the gradient checked using a simple levelling instrument such as an Abney. Then the path can be cut across the slope. If the width is not too great or the side slope too steep, the excavated material should present few problems for disposal. On steep side slopes it may be preferable to build up the path using rockwork so as to avoid too much cut and fill or problems of disposal of surplus fill.

The slope above the path should generally be cut to the natural angle of repose and shaped to prevent erosion. However, in soft soils it may need some work to prevent it from eroding. Stone revetment can be used for this, as can vertical timber shoring or woven willow branches fastened to the surface until vegetation can

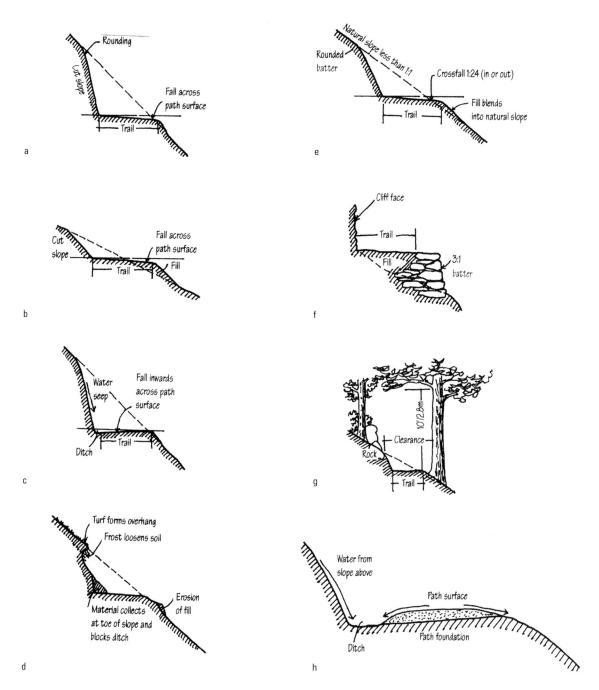

Path construction principles for side slopes: (a) On steep slopes, the path should be benched out of solid ground and excavated material taken away to be used elsewhere. Here the path is graded so that water is shed from it down the slope. (b) On less steep slopes, the cut material is used to make up the path formation on the lower side. This is acceptable where the fill will not erode away. (c) Where heavier rain is common or wetter soils are present, the path should be graded so that water runs to the foot of the cut slope, where all the water is collected in a ditch and discharged through culverts at intervals. This avoids the risk of washout and erosion. (d) The top of the cut slope should be rounded off to avoid the erosion problems shown here, and to allow quick colonization of the slope by vegetation. Fill left at too steep an angle also tends to erode, taking parts of the path with it. (e) This diagram recommends the maximum cross-falls and slope grades on which to construct a path using cut and fill. (f) In the steepest slope section the path may have to be built up using stone-retaining structures backfilled with rock and subsoil. An allowance for a safety edge is made. (g) When constructing a trail through a forest, the clearance should allow a reasonable space all around the walker to avoid the risk of collision with trees or branches. (h) This diagram shows that the path surfacing should be laid to a crowned shape on a general formation, which drains to a fall. This is especially important if wheelchairs or baby buggies use the path, otherwise they tend to keep being pulled down slopes into the ditch.

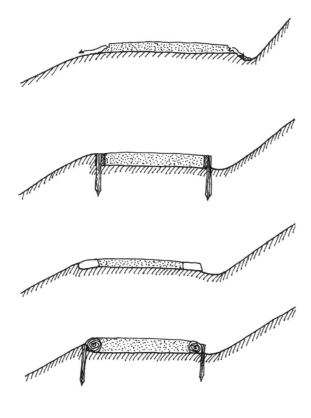

Path surfaces may need edges to retain them: (From top – a) An unretained edge begins to erode, washing material away. (b) Wooden rails held in place by timber pegs are functional, and have low impact, but cannot be curved very easily. (c) Stone is good, and can be laid to any shape. (d) Logs may be available on site, but the path becomes a series of straight sections, which look stiff and artificial.

An example of path edging made of concrete sculpted to resemble wood. This is a long-lasting solution but the material is generally not to be recommended. Mount Hakkoda National Park, Japan.

An example of a flat and well-constructed path held in place by log retaining edges. These also provide a tapping rail for blind or otherwise visually impaired people.

become established, either by natural colonization or by seeding, planting or turfing.

It may be necessary to retain the sides of the path surfacing to prevent it from slipping into the side drains and to enable it to be more easily used by blind and visually impaired people. Edges can be made from preserved sawn timber rails held by wooden pegs, round logs or local stone. The rails can be curved to some degree, but logs can be used only in straight sections, and this can look awkward. Stone is preferred if it is found on site, but it needs to be flat and capable of staying in place. Larger stones can also be used to vary the width of the path surface and tie it into other aspects of the local landform.

Surfacing is normally crushed stone, compacted with fine material or 'scalpings' on the surface. Occasionally other materials can be used. Sealed (paved) surfaces

Bark and wood chippings used for a path surface. This is not suitable for wheelchairs or buggies but it does make a comfortable and silent surface to walk on. Irving Nature Park, Saint John, New Brunswick, Canada.

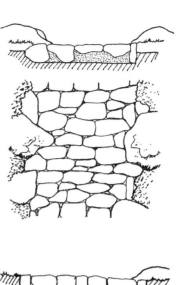

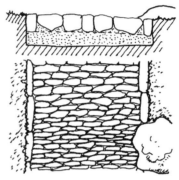

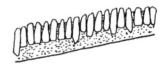

such as asphalt or tarmac may have a place in more urban settings or where other materials cannot be relied upon to stay firm and smooth for wheelchairs and buggies, but they should always be top-dressed in local stone.

Wood chips or bark can sometimes be used to give a softer, quieter surface. This might be useful in a wildlife-viewing area, where the noise from feet crunching gravel can disturb the animals. Soft surfacing can also be a welcome relief to feet fatigued by hard surfaces.

Stone paving is traditional in some areas. Dressed stone or crazy paving should be avoided in the outdoors for its urban or suburban appearance, but well-chosen stone can be laid to produce a hard-wearing surface, although probably not a smooth one. In rocky, mountainous terrain such paths may be easier to

Stone paving: (From top – a) A section and plan of paving using natural stone. A level surface is achieved by laying the irregular stones at various depths. The path is tied into the terrain by using occasional larger rocks along the edges. (b) Narrow stones set on edge provide a surface with plenty of grip on steeper slopes. This traditional method was used in mountainous areas such as the Alps to give sheep or cattle grip during migration to mountain pastures.

construct to permit better access and a more obvious route across boulder and rock-strewn areas where there are risks of damaging ankles. The rock needs only to be laid or rearranged *in situ*. Rock sections may also be useful where the gradient is steep and the surface vulnerable to washout. Stone laid to give an irregular

An example of a path constructed from stone across a very difficult area. Krkonoše National Park, Czech Republic.

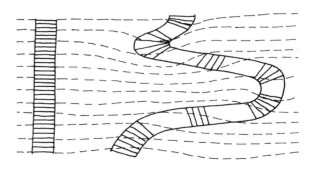

Step layout: (a) Avoid long runs of steps on a straight slope. These are daunting and tiring to climb. (b) Select a route where the steps can be divided into shorter sections with ramps and landings in between.

surface gives some grip and erosion protection when combined with a decent cross-fall and good drainage alongside.

Steps, ramps and changes in level

Every effort should be made to achieve reasonable gradients on trails to enable their widespread use by people with a range of abilities. In steeper, more rugged terrain and places where rock outcrops occur, there may be no alternative to the construction of steps or stepped ramps. However, long runs of steps going vertically up a slope are daunting to use and look out of place in the outdoors.

A slope where the gradient demands steps should be subdivided if possible into sections where different numbers of steps are needed, separated by landings and changes of direction to follow landform. In many areas, short sections of steps – perhaps three or five – can be used with ramps in between. This reduces the amount of construction and allows a more leisurely ascent or descent. The use of stepped ramps is another device, but these can be difficult for people with impaired sight to negotiate, and should be rarely used. The edges of the steps and ramps should be of a contrasting colour for such people.

Step dimensions should be generally bigger in scale than normal domestic requirements. The rise can be a little higher but the tread width should be significantly greater. This is because of the tendency to use larger movements out of doors. Also, footwear is normally

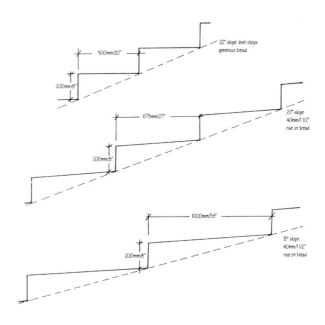

Typical dimensions of steps for the outdoors, where sizes can be more generous than in indoor or urban areas.

bigger, takes up more room, and is likely to overhang or catch on smaller steps.

Step construction should be carried out carefully, especially if using dry-laid materials. Loosely compacted material or unstable soil can mean that the impact of descending feet dislodges steps relatively easily. Foundations should be cut back to firm subsoil

A well-designed and well-constructed set of stone steps, which are blended into the boulder-strewn landform. Mother Walker Falls State Park, Maine, USA.

and drained properly (see above) before steps are laid.

The following forms of construction can be successfully used.

Natural stone

This is the best, most hard-wearing material, which blends into many landscapes. In the most rugged and mountainous terrain, steps can be very irregular in size and shape, so that they resemble slightly easier rocky pitches. In other areas the rocks should be chosen for a relatively even top and face, while the bottom and rear can be rougher, being dug into the foundations or packed level with smaller stones. Round stones are not suitable. Naturally bedded hard rocks, or those that split cleanly, are usually the best to use. Softer rocks may erode beneath heavy foot traffic.

The edges of the steps may need to be retained to prevent sideways movement. Larger stones can be used for this on the down-slope side, and can act as safety barriers or handholds in precipitous terrain. Such stone steps should be checked and repaired regularly, as sudden movement or disintegration of steps can cause ankle injuries. Stone steps can also be cut from the rock itself using a pneumatic drill (jackhammer) or similar tool.

Timber

This can be used in a number of ways. One version to be avoided is the use of round or half-round timber as edge retainers. These offer no grip, and under wet conditions they are extremely slippery and dangerous.

Steps have frequently been constructed of stout sawn boards laid on their edges to form a small retaining structure behind which hardcore or crushed stone is laid. These are dangerous, as the stone is liable to settle, wash out or collect water, causing the edge of the timber to stand proud and trip people, especially on their way down. If the wood is too narrow, it can wear down quite quickly. These should not be used.

Solid timber steps work best. These have often been constructed from old railway sleepers (railroad ties), which are of almost perfect dimensions when laid flat and sawn to length. There can be problems of pollution due to the leaching of certain preservatives such as creosote from the sleepers, which precludes their use in some places. Nevertheless, the same dimensions can be sawn from solid wood, but such steps tend to be expensive unless local rough logs can be used. Durable timber for use where preservatives are not possible includes cedar, oak and some eucalypts.

Any form of timber steps can be held in place by stout pegs or short stakes driven into the subsoil. Slots or notches for the pegs can be cut in the front edges of the steps to make a neater finish. If the steps overlap each other, a strip of timber along the underside near the front edge can help to hold them in position (see figure on next page). These steps are placed on excavated bases, on a layer of crushed stone to aid drainage and give a firmer support.

Alternatively, timber steps can be built as self-contained step structures similar to open staircases, perhaps placed against a low rock cliff or up a steep bank. Well-constructed, sturdy sections such as this can be anchored down and placed on rock bases to keep them clear of the soil to reduce rot. In the steepest of such steps a handrail up the side is desirable (see 'Handrails' below).

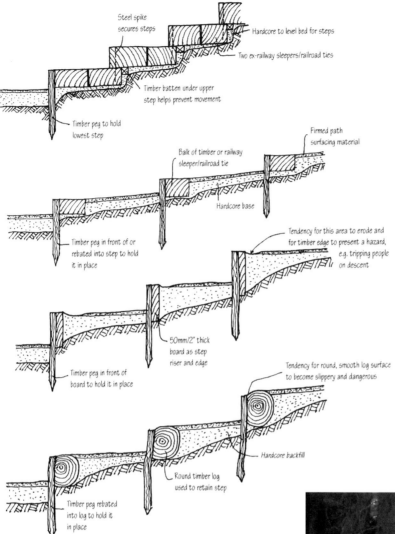

Steel spike
secures steps

Hardcore to level bed for steps

Two ex-railway sleepers/railroad ties

Timber batten under upper
step helps prevent movement

Timber peg to hold
lowest step

Balk of timber or railway
sleeper/railroad tie

Firmed path
surfacing material

Hardcore base

Timber peg in front of or
rebated into step to hold
it in place

Tendency for this area to erode and
for timber edge to present a hazard,
e.g. tripping people
on descent

50mm/2" thick
board as step
riser and edge

Timber peg in front of
board to hold it in place

Tendency for round, smooth log surface
to become slippery and dangerous

Hardcore backfill

Round timber log
used to retain step

Timber peg rebated
into log to hold it
in place

Various methods of timber step construction: (From top – a) Solid
steps made from sawn timber slabs or old railway sleepers/
railroad ties. (b) Steps edged with thick lengths of timber in-filled
with hardcore with compacted surfacing. (c) Boards set on
edge tend to stick up if the infill erodes, and people may trip over
them. (d) Round timber edges are likely to become slippery and
dangerous, particularly for people with visual impairment.

A formidable set of steps with an extremely long run without resting
places. Nuuksio National Park, Finland.

Other forms

Other forms of steps that are found in severe terrain include steel ladders bolted to rock faces, and iron steps set into rock. Such sections are almost always on pitches where rock climbing skills are needed. They are not for the faint-hearted, but they do give non-climbers a taste for exciting ascents and descents. Holes are drilled, and the iron or steel is held in place by molten lead poured in to fill up the space (traditional), epoxy cement (modern and extremely strong), or expanding bolts. However, such steps are also visually intrusive and dangerous, and so they should be used only if other methods of ascent or descent are impractical.

Handrails

Handrails serve two functions: (1) as aids to negotiating difficult sections of the trail, such as steep pitches or steps; and (2) as safety barriers to prevent people from falling. Along most paths, handrails should be unnecessary, but they are needed where steps are steep, where boardwalks or bridges are raised more than 500 mm (18 in.) above the surface of the ground, and where the path passes near a dangerous drop or cliff edge and over water. Handrails must be strong enough to support the weight of a person pulling or leaning on them as an aid to climbing, and to withstand the sideways movement of someone leaning or falling against them. Where small children use the trail, lower-level railings or an infill panel are also required to prevent them from slipping beneath the top rail. Older people may value a handrail more generally along a trail, as it helps them to walk further than they would otherwise be able to, so they should be considered a standard feature in some places, though not everywhere.

Handrails can be constructed from different materials and in a variety of ways. The simplest are aids to using steep stretches of trails and ledges on the most mountainous paths. These can include knotted ropes anchored to the rock with eyelets, steel cables held similarly, or galvanized steel handrails bolted to the rock. These are positioned on the inside of the trail and are intended for use with belts and clips to fasten the walker to them so as to prevent people from falling from the trail.

Handrails for support and safety must be sited along the outside edge of the path. Sturdy timber railings attached to wooden posts spaced at 1 m (3 ft) intervals are ideal in most circumstances. A substantial top rail looks good outdoors and gives structural strength, but it might also need a smoother, narrower handrail fixed

A viewpoint on a very high cliff with extremely heavy-handed metal safety barriers. While there is clearly a safety issue, a safety barrier could probably have been made to be less intrusive and just as safe. Walls of Jerusalem National Park, Tasmania, Australia.

proud on the inside, for people to hold onto. Beneath the top rail, narrower railings spaced horizontally prevent children from slipping through. An alternative to wooden lower rails is taut wire cables. These look lighter from a distance, and allow small children and people in wheelchairs to see through the barrier to the views beyond. In more urban settings, wooden walls made of vertical boards fixed to rails mounted on posts can be used. These are less easy to climb than barriers made from horizontal rails.

Wire mesh barriers on steel supports might seem stronger, but they look out of place in most wild landscapes. They are cheaper to maintain if galvanized.

Stone walls (cemented for safety) might be appropriate in more developed settings, perhaps at viewpoints and in mountainous areas where stone is the dominant material. The top of the wall should incorporate features such as pointed capstones to prevent daredevils from climbing on it. Panels of railings or tensioned wires can be inserted into the wall to enable viewing by smaller children or people in wheelchairs, who are unable to see over the top.

a

b

c

Climbing aids: (a) This knotted rope strung between two trees makes a useful aid for climbing up a steep rocky stretch on an otherwise easy woodland trail. Mount Orford Provincial Park, Quebec, Canada. (b) A sturdy timber handrail helps people to climb steeper steps, and is especially useful when the path follows a steep slope with a substantial drop to one side. (c) A steel cable fastened to eyelets fixed in the rock gives help and security for walkers along a cliff or ledge path in mountainous terrain. Based on examples from the Austrian Alps.

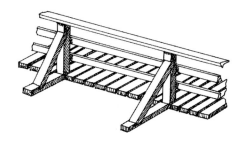

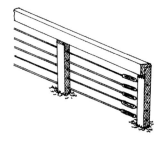

Some varieties of handrail for safety or support: (From left – a) Round timber used to give a strong rail. The bigger size of timber looks appropriate outdoors. (b) This design of heavy round rails set in uprights made of rock is based on 1930s CCC designs. It is strong, and can be constructed where posts cannot be dug into the ground because of rock. (c) Handrails on boardwalks or decking need to be given strength, to resist horizontal pressure, using outriggers and struts. (d) Tensioned cables used instead of rails can give less impact, and permit views through them by children or people in wheelchairs.

A handrail or barrier made from traditional zig-zag log construction. This is very solid and safe. Irving Nature Park, Saint John, New Brunswick, Canada.

A good example of a barrier at a viewpoint with good access for disabled people. The rail is low enough for a person in a wheelchair to see over the top. Pancake Rocks, South Island, New Zealand.

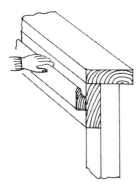

A handrail of an easier size to grip set beneath a heavier, stronger top rail combines visual appearance and function.

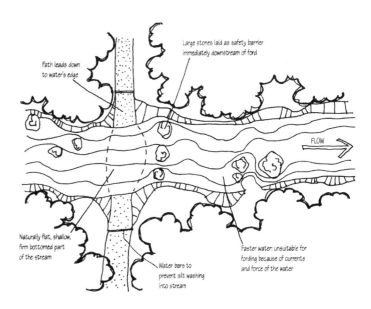

Path leads down to water's edge

Large stones laid as safety barrier immediately downstream of ford

FLOW

Naturally flat, shallow, firm bottomed part of the stream

Water bars to prevent silt washing into stream

Faster water unsuitable for fording because of currents and force of the water

The design of a ford must combine easy use with safety while ensuring minimal disturbance to the surroundings and preventing silt from washing into the stream from eroded paths.

Stream crossings

In most circumstances where water has to be crossed, special structures should be provided, such as culverts as previously described, some kind of ford, stepping-stones or other informal means, or bridges. In wilder, more rugged terrain, where primitive experiences and a greater expectation of self-reliance on the part of visitors are expected, crossing streams can be an exciting and challenging experience. Un-bridged crossings should be the normal practice, but safe crossing points must be selected, and warnings should be posted about the potential dangers of crossing rivers during floods, together with advice on alternative routes. However, where the water level can fluctuate quickly and torrent conditions are likely to persist for some time, crossing structures should be provided.

Fords

The walker must be able to wade through the water at a place where strong and turbulent currents are unlikely or absent, and where the water is usually fairly shallow. A section of stream where the water flows more slowly and the stream bottom is fairly even and firm should be chosen, and the path should be directed to and from it. If there is some risk from strong currents, and the ford is wide, large stones should be placed on the immediate downstream side of the crossing place to act as safety barriers. These give walkers something to hold on to if required, and can prevent people from being washed away. Although not designed as stepping-stones, they may be used as such if they stand out of the water, and are spaced reasonably close with a flattish surface.

In less wild areas, and for an easier crossing, the ford can be given a better bottom surfacing using large, flat, rough textured stones interlocked together. On popular routes, this may be advisable to prevent degradation of the crossing surface.

Stepping-stones

There may be natural areas of free-standing rocks, which allow nimble walkers to jump or step from one to another, improved if necessary by rocks placed to fill wide gaps. Such areas should be chosen where the rock is rough, and not colonized by slippery algae.

Stepping-stones can also be placed in stream crossings, where large rocks with flat surfaces can be laid to be stable and firm. The interval between them should allow the average person to step easily from one to another, and each stone should be wide enough to allow both feet to be placed on it at once. In an outdoor setting, the line of stones should be sinuous and appear naturalistic rather than formal.

A path constructed of stones crosses a steep stream using the rocks to form stepping-stones. Goat Fell, Arran, Scotland.

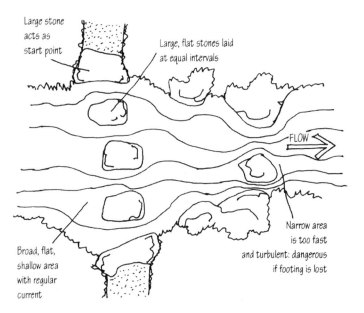

Stepping-stones should be sited in safe places and made of stable rocks with good surfaces to step onto.

Bridges

The main problem with fords and stepping-stones is how to cross the stream during high water. Although advice on alternative routes can be provided, if flooding occurs frequently and the trail is popular, it is better to have bridges. Where people with disabilities are encouraged to use the trail, bridges are a necessity.

Apart from the simplest, shortest spans, bridges are complex structures requiring engineering skills for their design, construction and maintenance. In a recreation context, their design also provides opportunities to enhance the enjoyment of visitors. To this end, consideration should be given to using multidisciplinary teams of engineers, architects and landscape architects as well as artists for the design and siting of bridges.

There are five main types that might be used in the outdoors, some more appropriate in some places than others:

- **simple beam bridges**, in which single or multiple beams are supported at both sides of the stream to be crossed;
- **trussed beams**, in which a larger structure is constructed from small sections joined together for strength;
- **cantilever beams**, in which the beams are supported at one side only, and where they rely on their anchoring and inherent stiffness to support the load;
- **arch bridges**, in which the construction technique forms an inherently strong structure;

- **suspension bridges**, in which the walking surface is suspended from tensioned cables fixed to supports on both sides of the stream.

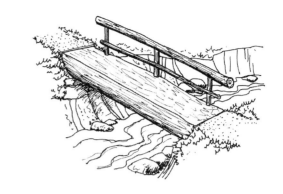

Simple beam bridges

These can vary from simple structures, such as a single log laid across a stream, to composite steel and timber construction. The form used will depend on the weight to be carried and the setting in which the bridge is to be erected.

In wild settings, particularly in forests, adequate and functional footbridges can be fashioned from large logs laid across the stream. The upper surface is sawn or chopped roughly flat to make a walkway. A handrail can be attached to one or both sides, being bolted directly onto the log. If the timber is durable or the log is very large, this type of bridge will last for a long time provided the supported ends can be kept dry. In such settings the weight of a few single-file walkers will easily be borne, but the bridge's strength (including the handrail) should be checked by a qualified engineer at regular intervals.

Logs used in construction should be straight and as cylindrical as possible; the bark should be removed, and surfaces chamfered to create parallel sides for neatness. Chunky, large logs will always look better, and this will usually help to ensure that they are sufficiently strong.

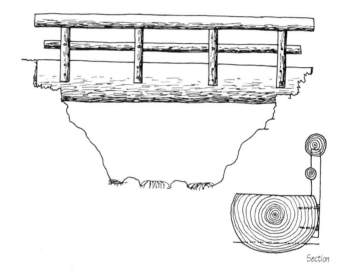

In the absence of a single large log, two or more may be laid side by side, and roughly squared on the top to give a flat surface. To prevent movement the logs should be bolted together at intervals. Handrails may be added (supported by outrigger beams – see figure right) for lateral strength. Narrow gaps between the logs should be left to allow water to drain away.

If a greater width of bridge is required, a decking may be added of planks sawn or split from logs laid across the log beams with narrow spaces between. The surfaces of the logs need to be level, otherwise the decking will be uneven. Durable or pressure-treated timber should be used for the decking, where maintenance is a priority.

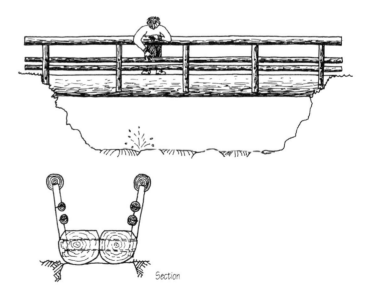

Two construction methods for log bridges: (From top – a) A single log, sawn across to give a flat walking surface with a round timber handrail bolted along one side. (b) Two narrower logs bolted together with a handrail on both sides.

This bridge between two stretches of boardwalk has made use of a naturally fallen cedar log. The upper surface has been levelled, and a railing has been fixed directly to the log using coach screws. Pacific Rim National Park, British Columbia, Canada.

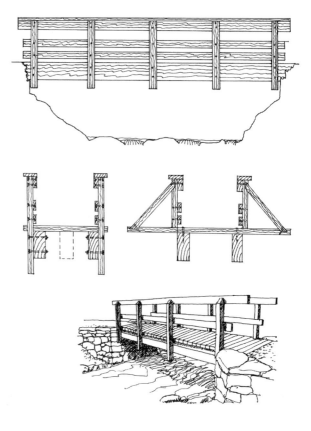

Designs of sawn timber beam bridges: (From top – a) Construction methods include handrails either fixed to the supporting beams or strengthened laterally using outrigger and strut. (b) A small beam bridge of good design and construction.

Sawn timber

This is more appropriate in less wild settings. Two or three beams can be sawn out of solid wood, being proportionately deeper than wide, laid parallel to each other with a decking of sawn boards fixed across them. Some bracing to prevent differential movement between the beams might be needed, with handrails bolted to the outer beams.

If beams sawn from single timbers are unsuitable, or unavailable for the loading or the span, then laminated beams can be used instead. These are made from narrow strips of timber glued in layers to form a single, very strong beam, which can be straight or curved. Once again, larger rather than smaller-scale sections look better in most landscapes.

Steel beams

Steel beams might be used where the span is too large to be bridged economically with timber. If these are made of 'Cor-ten' steel, galvanized and left to weather, or painted a dull earth tone, they can be acceptable. Wooden decking and handrails treated with preservative can be provided so that natural materials are more dominant when seen from the trail. Such bridges are very durable and have a long life compared with all-timber structures.

Steel decking and handrails may have a place in certain circumstances, where durability in harsh conditions is needed, or low maintenance is a priority and where a lighter all-steel structure might have less impact than a bulky wooden bridge. Sometimes non-natural materials can help to emphasize the drama of a natural scene. Expanded metal or steel grating can be used for the decking, with steel handrails and uprights infilled with tensioned wire.

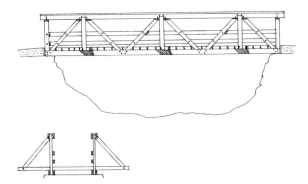

Truss construction is an acceptable form of construction. It uses smaller-dimension timber than the simple beam bridge. The truss also acts as part of the handrail.

An elegant arched bridge made of glue-laminated curving beams joined in the centre. Taeveskoja Forest, Estonia.

A bridge made of truss construction, using a combination of wooden beams – good under pressure – and steel – good under tension. Cradle Mountain National Park, Tasmania, Australia.

Trussed beams

Trussed beam construction can also use timber. Made of small wooden sections, bolted together on site, this type of bridge can be erected in areas where access is difficult. The handrail section becomes an integral part of the structure. Maintenance and repair involving replacement of individual sections are also possible without dismantling the whole bridge, as would be the case with a solid beam.

Cantilevered beams

In this construction the beam is not a single unit laid on an abutment at each end. Two beams are used, each fixed at one end with the other projecting over the stream that is to be spanned. The two beams meet each other and are bolted together, or for longer spans the central gap can be infilled with a short beam. The cantilever beams have to be made of stiff material and strongly anchored to bear the weight. This essential requirement can make this type of construction awkward to use. However, it has the advantage that two short beams can be used instead of one long beam, which might not be available.

Arches

Arches have traditionally been used in many places. Old stone arch bridges designed for use by packhorses and dating back centuries can be found in many remote areas. They need special skills for construction, and these are unlikely to be found nowadays. However, wooden arch constructions can be used. Similar in many ways to the trussed beam construction described above, an arch of timber latticework can form an inherently strong structure using small-dimension components, and can be erected on site. Laminated timber beams can also be fabricated into curving sections resembling arches.

Suspension bridges

These have been used as footbridges for centuries, for example, the rope structures used by the Incas of South America. There are several varieties of suspension bridge, depending on the setting and the amount of use expected.

The simplest and most challenging type consists of four cables slung across the stream. Boards are lashed across the bottom two to form a footway, while the

A simple suspension bridge makes an exciting crossing of a raging torrent. Coastal Mountains, Oregon, USA.

upper pair, loosely lashed to the bottom ones, forms the handrail. These bridges are unstable to use, as they tend to swing from side to side. They make an exciting crossing, but they are not recommended for the faint-hearted. However, for low use by experienced hikers in rugged terrain where materials are difficult to transport, such a bridge can be an option.

The usual kind of suspension bridge is a more sophisticated structure. The main cables are secured to the ground at each side of the crossing, and pass over tall uprights anchored into the stream banks. The footway decking is then suspended from these main cables by a series of 'droppers' placed at equal intervals. Beams connect the bottom of each pair of droppers and support the decking. A handrail can also be supported by the droppers. The main cables are tensioned to give

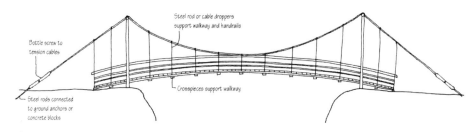

a

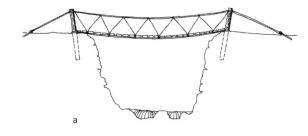

b

Suspension bridge construction: (a) A simple example, where one set of ropes supports the deck and a second pair provide the handrail. A good solution for wilder places. (b) A more sophisticated bridge with main support cables, droppers to support the deck and handrail and proper tensioning devices and ground anchors. (c) A view of a well-built suspension bridge from Ruunaa National Hiking Area, Finland. (d) A detail of the construction of the deck and handrail from the example at (c).

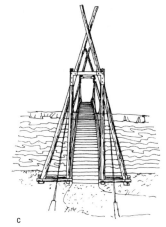

c

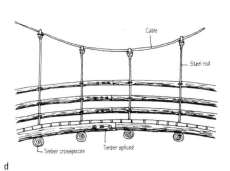

d

the decking its characteristic arched shape, while the cables assume a graceful series of curves.

It is clear that the complexities of design, construction and maintenance of suspension bridges must have an engineer's input. The size of the cable must be calculated, the anchoring needs to be determined, while the size and strength of the uprights are crucial for safe load bearing.

Steel cables tensioned by bottle screws will usually be anchored to concrete blocks or ground anchors, depending on the site, the strength of the subsoil, the loading and access for materials. The uprights can be timber frames with special anchor pieces at the top to connect the cables. Smaller steel cables or rods are used for the droppers, and timber can be used for the decking. All the steel should be galvanized, and the timber should be pressure-treated with preservative.

Bridge siting

Bridge decks must be set sufficiently above the water level to allow high flood levels, and to prevent them from damming the stream with debris and causing damage nearby or the collapse of the structure. Where the stream or river is in a region with extremes of climate, flash floods can cause water levels to rise quickly, and in mountainous areas these floods carry much debris.

Beam bridges, being horizontal or only slightly arched, frequently need abutments to raise them above the flood levels. If the height is more than 1 m (3 ft), ramps or low embankments will be needed to tie the ends of the bridge into the trail surface. Embankments might require culverts to release floodwaters, so they need to be considered carefully. Steps are sometimes used, but these are difficult to negotiate by visitors with disabilities. Other solutions include building the bridge on piers with more spans to enable it to start from higher places on the banks at either side. In other instances, suspension bridges might be sounder alternatives.

Abutments for footbridges are needed to support the structural beams and the deck. They must be constructed to give strength and anchorage. Wing walls may be needed to prevent erosion where the abutment meets the banks, or to contain any infill material used to make up the level. Abutments can be constructed in the following ways:

- **Natural stone**. If this is plentiful and part of the character of the landscape, stone abutments are ideal. Unquarried stones can be laid with concrete backfill or mortar to hold them in place. Recessed joints and grading of stones from large at the base to

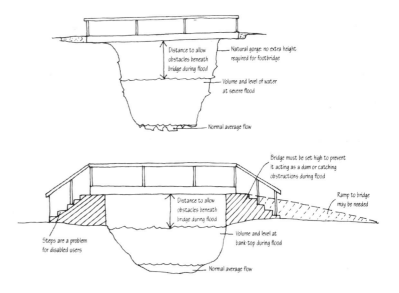

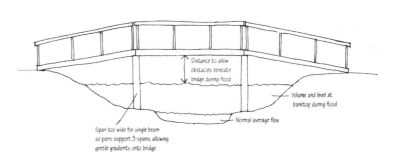

Bridges and stream-flow characteristics: (From top – a) A bridge can rest at ground level when a deep valley gives adequate clearance. (b) A bridge should be raised above flood level in a shallow stream valley. Steps or ramps link the path to it. (c) Piers support the central span so that the outer spans can slope to meet the natural bank level.

This bridge crosses a river and has been raised on piers to keep it above flood height. Tervete Nature Park, Latvia.

Three types of abutment: (From top – a) Natural stone construction, graded from the largest size at the bottom to the smallest at the top. (b) Gabion baskets made from galvanized weldmesh packed with stone from the site. (c) Log cribwork is a traditional method appropriate for use in forests. The cribwork is backfilled with stones and soil.

smaller at the top helps to tie them visually into the setting. There are opportunities for stone sculptors here.

- **Gabions**. Galvanized wire baskets are laid on prepared firm bases dug from the stream bank and filled with local stones, packed tightly and laid carefully against the face of the gabion mesh, ensuring that they will not fit through it. These give heavy weight and good resistance to erosion. The spaces between the baskets and the bank are backfilled with stone.
- **Timber**. Round timber piles, sawn timber planking or crib work (interlocked horizontal timbers) can be used to build up abutments. A piling or planking wall can be kept upright by cables fixed to ground anchors.
- **Concrete**. Concrete on its own frequently looks out of place. If needed for structural reasons, it can be cast to give it a coarse texture (using rough sawn timber shuttering) or jack-hammered to roughen the surface. If stone construction is not sufficiently strong, shuttering can be lined with stone facing and backfilled with concrete, which gives the main strength to the bridge foundation.

Bridge handrails are not always necessary, particularly for short log beam bridges in wild settings. However, for safety and reassurance, a single or double handrail is usually necessary. The same types are appropriate as described in the previous section on boardwalks and along paths against steep drops or cliffs. Others are depicted in the illustrations for the bridges described above. The handrail should extend a little way beyond the end of the bridge to lead the eye onto the structure and tie it into the setting.

Bridge maintenance is very important. Damage by floods, erosion of the area around abutments, corrosion of steel fixings or posts, damage to decking or handrails should be checked and repaired as soon as it is discovered. Regular inspections by a qualified engineer are essential except for the smallest, simplest bridges.

Waymarking

Many visitors to the outdoors are not experienced in the use of map and compass. They are apprehensive about following a trail unless they know where it will lead them, and that they will not get lost. Hence some kind of waymarking is frequently necessary to help visitors enjoy the experience of exploring the outdoors.

An example of a trail entrance panel showing routes and giving information about the length, average duration and path conditions to be expected of each trail.

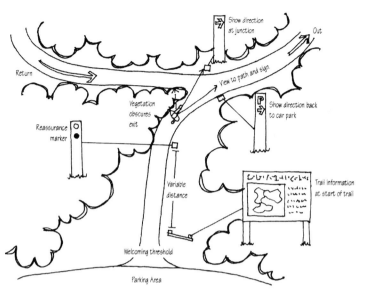

A diagrammatic layout of a trail entrance area. The path is designed to encourage walkers to follow the trail in one direction.

If the Recreation Opportunity Spectrum is adopted as a planning tool, or if a trail system graded for a range of ability levels is developed, then the map and compass enthusiast can be catered for by unmarked trails, while the inexperienced visitor can follow marked ones.

Waymarking systems will vary depending on the type of trail development. Often several trails are developed from a particular car parking area. These might be of different lengths, cater for different degrees of ability or lead to different points of interest. Often they might share sections of the route, with shorter paths diverting from longer ones and perhaps rejoining them closer to the end. Where such path systems exist, the waymarking has to differentiate between each path so that the points where routes diverge are obvious and not missed. One common and well-tried method is to colour-code each trail. A leaflet or board at the entrance to the trail (or trail-head) can be used to show, in map or pictorial form, the trail system, the colour coding, the difficulty, the expected duration and all the points of interest. The colours chosen should avoid those that people with colour blindness cannot identify – for example, certain shades of red and green – and should have a high contrast with each other and against whatever background they are painted on.

The method of waymarking also depends on whether the trail should be walked in one or either direction. This choice may be important if the gradients vary so that the steepest slopes are ascended rather than descended, or whether particular landmarks or attractive features should be seen in a particular order. Another reason for a one-way circuit is if there is interpretation along

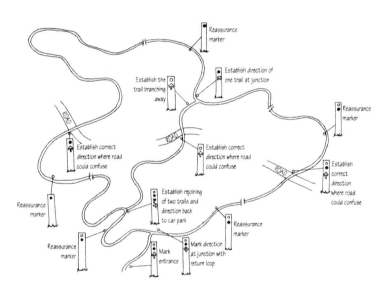

An example of a comprehensive waymarking schedule for a path trail layout. A plan like this should ensure that the minimum number of markers has been installed, taking into account the needs of visibility at junctions.

the trail that tells a story in a particular sequence (see Chapter 13). Finally, when trails are used heavily, a one-way route ensures that walkers are not always meeting people coming towards them so the route might feel emptier than it really is.

The design of the trail entrance is crucial to this: it can be laid out to steer people in the right direction, and if a one-way route is chosen, the waymarking need only be seen from one direction, perhaps reinforced by the use of arrow symbols.

If a two-way route is required, then the waymarking must be effective from either direction, and this is crucial at junctions. The position of waymarkers has to be planned from the walkers' point of view by walking the trail, resolving where there might be confusion (for example, at junctions), periodic reassurance of the route, and the best locations for signs in terms of visibility. A comprehensive map or schedule should be prepared, detailing every marker so that it is known exactly how many are needed, their particular function and their precise location.

Forms of waymarking

There are a number of methods of marking routes. Care is needed to ensure consistency in the form of waymarking used along the routes. This is particularly relevant if posts are used, as their design may need to relate visually to other artefacts such as information or interpretation signs. All methods must strike a balance between clear direction and avoidance of intrusion, especially in wilder or sensitive areas. All marking or symbols must be neatly made: for example, circles, ovals and squares with rounded corners relate easiest to natural forms:

- **Painting rocks**. In mountainous areas routes are frequently marked with paint. Bright colours such as red and yellow are often used. When the trail is indeterminate over rocks, the marks should be carefully positioned to catch the walker's eye. In Austria, for example, red and white patches are painted, on which are written trail numbers. In this way the marks are all the same, and they are easily repainted once a year or so. At key points the marks might be supplemented by small cairns that help walkers to locate the direction of the trail, although this practice is not advocated in Scotland.
- **Painting trees**. In forested countries, tree-trunks are often painted with markings. Sometimes circles of paint are used; a circular template is placed on the tree, and the marking is applied by spray can or brush. In other places, such as Sweden, smooth rings are shaved in the rough bark of pine trees and a complete ring painted around it. The shaved bark ensures a more solid colour and reduces the risk of the bark's flaking and losing the mark. This does not harm the tree.

Four examples of routed posts: (From left – a) A round stake with rings routed in it, each painted with the colour code for a trail. (b) The same method used on a square post. (c) Circles routed on the surface of a post may be more obvious but may not always be visible from every direction. (d) A symbol and arrow can be used for themed trails that are best appreciated by following them in one direction.

- **Fastening signs to trees**. Wooden or plastic signs can be fastened to trees with wire loops or nails. This may be unacceptable to some people because of damage to the trees, the need to tighten wire loops, or bark expanding to absorb nails and splitting off plaques.
- **Waymarking posts**. Wooden posts or stakes or stone slabs are driven or dug into the ground and markings are made on them. The markings might be in the form of discs painted onto flat sides, routed or sandblasted circles, arrows or symbols infilled with paint, or rings routed/sandblasted around the posts and filled in with paint. Several symbols can be used for stages where a number of trails follow the same route for a time. These posts can be round (peeled) or square sawn.

Markings that encircle the tree-stem or post are the most visible, being seen from every direction. Other types must be carefully orientated so as to avoid being missed by less attentive people. Markers set lower down must be kept free of vegetation, while ones on tree-trunks must not be so high as to be missed, especially if walkers are watching where they are going on rough tracks. In such conditions, rocks painted with markers on the surface of the route can be helpful. Marks set around 1.2m (4ft) above ground are ideal except for trails used in winter (see below).

At junctions where paths diverge, markers must be carefully placed. One at the junction and another a

This trail is waymarked by a series of square timber posts. Two grooves filled with different-coloured paint around the top of the post show that there are two routes. One branches away from the other further up the trail. The markings are highly visible, although the post is not a prominent colour.

short way along each path, which can be seen readily from the junction, will help to ensure that they are not missed. Another reassurance marker a little further on is advisable, particularly at a large junction. Fingerposts showing directions more strongly and giving distances might be used in larger trail systems. These should be 2.5–3m (8ft 6in–10ft) tall.

Short posts have disadvantages where snow lies thickly. Taller posts should then be used. Fingerposts need to be tall enough that they do not obstruct skiers on deep snow where this occurs. The height should be calculated to account for the depth of snow pack found in an average winter. Taller posts can be unsightly. They work best in forested areas, where they do not stand out as much as in more open landscapes.

Benches

On most trails, especially those used by families with small children, people with disabilities or elderly people, some resting places should be provided at fairly regular intervals. Where possible, benches should be positioned with good views or in attractive places.

As in all aspects of design, benches should reflect the landscape setting in which they are placed. This means that in the wildest areas it may not be

In countries which get deep snow, short posts can be buried. Cross-country skiers need visible signs: (Top) Arrow-shaped boards carrying the destination and route direction mounted in an upright post work well, and fit into the forest landscape. Finnish Lapland. (Bottom) A fingerpost using colour-coded diamonds, which is prominent in the view, marks the start of a trail system. Koli National Park, Finland.

A bench invites the walker to sit down, take a rest and admire the view. Koli National Park, Finland.

A natural bench made from a slab of rock set in a slope becomes part of the landscape.

A log has been cut to create a simple seat with a back to rest on. Glen Affric, Scotland.

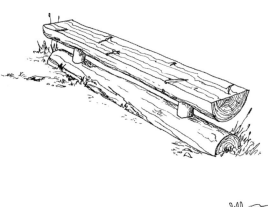

A range of designs for timber benches: (From top – a) This bench from Koli in Finland is made of two halves of a log and two smaller round posts. The bench is simple, stable, and suitable for a forest. (b) Two benches with backrests made from round timber. These work quite well, especially as they are set against some rocks and bushes. Central Germany. (c) A 'perch' makes a handy rest for a short time. Scottish Natural Heritage.

A bench with a back and arms but not too urban in design. This is easier for older people to sit in and lift themselves up out of. David Marshall Lodge, Scotland.

A bench made with the help of an artist. A back would have been more useful, especially as it is on a special sensory trail for disabled people. Mabie Forest, Scotland.

appropriate to have benches, and that the materials and styles of benches or perches will vary. In some places, conveniently positioned slabs of rock, logs with sawn-off tops or thick timber planks can be used. The edge of the trail might be excavated to receive one of these so that the bench becomes part of the landscape.

When elderly people or people with disabilities use the trail, the benches provided should be suitable for their use. This includes raising the level of the bench seat and providing it with arms and a backrest. Such benches should be robustly constructed with thicker sections to withstand the rougher conditions, contrasting with the style of benches found in urban parks. However, finishes should be smooth enough on the sitting or holding surfaces to prevent splinters, but paint and varnish should be avoided in favour of natural-coloured stains or leaving the timber to weather (see 'Picnic furniture' in Chapter 7).

An interesting approach to bench design in some landscapes is to create more sculptural examples. A scheme called Benchmark in Britain, for example, employs sculptors who take windblown timber and carve it into interesting and evocative benches, so that the experience of using them becomes something more than merely resting and looking at a view.

It is necessary to maintain a 'clear walking tunnel' along a path so that branches do not impede visually impaired people.

Trailside design and management

The small-scale landscape created by the vegetation next to the trail should be considered as well as the larger-scale landscape, the sequence of views and features of interest described in the section on trail design.

To be suitable for people with visual impairments, all branches and other obstacles should be cleared to create what is known as a 'clear walking tunnel'. This will need to be checked and maintained at intervals.

If the trail is in a forest, the first few metres/yards away from the path into the edge of trees define an enclosed landscape. If the trail route is merely cleared

The dense conifer trees along this path have been thinned out to improve the landscape along the trailside. Lionthorne Wood, Callander Estate, Falkirk, Scotland.

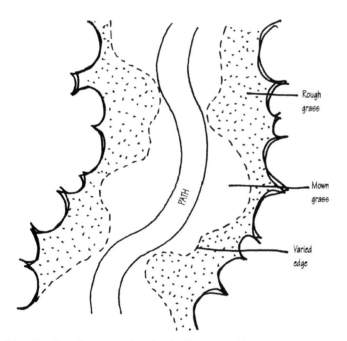

Rough grass

PATH

Mown grass

Varied edge

If the sides of a trail are mown, the edge should vary to avoid an artificial-looking parallel effect.

of obstacles and any awkward branches removed, this misses opportunities to vary the shape, size and sequence of smaller spaces. A survey along the route should be compiled to record such small detail. There may be special trees, pieces of rock, sunny glades or interesting flora that can be revealed. Thinning the trees or pruning some of them to lighten a dark section can

make a dense forest, especially one of plantation origin, less gloomy and oppressive for many people.

In open landscapes, the management of the edges may include some vegetation cutting to prevent too much encroachment on to the path surfacing. If the edges are cut to varying widths along the route, perhaps wider in hollows than on knolls, this looks more natural than a standard width. Sometimes a more structured design involving maintenance of different patches of vegetation at different growth stages can produce valuable wildlife habitat, perhaps for butterflies, as well as a visually more interesting landscape. Each of these patches can be cut in sequence to maintain short grass, herbaceous perennials, low shrubs or tall shrubs (see Chapter 11).

In places, wear and tear of vegetation might occur if the path alignment has caused corner cutting, or sections of path have failed and walkers try to skirt around wet areas. As well as path repair or realignment, the vegetation should also be restored. This will be easy in most areas where growth conditions are good, but mountainous, alpine or desert areas take longer to heal and probably need advice from appropriate specialists.

Viewpoints

Viewpoints, sitting places and wildlife-viewing areas should be included from the outset as part of the overall design of the trail system. There are several different kinds of viewpoint, each with its own requirements for design and maintenance to keep them open by removing overgrowing vegetation.

Panoramic views

These are usually obtained at high points such as cliff edges, mountain tops or the edges of steep escarpments. The broad sweep of the view should be unimpeded by foreground trees, bushes or artefacts. The immediate foreground to the view should be as simple as possible to avoid competing with the splendour of the scene. Vegetation management to maintain this is essential, especially where low growth impedes the view obtained by children or wheelchair users. If the view is from a cliff where a barrier is needed for safety purposes, then this should be designed as simply as possible so as not to upstage the landscape. The approach to a panoramic view should ideally conceal it until the last minute so that its drama or grandeur is emphasized. This can give a memorable first impression.

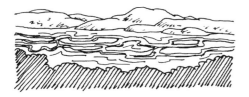

Different types of view: (From top – a) A panoramic view, where the foreground design is kept simple so as to avoid competing with the wide, distant vista. (b) A canopied view, where the overhead tree branches give an enclosed feeling in contrast to the open view beyond. (c) A filtered view, looking through a partial screen of trees. (d) A framed view, where the massive rocks frame the valley and view of a waterfall. (e) A focal view, where the ridges and lake lead the eye to the head of the valley. (f) A feature view, where a prominent landmark is visible across an open space.

Canopied views

At the edge of a forest, the canopy of tree branches can frame the view between the ground and trees. The foreground trees give a reference point to the scale of the view beyond, and provide a sense of safe enclosure looking out to a more distant landscape. To be effective, canopied views are best developed where mature trees with well-defined horizontal branching are present. Clean tree-boles and an unimpeded forest floor lend weight to the sense of an open volume.

Filtered views

Where trees are widely spaced with clean, straight trunks, they can form a partial screen or filter in the foreground. These views also offer safe vantage points, with a greater sense of being hidden from the external landscape. A path passing through dense forest and approaching its edge can exploit this device, contrasting the increasing light beneath the trees and the tantalizing view out. Filtered views can be used as an appetizer to other kinds of view, raising expectations in the walker's mind.

Framed views

These also use foreground features such as large trees or rocks to compose a view, add depth and give a sense of mystery or drama where parts of the view can be hidden from sight. Such framing can be quite narrow, helping to focus the line of sight.

Focal views

Sometimes landforms and woodlands help to focus views of landscape in particular ways. For successful appreciation, the orientation of the view should be controlled or guided by the direction of the path, the position of a seat or the use of foreground vegetation. As the composition is important, any foreground clutter

This is an example of a panoramic view on the Blue Ridge Parkway in Virginia, USA. The foreground vegetation should be simple so as not to distract from the more distant prospect. However, such vegetation can also grow and obscure the view, so often needs to be carefully managed.

or features that may distract the viewer should be removed.

Feature views

Where a particular landmark – a peak, a waterfall, a rock pinnacle or historic building, for example – is of special interest, the view should aim towards it. Framing the foreground can help to reinforce this, as can the position of a bench.

Many of these viewpoint devices can be combined. They are well tried, and were used as artistic devices by early landscape painters and later converted into real viewpoints by the pioneer landscape gardeners, particularly during the 'picturesque' period.

Viewing towers

In some landscapes, the landform and the presence of trees can make obtaining views difficult. Flatter, rolling topography and dense forests are examples of places where viewing towers or platforms can be provided. These are structures that require careful consideration, maintenance and advice from qualified civil engineers before they are built.

Viewing towers usually consist of a sturdy frame of timber or steel, steps (sometimes ramps), and a platform at the top. Climbing them can be quite exciting, and the view from the top is usually a 360-degree panorama. In the absence of any other large-scale views, the openness gained from a tower is often a welcome contrast.

Tower designs should be sturdy and stable, constructed of large materials such as peeled,

A viewing tower is an exciting feature, which elevates the viewer well above the tallest tree tops. Estonia.

cylindrical logs or sawn timber bolted together. Cross-bracing using timber bolted across the frame or tension cables will be needed for strength. Solid foundations to prevent overturning in high winds will also be required, and should be designed by an engineer. Steps and handrails are usually within the tower frame, ascending up the centre either as a spiral or winding in a series of right-angled flights. Some examples have the stairs winding around the outside, but these tend to look clumsy. Steps can be

A platform jutting out from a steep slope helps to give an elevated view, and is specially designed to be wheelchair accessible. However, the view from a wheelchair may be obscured by the railing in this example from Mount St Helens, Washington, USA.

made of timber, steel mesh or lattice, which needs less maintenance but which looks more urban. The same considerations apply to the decks, which must have handrails around the edges similar to those for bridges.

Viewing towers are expensive to construct, and need frequent inspection and maintenance. Their height depends on that of the surrounding trees or other features. If the trees are still growing, the tower should be built to anticipate their mature height, so that the views do not become obscured over time.

Viewing platforms

A variation on the theme of viewing towers is platforms constructed to jut over a cliff or steep slope in order to provide a better and safer view of an exciting feature by a number of people. Examples include a more dramatic view of a waterfall or a downward view into a canyon or river.

Viewing platforms can be cantilever structures jutting out from solid ground, often with struts underneath to give additional support. Their construction should be similar to that of bridges, viewing towers and railings, and involve structural engineers in their design, construction, inspection and maintenance. Platforms have the advantage of being readily accessible from trails by people with disabilities and generally of being more stable and easier to construct than towers.

A cantilevered observation deck on two levels – one wheelchair accessible – for wildlife observation over the sea. Irving Nature Park, Saint John, New Brunswick, Canada.

Tree-top trails

In forests, it can also be exciting to follow a trail up in the canopy of the trees themselves. If the trail ascends up into the crowns of tall trees this can be very dramatic and offer views out over the lower canopy and of details of the trees themselves and of wildlife inhabiting them. There are two main design solutions for constructing trails:

- **Suspended trails** made from cables stretched between tall, sturdy trees, rather like the simple suspension bridge described above. A walkway is laid across the bottom two cables and the upper two used for a handrail. Because of the height a netting infill between the walkway and handrail is usually provided. Steps, ladders of careful use of natural slopes can be used to gain access to the walkway.
- **Free-standing trails** constructed on timber trestles allow what is in effect a high-level boardwalk to be

A tree-top trail high in a rainforest, constructed using cables between giant *Dipterocarpus* trees. Taman Negara National Park, Malaysia.

A tree-top trail constructed of free-standing timber trestles at different heights to lead people up at a gentle gradient. Ringwood Forest, Dorset.

An elevated trail made of steel and timber which is easier for disabled people to use. Budderoo National Park, New South Wales, Australia.

constructed. This can ascend to the tree canopy more gently, allowing more people to use it than if steps or ladders are needed.

Both types of trail require input from civil engineers and regular inspection and maintenance, the same as for bridges and play equipment.

Trailside shelters

Along the length of the trail it might be helpful to hikers for shelters to be located at appropriate locations to provide shelter from inclement weather, shade in hot conditions, or camping opportunities. They can vary from simple roofs to give rain and sun protection, to simple walls to give shelter from winds, or to completely enclosed structures to give refuge from the worst conditions, or camping places or safety retreats.

The simple roofed shelters might be similar to the picnic shelters described in Chapter 7, except that in remoter places they should be less finished

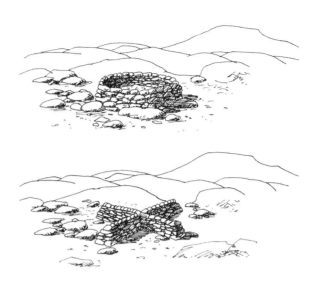

Some shelter ideas that look right in their respective landscapes: (From top – a) A simple overhead shelter of poles and twigs gives overhead shade in a hot desert climate such as Arizona or New Mexico, USA. (b) A shelter like a giant umbrella based on a 1930s CCC design. It is an all-wood construction set in a stonework base, which acts as a bench. (c) A shelter providing overnight accommodation in Kokanee Glacier Provincial Park, British Columbia, Canada.

Two designs for stone-built mountain summit shelters, which act as windbreaks whatever the weather.

in construction. A flat thatched roof of poles lashed together and covered in locally cut materials such as grass or twigs could provide shade in a desert climate. A mono-pitch frame of round timber notched together and roofed in shingles, split logs or planks will provide some shelter from rain and perhaps wind. The Lapp tent or other teepees, wigwams or wickiups modelled on indigenous or vernacular structures would work in appropriate places where more shelter is required.

In very exposed places, such as mountain tops, where the wind is severe, hikers are at some risk of

exposure when cooling off after the exertion of the climb. The windchill factor can be greatly reduced by erecting stone-walled shelters that enable climbers and hikers to sit in the lee of the wind to rest. Such shelters can be circular, creating a totally enclosed space out of any wind, or cross-shaped so that at any one time one quadrant will be entirely sheltered. Either of these types will work, but some skill is needed to build them well and tidily.

In very exposed conditions, or in places where the weather can change suddenly with low temperatures, refuge shelters could be provided for climbers and hikers caught unawares in a storm or blizzard. If the trail is above the tree-line in the open, buildings can be difficult to erect and keep weatherproof, as well as being intrusive in these sensitive places. One option is to find a hollow or low cliff beneath which a lean-to shelter can be erected, built from stone with a roof and door made from stout timber. The location must be in a place that can be found easily, marked on maps and on site and signed from the trail so that it cannot be missed.

A second option is to use a prefabricated structure designed to be weatherproof, which is taken up to the site and anchored in place with cables or Rawl-bolts of the type used to anchor climbing cables. Timber shelters of a 'beehive' shape have been developed for this purpose in Scotland, notorious for its changing weather and rapidly descending cloud, which reduces visibility extremely quickly. These shelters can accommodate

A specially designed beehive-shaped mountain shelter made of a curved timber pole framework covered and floored with sawn timber. Designed and built by Charles Gulland for Scottish Natural Heritage.

several people, who can stay overnight if need be, using the floor and benches provided to sleep on.

Where the trail is in the tree-line of a mountain forest, a log cabin style of building can be constructed on site and provided with a fireplace, as there is fuel nearby. The cabin should be primitive, to maintain the wilderness qualities while providing refuge for hikers.

Any overnight shelter can become a squalid place if not looked after by the users or by ranger staff. If it is in a remote location it is unlikely that rangers will be able to visit it very frequently. It is helpful if all users follow a code of conduct for such places, cleaning out food remains, litter and ashes, refilling wood stores and being hygienic when attending to personal needs. The provision of a visitors' book can help record incidents, weather conditions and observations about the state of the hut and the people using it.

Stiles and gates

At certain points along many trails there may be fences, walls or other barriers to be negotiated. Such fences may be needed to control livestock, to keep deer out of forests, or to prevent access by horses, motor cycles or all-terrain vehicles. Unfortunately, they can also be barriers to trail users, in particular people with disabilities or others unable to climb over them. Ideally all trails should be barrier-free, but this is not always possible.

Barriers such as fences or walls can be crossed either by climbing over or through them using some sort of stile, steps or ladder, or by a gate. Gates have the advantage of permitting wheelchairs, buggies or elderly people to go through, but they can be left open and allow stock to stray. Stiles are safer in this respect, but

mostly they cannot be used by people with disabilities or the elderly. Which method to use depends on the type of users expected and the importance of the barriers remaining intact in all seasons.

Stiles

There are several varieties of stile used: many form part of the vernacular construction used in different areas:

- **Slit stiles**. These consist of a narrow opening, tapering inwards towards the bottom, which allows a person to squeeze through while preventing stock from doing so. Made of wooden or stone posts, they are found in post and rail fences, hedges and stone walls. Modern variants also include metal self-closing stiles, which can be opened wide and are automatically closed behind by gravity.
- **Turnstiles**. These consist of cross-pieces fixed horizontally over a pole that rotates, thus allowing a person to slip through. They need to be strong and yet easy to rotate. A sturdy turning device can be made from galvanized steel.
- **Step stiles**. Wooden steps, either parallel or crossed at right angles, are built, which pass through the fence. They are used in wooden post and rail fences, hedges and wire fences. Any barbed wire should be covered by a wooden rail or plastic tube, or should be de-barbed. If one post is made taller than the others and smoothed, it can provide a useful handhold. Steps can be constructed as integral parts of stone walls, either using flat stones placed through the wall or built into the structure at wider sections.
- **Ladder stiles**. These are found in places where walls or fences (such as deer fences in the Scottish highlands) are too high for the step or slit types. Stepladders made from sturdy round or rough sawn timber are placed in an A-frame over the fence or wall, with extension pieces at the top for use as handholds.

Gates

There are many designs of gates suitable for use in most places, made of sawn timber with galvanized steel hinges and fasteners. If there is a risk of people leaving gates open, self-closing devices can be used, such as rising hinges, weights and automatic latches. Special leaning gates can be used in deer fences, but these can be heavy to lift, and there is a risk of their falling back onto people. One of the more reliable types is the kissing gate, which swings freely within a railed

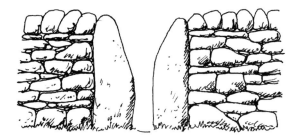

Stile designs: (From top – a) A slit stile in a wall made from stone uprights, which taper to a narrower gap towards the bottom to prevent livestock from passing through it. (b) A turnstile constructed of timber with a galvanized steel spindle. (c) A traditional step stile in a timber rail fence. The extended post makes a good handhold when climbing over it. (d) Stone steps set into the structure of a drystone wall is another traditional type of stile. (e) A ladder stile can be used to climb over high walls or deer fences. This one is in Ennerdale Forest in the English Lake District.

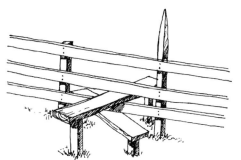

A gate with an easy to open catch so that wheelchairs or baby buggies can negotiate it. Threave Estate, Scotland.

enclosure. The user walks in, swings the gate past and walks out. It can be built to allow access by wheelchairs and prams without allowing motorcycles or horses to pass. It should be the standard form of gate for trails that are likely to be used by people with disabilities and others who may experience similar difficulties.

Fitness or trim trails

A special variety of trail much favoured in recreation areas closer to urban centres is the fitness or trim trail. This usually comprises a circular loop trail along which are positioned items of equipment used to exercise, tone and strengthen different sets of muscles. The equipment may be spaced around the trail or clustered at certain points. The jog around the trail, between the different pieces of equipment, warms the person using it, as does the order in which the exercise equipment is used.

Construction of the exercise equipment in the outdoors looks best in wood – sawn or peeled and

An area set out with various types of trim or fitness equipment. It is all made from wood to simple designs, and fits in well into this scene. Helsinki Central Park, Finland.

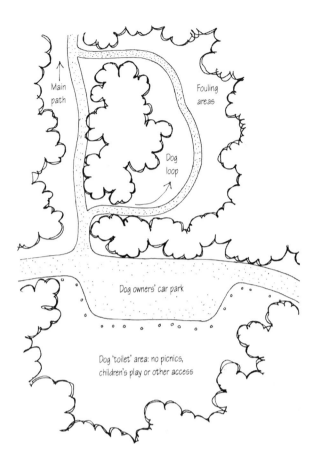

This diagram shows a couple of ways in which the problem of dog fouling can be reduced at a car park and trail area.

rounded. Metal tubing may be used for some pieces. Depending on the type of equipment it should be set in an area of hard surfacing to prevent wear and tear on the ground, or the surface should be covered in bark or wood chippings where falling from a height is possible.

Equipment should normally be set on one side of the trail so that it does not obstruct walkers who are not using it for fitness purposes. The equipment should be well spaced, numbered and provided with signs illustrating the way it should be used. Often each piece of equipment allows different degrees of fitness to be exercised, or is suited to different heights and ages of people. For example, lifting logs to make use of upper chest and arm muscles can range from light to heavy, or hurdles for jumping over can range from low to high.

Trails and dogs

Many people, particularly in densely populated areas, walk on a daily basis to exercise their dogs. This means that paths can be fouled by dog mess, presenting a hazard underfoot and a risk to health, particularly for children. Hence it is important to plan for dog walking from the outset, or redesign the trail system if it is currently a problem.

One method of coping with dogs is to devise special loops along which people can be encouraged to take their dogs when they first enter the recreation area. This enables dogs to do their business before a longer walk along the main paths commences.

The second method, more appropriate at car parks, is to set aside an area for dogs to use – a 'dogs' toilet'.

It should be clearly marked in order to let dog owners know that it is for their dogs to use, and to prevent other people from inadvertently walking over it. The area needs to be large enough so that dog mess decays before too much build-up occurs. The other method is to insist that dog owners collect and dispose of their dogs' mess. This is more common and easier to implement in urban parks than in remoter locations.

Dogs can also cause a nuisance by disturbing livestock, wildlife or other people. Management strategies may range from insisting that all dogs are under control at all times (preferably on a leash) to banning dogs in some areas at particular times of year, such as lambing or nesting seasons.

Horse riders along a special trail in the Amsterdamse Bos in Holland.

A trail for horses is provided with a hitching rail of simple but appropriate design and a set of mounting steps at places where riders may want to dismount to look at a view or have a picnic.

Horse trails

In many areas people enjoy exploring the outdoors on horseback. For some this will consist of riding from home, a livery stable or paddock into a woodland, across a common or along a bridleway. Some might take their horse to a particular destination by car and trailer, ride some trails and return home in a day. Others might go on a guided pony trek as part of a residential holiday or from a dude ranch. Finally, some will plan to ride a trail over several days, camping at places along the route where fodder and corral facilities are located. Whatever the way a trail is ridden, the route, the surface and the facilities, such as loading areas, hitching rails or corrals, need to be carefully considered in their planning and design.

The trail may be an established route such as a British bridle-path, where landowners are legally obliged to maintain the route in an open condition. It may be used by hikers as well as horses, which may pose problems when the way is narrow and heavily used. It is always preferable in busy areas to segregate trails, with special ones established for horses only, while keeping hiking routes horse-free, if this is legally permissible, depending on the access rights of a particular country.

Rough and steep horse trails are acceptable in places if it is expected that experienced riders will use them. Pony trekking or dude ranch operators may expect inexperienced or novice riders, and so they will want a range of trails from easy ones to those of a rougher nature. Riding for the disabled is a popular activity and requires extremely gentle routes.

The trail route should be laid out in a similar way as for hiking, when viewing the scenery is one of the purposes as well as exercise. The distances can be longer, as the horse is usually a quicker means of transport and the views gained from the higher position on the back of a horse are slightly more extensive than those on foot.

In areas of firm, freely drained mineral soils with rock, sand or gravel, the surfacing of the trail may need little or no attention. Sandy soils make excellent surfaces with a low risk of injury, so that stretches for a canter or gallop can be provided. However, poorly draining clay soils can churn up, and when hoof prints are deep, they can fill with water, become frozen and the surface turn into a quagmire. In such circumstances, it may be necessary to close the trail during very wet weather, restrict the overall amount of use, have alternative routes so that damaged ones can be repaired or given time to recover, or surface the trail with stronger materials to prevent damage.

If surfacing is used, the trail should be constructed in a similar manner to a footpath. The width should allow two horses to pass with ease. Trees should be kept back from edges so that riders' legs are at less risk of being injured as they pass. Low branches should be removed along the route. Additional surfacing can also be provided for a softer ride, to reduce the wear and tear on horses' shoes and to deaden the noise. Shredded bark or wood chips are excellent for this. Sand can also be used but is more likely to be washed off during rain on steeper stretches.

Water crossings can be forded in more circumstances than for hikers, thus reducing the need for bridges. Where bridges are needed, wider decking, solid planking with narrower gaps and possibly bark surfacing should be used. The handrails should be higher to prevent riders from falling over. Some horses do not like crossing bridges, so softer surfaces may help by reducing the noise and the risk of possible

An unloading ramp of two different heights allows for different trailers or vans to back up to it. Hitching rails are provided to tether the unloaded horses. Timber construction is used, with earth and hardcore infill behind the ramp retaining wall. Based on an example from the Alberta Forest Service.

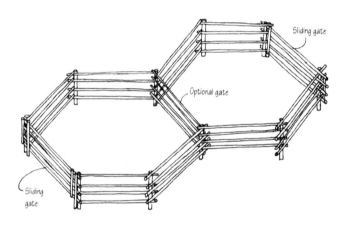

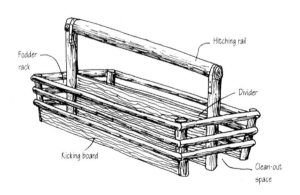

(Top) This design for a horse corral is in a traditional style with all pole ends outside the fence and an absence of narrow corners to reduce the risk of injury to the horses. Several corrals can be linked together to increase capacity in busy areas. Based on an example from the US Forest Service. (Bottom) A feed rack needs to be built where horses stay overnight. The hitching rail is incorporated into it.

injury if a horse shies. However, it is often prudent to lead a horse across a bridge.

At points where the rider may wish to stop to look at views, eat lunch or observe wildlife, hitching posts or rails are needed. A sturdy timber structure will suffice, but it must be securely fastened to withstand jerking movements by the tethered horse. A lay-by or flat open area away from the trail should be found so that the hitched horse cannot interfere with other riders passing by. If a group are out riding, then more rails will be needed. Steps for remounting horses might also be provided for the convenience of some riders. Such steps should use the type of construction suggested earlier in this section.

Where horses are brought to the area in a horsebox or trailer, special parking and unloading places should be provided so that the horses are kept out of the way of other cars and pedestrians. Hitching areas or a corral will reduce the risk of horses getting loose and causing problems elsewhere.

If camping takes place along a long-distance horse trail, overnight accommodation will be needed for the horse as well as for the rider. If a field, stable or paddock is not available, a corral is usually suitable and can be of post and rail or pole construction in a typical farm or ranch style. Corrals can be built for several horses or for single animals. Horse stalls can also be used instead of corrals. These are like open air stables, where the horse is tied in and provided with a manger. Water can be supplied from a spring or tap and fed into a trough made from galvanized steel. Fodder can be carried in a nosebag (oats or nuts), foraged around the area or provided at the campground as hay, nuts or oats. Hence storage and fodder supply has also to be provided, along with hay racks, mangers and water troughs. All structures can be made out of rough sawn or round timber, which should be untreated to avoid poisoning the horses if they lick or chew it. All bolts or nails must be recessed, cut off or otherwise hidden. Sharp corners or angles should be removed from post ends and sawn planks to prevent injury to the horses. Horses can be hobbled or tied to a long rope secured to a post, but this can be risky.

The location of horse facilities should be downwind of the camping area to reduce smells, but should be sufficiently distant so that smoke from campfires does not affect the horses. The facilities should also be placed away from any streams to minimize the risk of pollution from horse droppings and urine. The soil on which they are constructed should be suitable for horse use, as described earlier.

Horse trails, like other trails, may have to pass through fences or other barriers. Traditionally, gates have been provided that can be opened from horseback by hand or by using a whip or crop handle. Self-closing devices such as rising hinges and spring-loaded catches are fitted, as it is easier to lean forward from a horse to open a gate than it is to lean back and close it. If the main purpose of the barrier is to keep motorcycles out, a gate is inadequate. Instead, spaced horizontal logs set on posts about 1m (3ft) above ground level allow horses to step over them, but are too high for motorcycles to be lifted or wheeled over.

Where riders want something a little more exciting than a ride along a trail with perhaps some cantering or galloping, a special route with obstacles and jumps can also be provided, similar to a route used for the cross-country stages of three-day events. Steep slopes, water splashes, jumps and other obstacles can be laid out along a special trail or alongside a regular trail for this. The landowner will need to take special precautions with regard to legal liability for injury in case an inexperienced horse or rider falls along the route.

All-terrain cycle trails

One of the growth areas of outdoors recreation is that of all-terrain cycles or mountain bikes. These can go almost anywhere, can attain quite high speeds on downhill stretches, and can cause severe wear and tear, especially on soft ground. As the sport has developed there are three different main types of mountain bike use to consider:

- **General cycling** along trails with mountain bikes, coping with some steep slopes but mainly using them as a means of exploring the landscape.
- **Intermediate mountain biking** using more challenging trails and requiring more skill and fitness, where the excitement of the ride is an equal or greater element of the experience than the enjoyment of the landscape.
- **Extreme mountain biking** where the aim of the ride is the experience of following routes of different grading, plunging down steep slopes at speed, negotiating difficult, often specially constructed trails and needing special bikes, a high level of skill and a need for an adrenaline rush.

In general, where the trail system is well used by walkers, mountain bikes should be kept separate in order to avoid accidents. Codes of conduct for cyclists

All-terrain bikes are increasingly popular, but they can cause erosion, and they do not always mix well with other trail users because of their speed. Gauja National Park, Latvia.
Source: Courtesy Janis Strautnieks.

A section of trail made specially for mountain bikers so that they have more challenges. Dalbeattie Forest, Scotland.

should be encouraged. As for hiking and horse riding, the cycle route for the general cyclist should be chosen with the overall experience in mind, including physically challenging sections, interesting features and views.

Routes for general cycling should be chosen to avoid soils that are easily eroded, and should be aligned where possible to prevent washout during rainy periods. Some surfacing may be needed in soft or wet places, where these cannot be avoided. Cyclists might also be encouraged to use forest or park roads for some stretches. This will reduce wear and tear elsewhere.

For intermediate and extreme cycling, a network of graded routes can be developed. The grading system

A set of signs explaining the different kinds of routes available for mountain biking, graded to different levels of difficulty. Mabie Forest, Scotland.

A bicycle lock made from a large log with slots cut from it and large eyelets to lock the bikes to.

used for skiing has been adopted, using colours to indicate runs, such as green, blue and black. In partnership with cycling organizations and in order to provide adequately graded challenges yet preventing unacceptable erosion, considerable construction might be incorporated into the route.

All routes should be waymarked where there may be doubt about the direction, so that cyclists do not stray into more sensitive areas and follow the relevant grade of trail. However, in many places, especially if the use is light and the terrain robust, unrestricted access to roam around might be permitted for general cycling.

In cases where the trail surfacing has collapsed, remedial action should be taken as quickly as possible. Routes may have to be diverted, the surface reinforced and drainage laid.

Cyclists can usually use the same water crossings as walkers, carrying their cycles if need be. This reduces the number of bridges and fords that are needed. If cyclists and hikers or horses have to cross or share a section of route, the layout should allow plenty of passing room, and the code of conduct should explain who gives way to whom. Signs should give warning of the section, especially crossing of one path by another, and the trail layout should ensure good visibility, a crunchy surface to warn of cyclists' approach, and possibly barriers to keep users separate in unavoidably narrow sections.

Bikes can also be carried over stiles in most instances. Where there are kissing gates, it is possible to insert a special slot in the enclosing fence that will allow a cycle to be passed through but not an animal or motorcycle.

As cycles are valuable and easily stolen, racks that can be locked should be provided for them at car parks or other risky places. A design suitable for the outdoors consists of a log with slots cut out of it. Each slot has a strong eyelet screwed in next to it. The cycle wheel or frame is placed in the slot, and the cyclist can lock it to the eyelet using their own lock.

Cross-country ski trails

Another growth area of trail use is cross-country or Nordic skiing, used to follow trails during the winter season. The same principles of trail route design should be followed as have already been described, as one of the enjoyable aspects of such skiing is the chance to see wildlife, frozen waterfalls and lakes and splendid snowy scenery. Routes through forests are frequently preferred, as the trees catch the snow, and the day-long shade in the winter reduces the thawing. There is also less chance of the snow being blown off the trail. Since the landscape is experienced at a faster pace than when hiking, and as uphill or downhill sections imply either extra effort to climb or greater speed on the descent, these sections should remain simple, with more consideration for the landscape variety along the more level or undulating stretches.

In many urban fringe and accessible forests in Scandinavia or parts of North America, extensive systems of specially prepared trails are provided. These are of

Cross-country skiers enjoying the wide spaces and rich landscape of Trollheimen in Middle-Norway.
Source: Courtesy Jørund Aasetre.

A cabin in Lapland used for shelter and to warm up after skiing in Lapland, Finland.
Source: Courtesy Tuija Sievanen.

different lengths and for different levels of proficiency. Usually the prepared trails are wide enough – up to 3m (10ft) – to permit one or two sets of parallel tracks for the traditional method of skiing side by side with room for speed skiers using the skating technique. Lighting might also be provided in northern latitudes where daylight is short or nonexistent in winter months. These routes should be waymarked like hiking trails, with information provided at the start on length, difficulty, expected duration and any special features to be encountered.

In wilder places, the chance to ski on new, unprepared snow and experience the stillness of the winter forest provides a marvellous experience. Forest roads covered in snow have far less visual impact than at other times of year, and make excellent routes from which other trails can be chosen. Hiking trails may also be used if the gradients are not too steep or dangerous.

Along the route it may be appropriate to locate benches and shelters such as those described for hiking trails and picnicking. In remoter areas many people enjoy skiing to a cabin, cooking food and camping before skiing back the next day. Shelters with fireplaces and fuel are provided along such networks in Finnish Lapland, for example, where sausage roasting over a fire is a traditional experience after a day's skiing.

Other artefacts that are needed are racks where skis can be stacked when taken off and for leaning them against to apply resin coatings. In busier places, toilets might be needed (see Chapter 6).

Ten

Water-based recreation

Water in almost any form is an attractive feature in the landscape. As well as its aesthetic qualities, it is highly valued as a recreation resource for fishing, bathing and boating.

Planning for water-based recreation to cater for the often conflicting demands of various activities is essential. This is a large subject, and this chapter is not intended to explore it in any detail. Its purpose is to consider the design of facilities needed by the main forms of water-based recreation, and measures needed to prevent site damage at the vulnerable land/water interface. Site layout should consider the segregation of different uses, such as boat launches and jetties, fishing from the shore, sunbathing and swimming, together with the protection of sensitive shoreline habitats. Zoning of a lake or river for these uses is frequently the main result of water recreation planning, which in turn determines the general layout and site design criteria for the area. The requirements for structures and artefacts to enable visitors to enjoy their activity to the best of their ability and in safety will be determined by this set of considerations.

Fishing

Fishing is a very popular pastime, enabling many people to enjoy an absorbing activity in the outdoors, as well as an appreciation of nature.

In general, the facilities described in this section are extra to the basic requirements already covered in previous chapters, such as car parking, picnic areas, paths, toilets and shelters. In many areas there is no design for fishing facilities: they look scruffy and badly constructed. Nor is there much attention to the site, so that common problems are bank and access route erosion, damage to sensitive habitats, litter, human hygiene and the danger of fire. There are different requirements for game (trout, sea trout and salmon) and coarse fishing, and differences between riverbank or lakeshore fishing and fishing from a boat.

Fishing from a riverbank or lakeshore

Game fishing involves access to the bank or shore and wading into rivers. Access routes and paths need to be planned and designed unless the use is low enough to involve little wear and tear. The wilder character of many rivers and lakes may suggest as little path construction as possible. The next requirement is for vegetation management to maintain space for casting flies. This may involve removal of trees or trimming of branches, which should be carried out so as to prevent unsightly disfigurement to trees or bushes. If boats are used, launch areas and jetties are required (see below for details).

People who go coarse fishing (that is, for fish other than trout, sea trout or salmon) normally sit on the bank of a lake or stream, or use a boat. Small platforms are needed if the soil is wet, soft and sticky. Timber planks nailed to a frame will spread the weight of a person and enable stools, umbrellas and tackle to be organized more easily clear of mud and weeds. A boardwalk or strengthened path may be needed to provide a better route to the fishing areas (see Chapter 9).

A jetty over the water will give access for visitors with disabilities. Railing may be necessary if the water is deep, or for other safety reasons, but raised edges

Fishermen can cause a lot of wear and tear to the ground, so they often need paths, platforms and other features along the edge of the river, lake or pond.

A fishing jetty where anyone, including people with disabilities in wheelchairs, can gain access to the water for coarse fishing. Finnish Lapland.

A life-ring and instructions near a lake where many people, including young children, visit. David Marshall Lodge, Scotland.

A fish-cleaning station with cutting surfaces and vermin-proof lids over plastic buckets, which can be used to collect and dispose of fish guts. Derived from a design by the Alberta Forest Service, Canada.

to prevent wheels from slipping off may be all that is required. The jetty can be cantilevered from the bank, built on piles, or floated on the water.

Where visitors are permitted to venture close to water, however deep, especially when paths lead them there, safety must be considered. Life-rings should be provided, located close to the water's edge in visible places that are easily accessible. Spacing between life ring stations should be close enough to require only a short dash to one once a person is spotted in difficulties. The usual plastic floating rings are adequate, with a length of line attached by which to pull the rescued person back to the shore. The line should be rot-proof (polypropylene), and long enough to reach beyond the distance out from the shore that people are

likely to fall in. Regular and frequent checks of safety equipment are necessary to ensure that it is in good condition. The life-ring stand should relate visually to other artefacts and be of simple design. A vertical post of large dimensions can be used in many situations.

It is enjoyable to eat freshly caught fish, so picnic areas with fireplaces should be provided nearby if appropriate to the character of the landscape, or where fire risks from uncontrolled fires are too great (see 'Fireplaces' in Chapter 7).

Fish for cooking have to be cleaned. The odd remains of cleaning one or two fish for cooking in a remoter place can be disposed of by packing it out, burning it on the fire or burying it so as not to attract wildlife. However, in well-used places, in hot weather and by lakes used

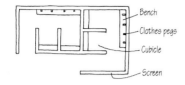

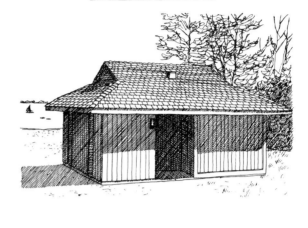

Changing-room designs: (Clockwise from top left – a) A monopitch building with high-level windows provides facilities for segregated male or female changing. (b) Individual units to be used by anyone. Light can get in above and below the doors. (c) Combined changing rooms and toilets in one building. The rooms are ventilated by louvres, but they do not receive sufficient natural light. Williamson Lake Provincial Park, Alberta, Canada.

for other activities, fish residues should not be left lying around. They smell, attract flies and other wildlife, such as bears in much of wilder North America. Therefore, cleaning stands should be provided. These can be made to workbench height with surfaces equipped with cutting boards that can be scraped off into plastic buckets or bins with lids to prevent seagulls, flies and, if need be, bears from getting in. Hard ground surfacing all around and water available for regular hosing will keep the stands clean. The buckets or bins should be regularly removed along with litter and garbage from elsewhere on the site. Such cleaning stands are especially needed when people land numbers of fish

from boats and clean them before taking them home. As with all artefacts, they should be simple structures designed to fit in with others on the site, and positioned to be screened from attractive views, perhaps in spaces at one side of the main access routes from the shore or boat landings.

Freshwater bathing areas

In the summer months, especially during long periods of hot weather, lakes become warm and rivers and streams present tempting opportunities for cooling off. In the wilder places people may wish to swim in a lake

A lake beach where a low retaining wall has been laid in order to reduce the wear and tear of the grass edge along the beach. Whistler, British Columbia, Canada.

A river can also be popular for bathing and the movement of water offers excitement but also danger. Black Water of Dee, Scotland.

or stream and delight in the remote, solitary nature of the place. Other more gregariously used places may become busy and subject to potential problems of hygiene, litter, safety and site damage, which reduce the pleasure and spoil the setting.

Hygiene requirements may include toilet blocks, showers, changing cubicles, drinking water supplies, litter management and restrictions on taking pets into or near the water. Ideally, bathing facilities should be grouped within a single building to reduce the impact of several structures in the landscape. Toilet blocks have been dealt with in detail earlier, and can include showers and changing cubicles.

Where separate buildings are needed to house changing cubicles, these should be designed to match the toilet blocks and picnic shelters used elsewhere; they can also include showers. Basic shelter structures can be modified easily with partitions, screens and benches. Their design should include non-slip floors, which are sloped for ease of washing down and draining. Partitions must be high enough to ensure privacy, with sightlines into entrances screened off. Materials should not splinter or be of an abrasive nature. Pegs or hooks should be provided for hanging clothes. Lockers are occasionally provided at the larger sites but not at smaller ones, where cars or family picnic spots are within easy reach. Changing cubicles can be individual, unisex arrangements or communal separate-sex areas with appropriate signage. If demand increases at the site, it may be necessary to increase the number of changing units, so designing a building

that can be extended easily or internally remodelled is an advantage.

The site layout should also include signs to orientate visitors to the changing facilities and toilets, and to guide their behaviour: for example, reminding them that glass bottles should not be used anywhere on the site.

Lakeshore protection

Constant wear and tear along the landward edge of a beach should be prevented. This can be achieved by access control in the most vulnerable places such as wetlands, stream mouths and steeper banks, and by edge reinforcement where access is permitted. Low, rockwork walls or timber edges help to define the edge and stabilize it.

Rockwork walls can vary from the use of locally obtained natural boulders laid fairly roughly to maintain a natural character, to well-laid drystone or mortared construction in keeping with a more rural or urban character, and where use is heavy. Ramps and steps should be provided along obvious access lines from parking areas to the water's edge. The rockwork can act as seating, places to dry towels and bathing costumes, can give some shelter from wind, and can provide warm areas for sunbathing.

Edges might also consist of stout baulks of timber laid end to end, possibly built up in horizontal layers to form low walls. Higher walls can be made by vertical round timber driven in side by side and topped with horizontal sawn planks. If the wall is taller than 1m (3ft), protective handrails are probably needed (see Chapter 9).

Lake bathing areas

That part of a lake set aside for swimming should be planned and laid out for safety and to give people an enjoyable experience. The choice of swimming area should take several factors into account. The suitability of the water is important, particularly its cleanliness and temperature. The shelter or exposure of the area and the likelihood of insects if it is too sheltered should be considered. The character of the lake bottom is also important. Firm sandy or gravelly conditions, gently sloping with no sudden drops, are essential so that inexperienced swimmers do not suddenly find themselves out of their depth. Sand or gravel beaches are more likely to be backed by grass or forest vegetation instead of cliffs, sand dunes and other coastal features. This means that they can be less vulnerable to damage than sand dune areas are, but they can also be muddier when worn.

If sailing and powerboats also use the lake, they must be separated from general bathing in order to avoid serious accidents. This can be achieved by a line of buoys demarcating the outer zone at around the 1.8m (6ft) depth. These buoys are spread along a rope or cable anchored in place at intervals, with a depth marker at each corner or change of direction. The ends of the cable are attached to adjustable fixings on the shore, such as posts or anchors.

Within the demarcated swimming area, a second area should be divided by another line of buoys along the 1m (3ft) depth line. Again, this should be provided with depth markers. This inner shallow area can be further divided into a safe area for children and non-swimmers to use.

Depending on the degree of use, and on any national, state or provincial regulations, safety equipment and personnel should be stationed at regular intervals along the beach. A lifeguard station may be present, and equipment such as a small boat, surfboard, radios, life-rings and first-aid kit should be kept there. A secure shed for the equipment other than the boat and a high seat for the lifeguard should be constructed in the same design character used elsewhere on the site.

River bathing areas

If rivers are to be used for bathing, planning must address issues of zoning for different users along different stretches, such as boats fishing and swimming, which may conflict with each other or require particular qualities of river water depth, speed or riparian vegetation.

Rivers may provide good swimming opportunities, although the water is usually colder, which, together

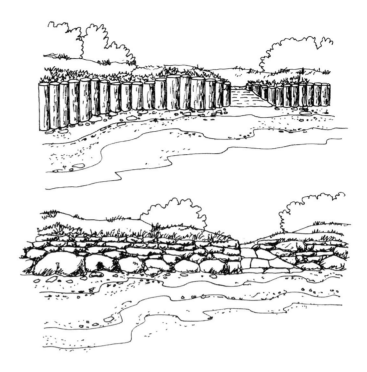

Two methods of protecting lake shores: (Top) Timber piling trimmed off to follow the profile of the land. (Bottom) Rockwork, with large rocks lower down, grading to smaller ones at the top. Both methods allow the inclusion of an access ramp.

with currents, may make them less safe for children or inexperienced swimmers in an unsupervised location. Shallow pools with gravel bottoms and stretches of potholes, natural chutes or slides and ledges are very attractive, allowing safe and exciting activities. Some of the best swimming is to be found in places where glacial meltwater torrents have eroded solid rocks into dramatic forms, but where the river is now much less than it once was.

As with lakes, riverbanks can be easily eroded by overuse, so that retaining and reinforcing structures of a similar nature might be needed. As erosion is also a natural process, it is worth looking at the pattern of currents, so that access and use are not concentrated on the most vulnerable areas. This depends on the rock type and the character of river. A faster mountain stream is more erosive than a sluggish one meandering across a flatter area. Erosion is mostly concentrated on the outsides of bends, while shingle banks occur on the inside. Hence creating access to the inside areas is less likely to cause damage.

As with lakes, safety features such as depth markers, life-ring stations, ropes across the stream to delineate deeper areas and to hold on to, or rocks placed across

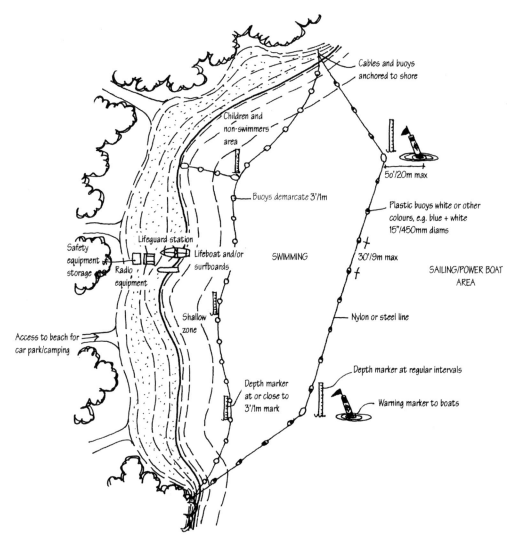

Cables and buoys anchored to shore

Children and non-swimmers area

Buoys demarcate 3'/1m

5o'/20m max

Plastic buoys white or other colours, e.g. blue + white 15"/450mm diams

Safety equipment storage

Lifeguard station

Radio equipment

Lifeboat and/or surfboards

SWIMMING

30'/9m max

SAILING/POWER BOAT AREA

Shallow zone

Nylon or steel line

Access to beach for car park/camping

Depth marker at or close to 3'/1m mark

Depth marker at regular intervals

Warning marker to boats

A diagram showing all the requirements for a lake bathing beach to be used by many people.
Derived from the US Forest Service.

faster areas for the same reason, should be provided. Warnings about places where it is difficult for children or less fit people to get out of the water should also be considered.

Boating facilities

At many sites with water access, people want to be able to launch boats. These may range from small kayaks and canoes that can easily be carried from a car roof rack to the water, to larger sailing or motorboats, which need ramps into the water to launch them. In remoter locations it might be appropriate to allow only those craft that can be manhandled, while in the busier areas nearer cities boat launch areas, mooring jetties or

even fully fledged marina facilities with refuelling places might be provided. This is partly to reduce the degree of development, the number of artefacts and the use of motorboats in wilder places. The use of materials should also reflect the environment. However, good, simple, well-constructed facilities are needed for durability, appearance and safety. When planning for boat use, the launching ramp or jetty should be chosen for the landscape setting as well as the type of boats, site requirements and safety.

Boat launches

One of the simplest and most effective forms of boat launch is a sloped ramp descending at a shallow angle into the water. Boat trailers are reversed down this, and

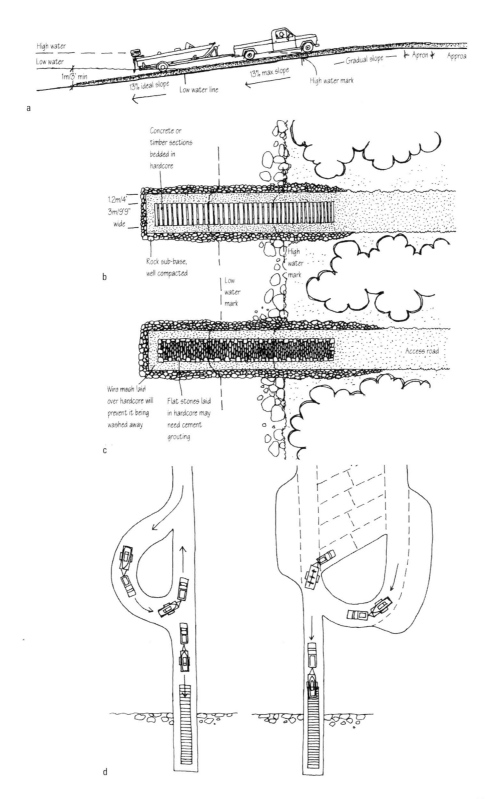

Boat launching-ramp designs: (a) The basic requirements of gradients and water depths for a functional and safe boat-launching ramp. (b) A ramp layout using prefabricated concrete or timber slabs bedded into hardcore laid on a compacted rock sub-base. (c) A ramp constructed from flat stones laid in hardcore retained by an edge of larger stones, which are embedded in the base. (d) The layout of the road to and from the ramp allows the towing vehicle to turn to reverse down it and then to park, after launching the boat, in a pull-through parking area nearby.

A boat launch on a lake in British Columbia, Canada, with a ramp made of concrete slabs laid on hardcore.

A launch place for canoes or kayaks, enabling them to be carried down the bank and lowered into the water. Columbia River, Oregon, USA.

the boat is slid by hand or let down by cable under its own weight into the water. It can then be moved to a jetty nearby, where passengers can board and supplies are loaded. The trailer and the towing vehicle are then moved to nearby parking, which does not intrude upon the water setting.

Launch ramps can be constructed from the following materials:

- **Poured concrete**, which is prone to cracking, especially in areas where severe winter temperatures are likely. If damaged, it is difficult to repair. It can also look most urban and too finished for wilder locations. Exposed aggregate varieties of concrete that use local types of stone will blend in better.
- **Reinforced concrete** slabs laid side by side and linked with steel couplings. A small space is left between them and filled with gravel. These are flexible to lay, easy to replace, and can be pre-cast off site. The gaps between them give good grip for shoes and vehicles in wet conditions. The coarser texture and gravel infill helps, this type to blend into the landscape. Exposed aggregate concrete looks better and helps give a good grip.
- **Timber slabs**, laid in the same way as the concrete slabs. These do not last as long, but they are easy to lay and replace, and they do less damage to the bottoms of boats when they are hauled out of the water. Preservatives cannot be used on the timber because of the risk of the chemicals leaching into the water. The timber may become slippery where it is most frequently in contact with water.
- **Flat rocks**, which can be laid *in situ* on a firmed base in-filled with gravel. These may depress under

the wheels of heavily laden trailers but they tend to blend with the landscape better than the other varieties, and are easier to fit and re-lay.

Jetties

Jetties are needed for mooring boats and seaplanes that land on lakes in the remotest locations. Jetties should be located in sheltered places out of the way of currents and in places where the water is naturally deep enough for the types of boat or seaplane intended to use them. The design of jetties must reflect the qualities of the landscape while being planned to be fully practical.

In shallow water where levels do not fluctuate, a jetty can be constructed on piles made of durable timber connected by a framework with a surface deck. Rocks can be used to infill between the piles and give some shelter and breakwater to the mooring area.

In deeper water, floating jetties may be better, particularly where water levels vary significantly. Floats can be made from well-cleaned petroleum drums (metal or plastic), blocks of polypropylene, or special proprietary floats made from plastic with flanges to fix them to frames.

The deck of the jetty can be constructed from sawn timber frames surfaced with planks. If preservatives are used, care must be taken to ensure that it is not toxic to fish or other aquatic life (see section on boardwalks in Chapter 9). Any metal fixings should be of galvanized steel. Small jetties can be taken out of the water and stored on shore over winter for repair and maintenance. Jetties can also be prefabricated, which is an advantage when they are to be transported to remote locations.

A small jetty for tying up boats made of timber piling along the edge of a lake.

A small marina made of floating prefabricated sections, which are linked together and connected by a hinged ramp to a floating fuel store and then to the shore. The whole system is flexible, and allows changes in water level and swell on the water surface. A reservoir near Portland, Oregon, USA.

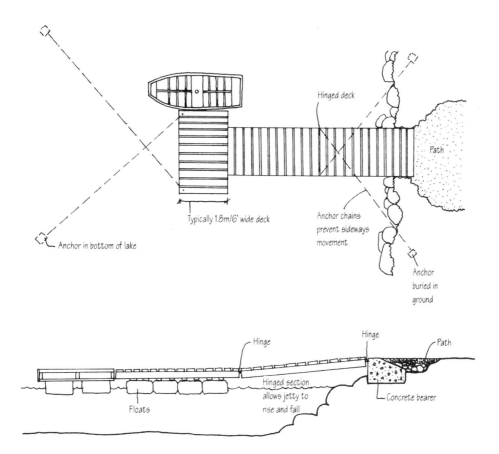

(Top) A plan showing the layout and general dimensions of a simple timber jetty and the way it is stabilized using anchor chains. Based on Alberta Forest Service designs. (Bottom) A section through the jetty shows the general method of construction, connection to the shore and the floats fixed beneath it.

The jetty must be anchored to a fixed base on dry land, usually a concrete block, by hinges or short chains, which allow it to rise or fall with the variations in water level. The jetty consists of an access ramp or gangplank section, whose angle varies with the water level, to walk along; this joins by another set of hinges onto a floating section used to moor boats. To prevent sideways movements and twisting or buckling in waves and winds the ends of the gangplank and the offshore end of the floating jetty section should be anchored with diagonally arranged cables or struts.

Steel and timber can also be used. This is more durable and stronger, which may be required in busier locations and for less experienced boat users where buffeting is more likely. Galvanized steel frames can be prefabricated; floats can be made of metal tubes with timber decking bolted on. In places where less experienced sailors, passengers and swimmers are expected to use the facility, or where the gangplank can be steep due to low water levels, handrails should be fixed to it. This variety is a low maintenance one, but it can also be hauled out of the water if need be. It must also be anchored to the shore as described above using cables or steel struts, which give added stiffness as well as securing the ends to prevent sideways movement. The metal frame construction is a more highly finished design appropriate to busy sites. Its more urban appearance is out of place in wilder, more remote locations.

All-metal jetties of pontoon construction are also used in marinas. Hollow metal watertight boxes are the basic unit, with or without timber decking, and bolted together in various combinations, which can be expanded as demand increases if the lake can support the number of boats. This type of design is at the most urban range of the spectrum from the simple wooden structures described above, and is appropriate for the most gregarious locations.

Eleven

Wildlife viewing

One of the most exciting aspects of visiting the outdoors for many people is seeing wildlife, especially unusual or large mammals and birds. Sometimes driving along roads provides opportunities, as some animals use the verges to graze, or they cross roads *en route* from one place to another, and do not seem disturbed by the presence of vehicles. Birds of prey can be observed hunting along road edges for small mammals, taking carrion in the form of road kills and using utility poles and wires as perches.

Often road traffic hits and kills wildlife, while large animals such as deer can inflict damage to vehicles and injury to passengers. Where scenic or tourist routes encourage wildlife viewing, the wildlife should be protected from injury by traffic by a range of measures. These include wildlife warning signs for motorists, passages beneath the road to allow wildlife to cross the route in safety, fences and small roadside mirrors to reflect headlight beams off the road to warn wildlife at night.

Some drivers will stop and leave the vehicle to take photos of wildlife, which may not be as oblivious to the presence of a human as they might be of a car. Hence an attractive alternative is to view wildlife in more natural settings, in circumstances where there is no risk to either the animals and birds or to the people who have come to look at them. Moreover, the hint of mystery and element of surprise on arriving at a place where a herd of deer or bison or flocks of birds can be seen adds greatly to the experience of the visit.

Hide layout and design

One of the best ways to identify and observe wildlife is from a hide (blind) where the approach is camouflaged and from which a good, clear view can be obtained. Benches to sit on, an aperture to look through, and the knowledge that the animals or birds are undisturbed by the human presence – all add to the enjoyment.

Many organizations have developed facilities to enable visitors to observe wildlife in this way. Occasionally the observation is also used to protect rare species, especially birds, during the nesting season. Thus, visitors appreciate the sight of birds feeding their young and understand something of the need to protect them from egg thieves or unscrupulous hunters.

As with any facility, places for wildlife observation will need some design consideration and input. If the site is particularly attractive, large numbers of visitors might arrive to see breeding, migrating or over-wintering birds or animals. Hence there might be a need for large-capacity hides, good paths, well-designed car parking and toilet facilities. All of these, except the hide, have been dealt with already. The design of the hide or observation point is the next thing to consider.

The approach to the observation point should be designed so that the visitor is downwind and out of sight. Landform can be used to ensure that the trail is below a ridge or behind a slope. Thick vegetation can also be used to screen the access, and is ideal in most cases. Screen fencing, preferably as a temporary measure, can be used to fill any gaps or to cover the last stretch before the hide itself. Woven hazel fencing or any visually opaque material taller than head height is satisfactory. If people with disabilities are to look at

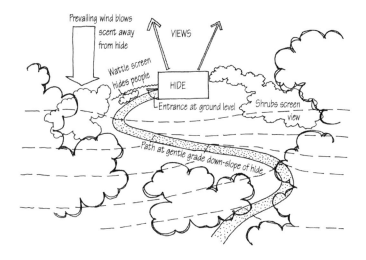

A layout of a wildlife observation hide area, showing the factors that should be included in the design.

A hide with a hidden approach path using dense trees. The hide is also reached by a boardwalk, which is ideal for access by people with disabilities.

the wildlife, the approach path will have to take account of the gradient and the surface needed by them as well as the hidden approach.

In its simplest form, the hide can consist of a section of fence with viewing slots or holes through which people can look. The slots can be at different levels to permit use by smaller people, children or wheelchair users. If the hide can be orientated so that the sun is usually behind it, the wildlife will be front lit and easier to see and better to photograph. Lenses of binoculars or cameras will not catch the light and alarm the wildlife, and the shady, back-lit face of the hide will be less obvious.

In order to be used all year round and in all weathers, an enclosed building should be constructed. A neutral, simple form that merges into the background will cause the least intrusion. Often a wooden structure will suffice, either square, rectangular or polygonal in shape with a mono-pitch roof, perhaps covered in turf, thatch or branches, accessed from the rear either at ground level or from a gently graded ramp. Its capacity and sophistication should reflect the degree of use expected. If coachloads of ornithologists or school-children are regular visitors, then a large building may be needed, with raked seating and a large window through which to see the wildlife. A big window means that the interior of the hide should be kept dark to avoid the sight of moving people. A screen or shutter can

cover the window while people go in and out with a light on and then be opened to reveal the wildlife. An overhanging roof will ensure that a shadow is cast over the window to keep it darker still. For winter observation in cold climates, double glazing, insulation and heating may also be required. Benches and ledges to rest binoculars or cameras on will assist people staying to see more elusive wildlife. Posters showing the characteristics of the different wildlife can be put on the walls.

Aquatic wildlife such as fish can be viewed in several ways – from below or from above. There are examples of submerged structures equipped with windows of strong, thick glass through which views into the river or lake can be obtained. These are expensive to construct but they give an unusual and exciting view of fish from within their own habitat. A boat with a clear plastic or toughened glass panel in the bottom of the hull is another method.

Viewing platforms can also be constructed that jut out over a river or lake. In places where migratory fish come up to spawn, the sight of thousands of salmon or sea trout can be awesome, especially as they try to jump up rapids, and such platforms give more people a better view. The type described in Chapter 9 can be used for this purpose.

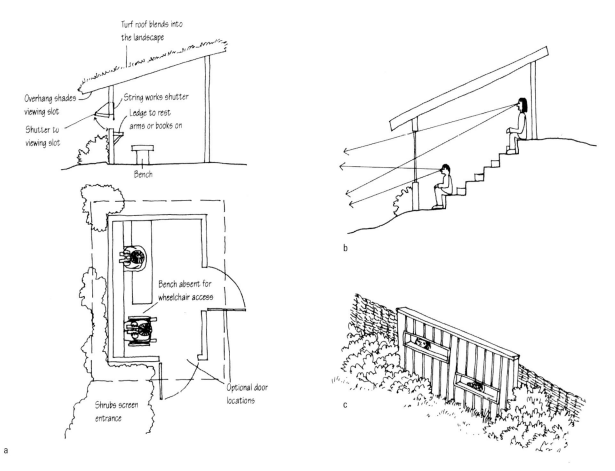

Some considerations in wildlife observation hide design: (a) The layout of a simple hide with access for wheelchairs.
(b) A larger-capacity hide with tiered seats to accommodate larger groups of people such as a school party or a bus
trip. (c) A simple hide made from a timber screen wall with viewing slots is cheap but effective.

Design of wildlife areas

As well as bringing people to the wildlife, it is possible to bring wildlife to the people. Areas can be developed into open glades, wetlands or ponds that attract deer, birds, butterflies and other wildlife. Such areas should be designed not just to provide good habitat but also to look as natural as possible.

- **Open glades in a forest**, where sunny edge habitat, good quality forage, water and mineral licks are provided, can attract shy creatures such as deer regularly enough so that visitors have a high probability of seeing them. The edge design of such glades, their shape, size and the impact of management activities should be carefully considered. Irregularly shaped areas where the open space tends to be in the hollows among landform will

often look more natural. For similar effects, groups of shrubs planted for browsing should be placed at irregular intervals and be of varied sizes, while trees pruned to let more light into the edge or to open up the edge for a view should have the height of the pruning level varied.

- **Glades in a woodland** can also be developed for butterflies and insects, which do not usually move away from humans like animals or birds. Vegetation management is the key here. Edges of trees, patches of shrubs of different varieties and heights, herbaceous vegetation and grassy areas maintained on a cycle of cutting and mowing will provide the food plants of indigenous species for butterfly larvae and the nectar-giving flowers for the adults to feed on. The design of these glades can be developed by varying their width, the shape of the space and their

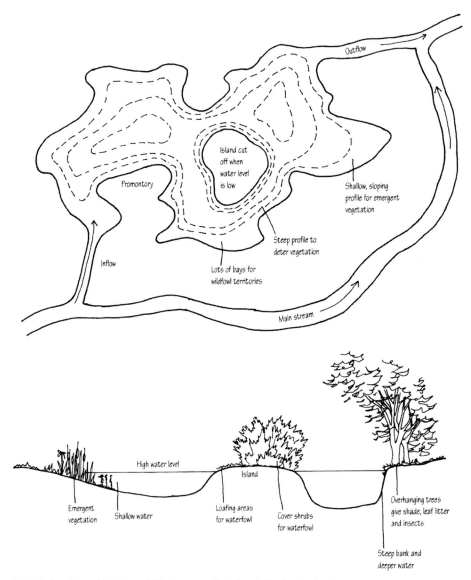

Labels (top diagram):
Outflow
Island cut off when water level is low
Promontory
Shallow, sloping profile for emergent vegetation
Steep profile to deter vegetation
Inflow
Lots of bays for wildfowl territories
Main stream

Labels (cross-section diagram):
High water level
Island
Emergent vegetation
Shallow water
Loafing areas for waterfowl
Cover shrubs for waterfowl
Overhanging trees give shade, leaf litter and insects
Steep bank and deeper water

Considerations in the design of a pond to attract wildlife to an area. Variations in depth and edge shape are important in order to give a range of pond habitats.

direction to create wonderful linear habitats as part of a trail through the landscape.

- **Wetlands and ponds** should be made to look natural with varying water levels, curvilinear shapes and graded edges to allow different vegetation types to be developed in different places. Irregularly shaped islands placed off-centre in ponds will help to protect waterfowl from vermin. Bays and promontories will increase the territories available for different birds and add to the natural effect.

If dams are constructed to convert a stream into a wildlife pond, these should be designed to blend into the surrounding landform as well as possible. Engineered, trapezoidal retaining walls stand out artificially in the scene, and should be modified with naturally shaped earth mounds and plenty of shrubs and trees.

- **Old gravel workings** often make excellent habitats for a wide range of wildlife in areas close to cities, where excavation can leave well-shaped areas that colonize quickly. Wildlife observation can go hand in hand with environmental education in these circumstances, particularly when schools are close by.

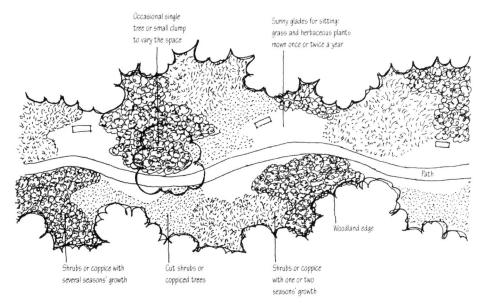

A glade area with a path through it and a varied edge habitat developed to attract wildlife, particularly birds and butterflies.

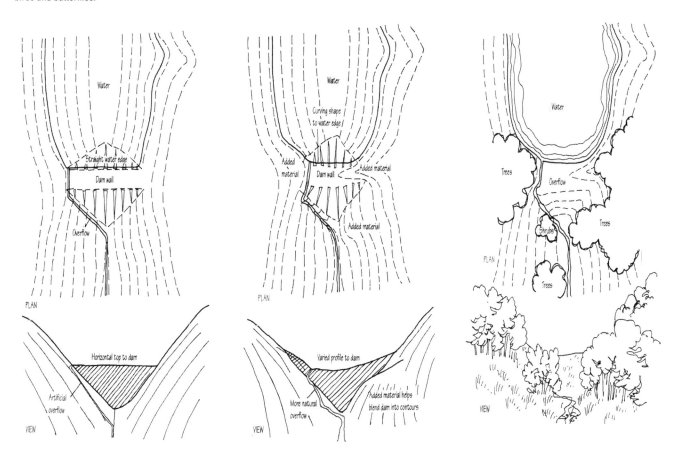

The design of dam walls for wildlife ponds needs care: (From left – a) A basic dam wall with a symmetrical profile and flat top. (b) Earth has been added to the dam to vary its profile and to blend it into the nearby contours. (c) Vegetation on the parts with extra soil helps to blend it further into the surroundings, as long as the roots are prevented from damaging the clay core of the dam.

Small jetties can be extended over a pond to allow activities such as pond dipping.

As well as the more obvious larger animals, birds and fish, viewing opportunities for other wildlife are possible. In wet areas, small jetties can be erected from which pond dipping can take place. This allows children as part of their education or play (see Chapter 8) to see frogs, snails, newts, water beetles and small fish, which are just as useful and fascinating to study. Shallow places can be used for wading with nets for the same purposes.

Twelve

Design for overnight visitors

Previous chapters have concentrated on designing for visitors who go to an area primarily for a day trip and leave before the evening. However, the outdoors can be particularly attractive at other times of day, especially at dawn and dusk. There is also something special about staying longer at a place, when there is time to know it better, to explore remote places and absorb the atmosphere. Nights spent in wild places, whether unrolling a sleeping bag beneath the stars, camping in a tent, a trailer caravan, a motor home or staying in a cabin, can complete the sense of closeness to nature, extend the period of unwinding and relaxation, and permit more extended routes on foot, horseback, all-terrain cycle, skis, boat or kayak to be explored. Some of the facilities needed for overnight stops – fireplaces, toilet blocks, horse corrals, boat jetties and shelters – to some extent have been covered in the previous chapters. In this chapter, the specific requirements of a night's stay in the outdoors will be discussed. Tents, touring caravans or camper vans/recreational vehicles and cabins will be covered. Static caravans could also be considered in a similar way to cabins in terms of the design considerations for their layout.

Desirable qualities for an overnight visit

Staying overnight in a wild, remote and scenic place offers a rather different experience from staying in a motel, hotel or bed and breakfast. Sometimes the discomforts associated with some forms of camping can be so acute – burnt and smoky food, biting insects, inadequate washing facilities, uncomfortable sleeping arrangements – that the experience of the outdoors must far outweigh these and the perception of home comforts available in more usual overnight accommodation. Hence there are two key elements to the overnight experience. One is the level of home comforts to be provided, and the other is the quality of the setting and the atmosphere and its enjoyment.

Home comforts can increase with the type of accommodation available, but there can be a consequent reduction in the quality of setting, the atmosphere and its enjoyment. The Recreation Opportunity Spectrum tends to favour backpacking with a bedroll or small tent in the wildest areas to fit in with the setting of remoteness and lack of human presence, whereas trailer caravans and motor homes set in developed areas supplied with electrical hook-ups and on-board bathrooms would be more typical of less remote, more gregarious settings. At one end of the scale, there is the added thrill or tension of being among wild animals, some dangerous to humans, while, at the other, the risk of attack is minimal.

Nevertheless, there can be a wide range of experiences. Dispersed camping sites can mean that it is possible to be alone in a motor home and feel away from others, while at some busy backpacking sites campers can feel very crowded. Therefore, it is important to design to sustain the qualities of being close to nature but not too close to other people.

Market demand should be assessed before deciding what to provide. Provision might be segmented, allowing different sites or different parts of the same site to be developed for different categories of user in varied ways. For example, backpack hikers are likely to seek a remote, wild experience where some element of self-reliance is needed. Alternatively, they might be on a low budget for their trip and wish to camp cheaply in a field by a farm that may be near to a pub or bar. Remote long-distance trails in the Rockies of North America or New Zealand will suggest the former, the West Highland Way in Scotland the latter. There is nothing wrong with either, except that both markets should be catered for if possible.

Family groups may camp because they also seek a wilder experience, except that issues of vehicular access, safety and entertaining young children have to be accommodated. Camping has also traditionally been a cheap way for less well-off families to have a holiday or vacation, so that wilderness may not necessarily be what they want. Families often prefer or will tolerate busier campsites, where they can mix with like-minded people and where the children can play easily and safely together while the adults socialize.

Trailer caravans may also attract a particular user group. In some places, the users may return regularly to the same site and even the same pitch, spending several weeks there and meeting old friends from past years. This social side becomes difficult if the units are widely dispersed around a large area. There may also be another category of people who tour from place to place, staying one night at a site and then moving on. For them, the social contacts outside the family or couple may well be secondary to the solitude and the variety of settings experienced.

Motor homes, because of their mobility, are most likely to be used by people who like to spend a fairly short time in one place. In the USA and Canada, the biggest of these RVs (recreation vehicles) may be seen towing a car with a boat loaded on a roof rack. They stop at sites, and use the car for local expeditions and the boat to fish or sail on a nearby lake. Such a versatile vehicle requires plenty of space, and needs good roads.

Cabins, by contrast, can be owned by a family who use it for their vacations; or sites with a number of cabins may be built to be let or co-owned. In many places with lakes, such as the Okanagan region of British Columbia, almost every lake is ringed by cabin sites set down near the shore and tucked in among the trees. In Finland, the recreational use of lakeside cabins is part of the national culture. Cabins for rent are increasingly popular. The quality of accommodation can be high, while the self-catering aspect attracts people, especially families, for whom eating in restaurants is too expensive or detracts from the experience. Cabins can be used all year round, and in some places such as

ski resorts the high season is the winter; they provide the security of home comforts within an outdoor or wilder context.

A further user of camping facilities is the organized group such as the Scouts, Girl Scouts/Guides or other youth organizations. These offer youngsters the well-tried formula of fresh air, exercise, an introduction to nature, team building and pioneer skills such as open-air cooking, building things from materials found on the site, and exploring. As well as the supervision of large numbers of one age group, there are requirements for segregating the sexes, formal activities such as parades, open-air services and separate areas for patrols or subgroups within the main camp area.

Camp layout and planning: general considerations

Observation of established campgrounds in various countries and locations suggests that there are different varieties of layout to suit different user groups. Sites can be designed to cater for one group or be varied so as to offer different settings to suit different preferences.

Open sites with free or flexible access

In much of Europe, especially Britain, the Netherlands, Denmark and Germany, more open campgrounds often seem to be preferred. The populations of these countries are high, space is at a premium, distances to sites are not great, wild or remote places are relatively rare, and more gregarious layouts seem to be acceptable. In Britain and the Netherlands, where woodland cover is quite low, open sites frequently cannot be avoided.

An example of a camping and caravan site in a relatively open setting. Each pitch is equipped with cable television and internet as well as electricity. Garmisch Partenkirken, Bavaria, Germany.

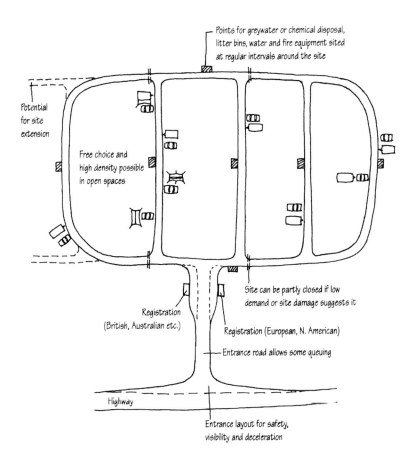

Points for greywater or chemical disposal, litter bins, water and fire equipment sited at regular intervals around the site

Potential for site extension

Free choice and high density possible in open spaces

Site can be partly closed if low demand or site damage suggests it

Registration (British, Australian etc.)

Registration (European, N. American)

Entrance road allows some queuing

Highway

Entrance layout for safety, visibility and deceleration

(Top) This typical layout used in many places, particularly by commercial operators, is efficient in using the ground. The vehicle circulation can be confusing, leading to some areas being over-filled and others left relatively empty, depending on whether spaces are allocated at registration or are freely chosen. (Bottom) The same area can be laid out better as a series of self-contained loops leading from the main entrance. This layout also helps pedestrian circulation and the siting of toilets and ancillary fixtures.

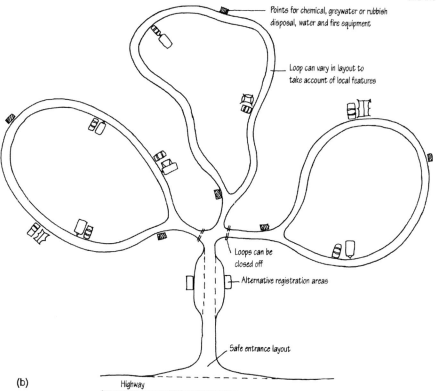

Points for chemical, greywater or rubbish disposal, water and fire equipment

Loop can vary in layout to take account of local features

Loops can be closed off

Alternative registration areas

Safe entrance layout

(b)

Highway

It is typical for a site to be laid out with an entrance road leading to a loop or series of loops from which access is freely available to pitch a tent or park a vehicle and caravan on a grassy surface. At peak times such sites can be very densely arranged. Open campfires are not usually found there, so most people bring gas stoves or charcoal barbecues for cooking. In partially wooded sites, such as the New Forest in the south of England, the trees help to disperse camping or caravan units and reduce the impact of a large site.

One advantage of open sites is the flexibility to increase densities at peak times if the users are tolerant of such close proximity. If use is dispersed at other times, parts of the site can be closed off to allow vegetation to recover or to reduce the area of the site to be maintained and supervised.

Open sites can be windy and exposed to external views, whence they may appear very unattractive. Planting of small trees or shrubs and the use of landform can lessen the wind and help to screen the impact of the site, as can the use of landform. Using the same techniques, the site can be broken down into smaller and pleasanter spaces with some increase in privacy. On the other hand, windy or at least breezy sites can be advantageous in insect-ridden places. Midges and other pests cannot fly in a stiff breeze, and the speedier drying of open sites after rain can further reduce their incidence as well as making the site drier underfoot.

As well as the tents, caravans or mobile homes, there will be other structures or items needed around the site, such as fire hydrants, extinguishers or sand buckets, taps or stand pipes, rubbish bins, grey water or chemical toilet disposal points, electrical hook-ups, information signs and ablution buildings. These will be more visible and potentially have greater visual impact on open sites. Enclosures or clusters of these facilities should be considered, and a comprehensive approach to their design should help lessen the impact and visually unify the site.

Spur sites with controlled vehicle access

In North America, it is more common to disperse the camping around a site into individual or sometimes dual or family units well separated from their neighbours. A short spur is made off the loop access road, into which the trailer, motor home or car can be reversed. An area next to this is laid out as an open area equipped with a fireplace and table.

The setting for many but not all of these sites is forest or woodland, providing a strong sense of

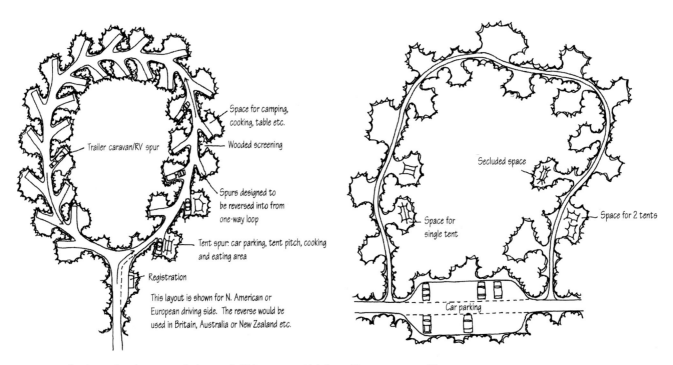

Good examples of spur campsite layouts: (Left) A one-way vehicle loop with spur areas set off it at intervals. (Right) A walk-in tent loop where parking is restricted to one area and tent spaces are spread out along a loop trail.

enclosure, screening from neighbours, increased privacy and reduced fire risk. Some sites are zoned into tent or trailer/RV areas. In the tent zones there are car spurs next to a prepared area that is level, well drained and smooth, on which to pitch a tent. In the trailer caravan/RV zone, the surfaced spur usually needs to be larger, and the open space does not need to be as level.

In Britain and Europe, there are examples of woodland sites of a similar nature, but they do not seem to be as popular. This may be partly because people are not used to enclosed forests and so tend to favour more open landscapes. They might also be more worried about trees falling on their tent or vehicle. Southern Europe is an exception, where shade is needed. Tall trees such as umbrella pines can provide shade yet the space beneath can be quite open and not very enclosed by shrubs, for example.

Wooded sites offer shelter and shade, but they may also be more prone to biting insects, especially in damp, shady conditions during the summer months. The choice of site should try to avoid places where insects are a problem, such as low areas next to boggy or marshy ground.

Walk-in, boat-in or fly-in sites

Some campgrounds for tents only can be laid out so that there is no direct vehicle access to the pitches. A central car park is provided next to an open area or with walk-in loop trails leading to small clearings in which to pitch a tent. These give a slightly wilder feel than those where the tent is next to the car, but they do require all the equipment to be carried in. This type of site might be more attractive to people who travel light and prefer a more 'backwoods' atmosphere.

As well as campsites where vehicles are used for access, there are those on lakesides, where a number of campers arrive by boat or seaplane. Although these are located in some of the remotest settings, the number of people attracted to the area justifies laying out a campground in order to reduce impact or pollution risks.

Pedestrian circulation

Pedestrian circulation around the site must be considered in the layout from the outset. Routes to toilet blocks, rubbish disposal points, to shorelines, trails, boat launch places or moorings, and so on, need reasonably direct access from various parts of the site without people interfering with the privacy of other pitches. The concept layout can be tested for possible route lines, and where possible conflicts occur, the design can be adjusted.

Vegetation, landform and water or wet areas can be used to help guide pedestrian use. Based on an agreed design, paths can be constructed and signs and information panels erected to help new arrivals find their way around, particularly when the site is widely scattered and views around it are curtailed by shrubs and trees.

Provision of facilities

It may be necessary to provide a range of facilities at campsites. The level and type of provision will depend on the character of the campsite, the type of users it is aimed at, and its robustness. This may be related to the ROS, to national, state, provincial or local regulations concerning public health and fire safety, and the demand for various activities by the users.

Toilets

Most campsites for tents should be provided with toilet facilities. The type and the amount of provision should follow the same concepts and specifications as those described for toilet provision at day-use sites in Chapter 6. Any of the types described will suffice, depending on the size of the site. To minimize the distance that people have to walk to the toilets, it may be better to erect several small blocks in key locations around a scattered site instead of a large and more economical central block. There may also be regulations determining the maximum number of pitches per toilet block that can be provided.

Showers and laundry facilities

Buildings with toilets and showers in single-sex sections with a laundry room attached may also be provided. The design and layout can be based on some of the toilet designs, modified as necessary. Laundry facilities may be restricted to hand washing, or may include coin-operated washing machines and tumble dryers. The latter may be appropriate if people are staying for any length of time and there are no alternative facilities within easy travelling distance of the site.

Community buildings

In many places where the weather can be unpredictable, a hall or community building can be provided to give campers a chance to keep warm and dry, to cook under a shelter or to meet other people. This can be a simple

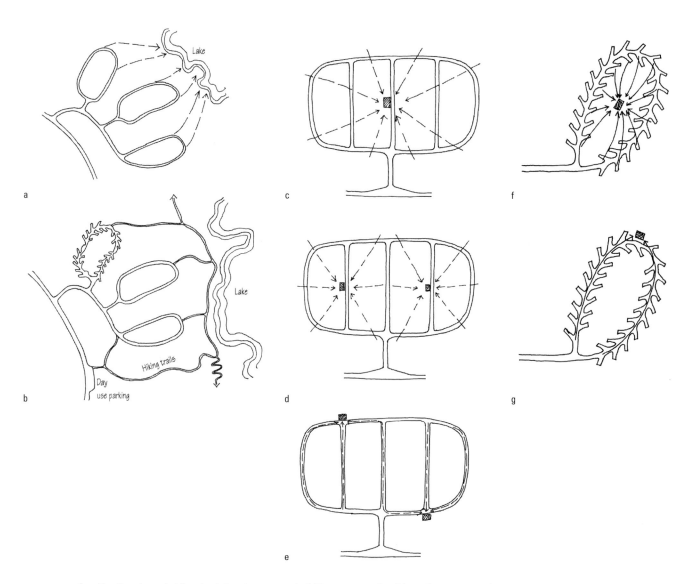

Considerations for pedestrian circulation at campgrounds: (a) Loops arranged at right angles to an attraction such as a lake enable people to use the roads without crossing through campsites. However, this can put pressure on the nearest part of the lakeshore. (b) Separated day use with controlled circulation to provide access and site dispersion should be considered. (c) Circulation within an open site can cause problems where there is, for example, a central shower and toilet block. People will tend to take the shortest route, reducing privacy and security and possibly causing disturbance. (d) Two shower/toilet blocks reduce the overall traffic but at possibly greater expense. However, the siting still causes similar problems to (c) even though all campers are equidistant from them. (e) In this layout, the toilet/shower blocks are placed so that the roads are naturally the easier routes to follow. (f) Circulation problems can occur with spur layouts. Centrally located toilets or showers should be avoided for this reason. (g) Placing toilet/shower blocks at the end of the loop makes it easier to follow the road to them, and reduces impact elsewhere.

A campground community building based on a 1930s CCC design. It contains a large room with a generous fireplace. The log and rough stone construction is visually attractive and of extremely good workmanship.

affair such as a shelter with a fireplace and some benches or a more sophisticated enclosed building with several rooms.

Any of these buildings, if provided, should be carefully sited and the camping loops/spurs so arranged to give the shortest route to the toilet blocks for pedestrians.

Other facilities

The same criteria of siting apply to water supply, litter bins, fire extinguishers and other safety equipment. If possible, the toilet block should act as the focus for positioning all these facilities so that drainage, litter collection, sewage pumping and other servicing needs can be achieved at one place with minimal travelling by service workers around the site. Furthermore, there may be office/shop buildings and storage to be considered at the entrance area to large, more commercially operated sites.

Campground layout design

Given the range of considerations described above, together with the requirements for daily activities at or near campgrounds, their design is a complex task. The layout should try to fit the desired number of camping or caravan pitches and the best vehicular and pedestrian circulation (separated if possible) into the landscape while accommodating the wide range of additional structures needed. Different landscapes will offer different possibilities, so a thorough survey

is needed to establish the main features and limiting factors before design is undertaken:

- **Slope and landform**. Tents and caravan trailers need to be on a level surface, wherever possible. Naturally level areas such as hollows or spurs in hilly places should be identified so that the pitches can take the fullest advantage of natural places and minimize excavation or filling of side slopes.
- **Drainage**. Wet areas breed insects and are unsuitable for tent camping, so the provision of some drainage might be desirable, especially if natural drainage has been disrupted by excavations for the roads, paths and pitches. Water may flow onto a pitch site unless cut-off drains are laid. Run-off from surfaced or cut areas collected in drains may carry silt into watercourses or lakes unless silt traps or soakaways are provided.
- **Trees and vegetation**. In more open sites, the existing surface vegetation such as grass may not be robust enough for heavy use, so that consideration should be given to alternative surfaces for vehicle control. Shrubs and trees with extra planting as required may offer ideal opportunities for screening to reduce the impact of the mass of tents or vehicles, separate pitches, create shelter or shade and guide circulation. The design concept for the site may be based on the opportunities provided by different vegetation types and the amount of enclosure they provide.
- **Linkages**. The various linkages into other parts of the campsite and its surroundings have to be established. If the site is near a feature such as a lake where there is significant day use, it is often preferable to separate the two types of facility for access and parking. However, links from overnight and day use into a trail network could be worthwhile so long as day visitors do not become enmeshed in campground circulation and activities.

The whole site can be split into areas for different kinds of camping as described above, and can also take account of different landscape types within the overall site: flat versus hilly, open versus wooded, near attractions versus remote, and so on. It is also possible to vary the character in terms of the degree of finish to the camping area to reflect the ROS ranges. This is also relevant in Britain and Europe, where different sites and diverse camping environments are difficult to obtain.

The detail of some layout designs for different environments and categories of users is now considered.

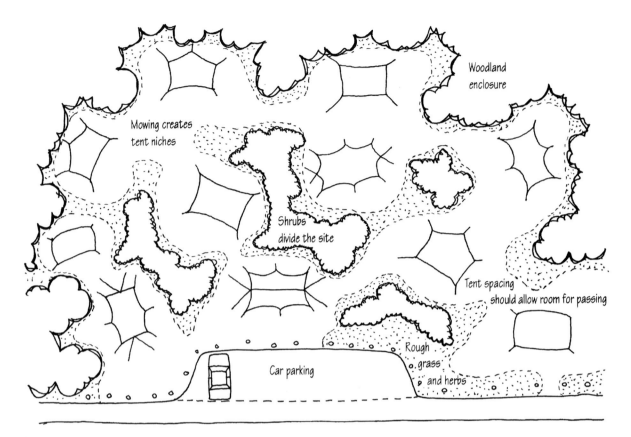

Woodland enclosure

Mowing creates tent niches

Shrubs divide the site

Tent spacing should allow room for passing

Rough grass and herbs

Car parking

A layout for a tent area in an open site. Car parking is restricted to a central area. The site is divided into pitches separated by shrubs and rougher grass. This helps to give campers their own spaces. No fires are accommodated here, although it would be possible in a roomier layout.

Open sites for tents

The ground needs to be level, reasonably smooth and with a good dense grassy sward. The soil should be freely draining, relatively easy to drive tent pegs into, and unlikely to stay wet or become muddy. Noise insulation is non-existent in tents, so some physical separation between pitches is desirable. Unless tent pitches are marked in some way, such as by a numbered post, or each place has its own fireplace or hearth, a practical way is to let people choose their own site. They will probably tend to select the widely spaced locations first and fill in until the space seems as full as it can be given the need for private space. Dividing the space up with irregularly shaped shrubs or trees will create pitches for a given area that feel more private.

Fireplaces of the circular 'campfire' variety can be provided for some or all of the pitches (see Chapter 7). Strict regulations about distances between pitch and campfire need to be indicated and implemented to avoid fire risks, as most tent materials are highly flammable.

The grass should be mown fairly regularly. This can also be used to demarcate pitch layouts, by mowing some areas and leaving others to grow tall and thus deter camping.

There are two main options for car parking design. Either cars drive to the pitches, so that tents can be pitched next to them, or else cars are parked at a central parking area around which the camping sites are arranged, and campers carry their equipment to their pitches. The latter option has several advantages: cars are confined and cannot spoil the surface in damp or wet weather; it is much quieter, as some campers can use their cars without disturbing nearby pitches.

Open sites for trailer caravans/tent-trailers/RVs

The sites should be laid out so that access roads in the form of loops have pitches set alongside them numbered with marker posts. The trailers or RVs are then reversed onto the grass at right angles or obliquely to the road at set distances. Where required, the area

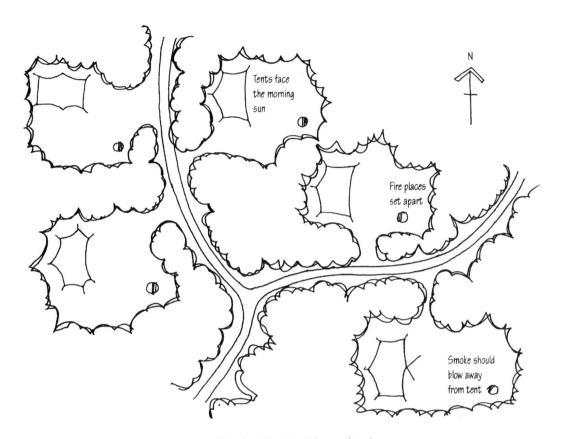

Tents face
the morning
sun

N

Fire places
set apart

Smoke should
blow away
from tent

Thought should be given to the layout of tent sites within a loop. Here the pitches can face the
morning sun; fireplaces are set apart to reduce fire risks to tents or vegetation, and to reduce the
drift of smoke.

can be subdivided by trees and shrubs to create smaller
spaces and to allow some small clusters of family
groups to establish themselves.

One advantage of an open layout in Europe and
Britain is that it can more easily cater for cars and
trailer caravans, whose doors open on different sides,
depending on whether the vehicle is driven on the right-
hand or left-hand side of the road. Thus the layouts
must be flexible in terms of space and orientation, for
camping extensions to trailer caravans and the location
of picnic tables or fireplaces.

Where electrical hook-ups are supplied, their
number and position set the limit for the capacity of the
area and the spacing for the pitches.

Spur sites for tents

In this layout there are three further options:

- **Loop road**. The tent area is accessed by car from
  a loop road. Each pitch is provided with a parking

An ideal woodland tent camping area provided with a parking place,
flat tent base, picnic table and fireplace. The trees screen sites from
one another, giving privacy and security. Baxter State Park, Maine,
USA.

A camping shelter, known in the USA as the 'Adirondack Shelter'. The fire in front of the open shelter gives warmth. Baxter State Park, Maine, USA.

where trees and shrubs come close to the tent, providing effective separation between units in terms of sight and sound. Rubbish is either taken out completely or left at a receptacle by the car park, where a standpipe and vault toilet will also be provided. This layout is also suitable for those remote camping areas where access is by boat or seaplane. Instead of the car parking area, there is a jetty, or use is made of a gently shelving beach. This option is likely to be more suited for those people seeking a quieter, more solitary, wilder experience, and who do not require so much equipment.

- **Camping shelters**. Instead of tents, wooded sites can be equipped with open-fronted camping shelters. These are constructed from timber with asymmetrically pitched roofs. They have a wooden floor, and are raised off the ground. In front of the open side is placed the campfire. In the USA, these are often called 'Adirondack' shelters after their origins in the Adirondack Mountains of New York State.

Spur sites for trailer caravans/camper vans/RVs
This layout is similar to that for tent spurs accessed by car, except that the spur has to be longer to accommodate the larger vehicle combinations, but adjoining space does not have to be so large or so flat. Spurs must have gentler gradients, and should be set out to be reversed into at an oblique angle to a one-way loop, or be arranged parallel to the road to allow vehicles to pull through them to leave. Because of the increased length, extra cut and fill may be necessary on steeper or more variable terrain, and so careful surveying of sites is prudent.

In North America, all camping spurs of this kind can be arranged so that the caravan/trailer/RV doors open onto the picnic and fireplace clearing or access to it. In Britain and Europe, because of the variations in position

spur. Next to this is a tent area, a picnic table and a fireplace. In the most primitive type the pitch can be an open space, a little distance from the car, cleared of stumps and stones, and with a grassy surface. Logs can be provided as simple benches, and a circle of boulders for a hearth. A slightly more improved variety can be given a better surface, nearer to the car, with a hearth equipped with a grill or kettle hook and a sturdy bench. A further upgrade could have special pitches of level, smooth surface provided with a steel hoop fireplace or a steel altar fire and a picnic table. Toilets, showers, water and rubbish disposal will be concentrated at a focal point of one or more loops.

- **Central parking.** Cars are left at a central parking area and campers walk into the camping area carrying their kit. The pitches are sparsely equipped ones, as described in the first option above. Small paths lead from the main trail into secluded spaces

A series of camping spur layout designs: (a) General dimensions and road geometry for parking at a camping spur (left-hand drive vehicles.) (b) A design for level ground. (c) On side slopes some excavation may be needed. The camping/picnic area has been placed a little distance away from parking to take advantage of the setting. (d) A pull-through spur parallel to the access road may be better on steeper side slopes, to reduce excavation. (e) Two vehicles and two tents are accommodated for a larger family in this design. (f) Another design for two cars and one large or two small tents. This layout can be used for right-hand or left-hand drive vehicles. (g) In this layout, the table and fire are set away so that an awning can be erected for a trailer caravan or RV. (h) This design allows caravans or RVs of left-hand or right-hand drive to be accommodated, together with awnings or extensions.

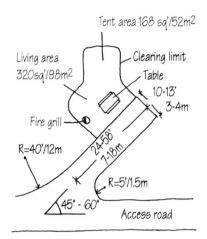

Tent area 168 sq'/52m²

Living area
320sq'/98m²

Clearing limit

Table

10-13'
3-4m

Fire grill

R=40'/12m

24-58'
7-18m

R=5'/1.5m

45° - 60°

Access road

a

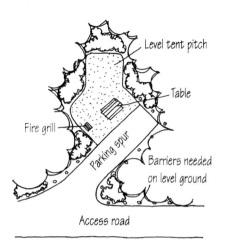

Level tent pitch

Table

Fire grill

Parking spur

Barriers needed
on level ground

Access road

b

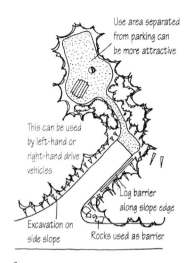

Use area separated
from parking can
be more attractive

This can be used
by left-hand or
right-hand drive
vehicles

Log barrier
along slope edge

Excavation on
side slope

Rocks used as barrier

c

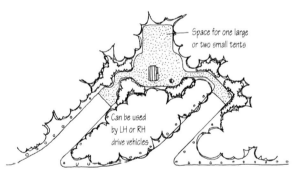

Pull-through spur

Can be used in either direction
depending on drive side of vehicle

Rocks used as barrier

d

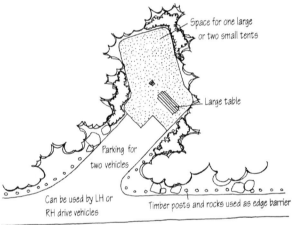

Space for one large
or two small tents

Large table

Parking for
two vehicles

Can be used by LH or
RH drive vehicles

Timber posts and rocks used as edge barrier

e

Space for one large
or two small tents

Can be used
by LH or RH
drive vehicles

f

This option uses
more space but
allows both RH and
LH drive trailer
caravans to erect
awnings

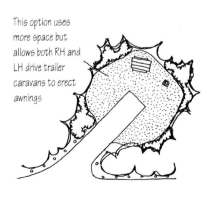

Area close
to trailer
caravan or
RV allows
space to
erect awning.
Can also be
used for tent

For RH drive vehicles, reverse the layout

g

h

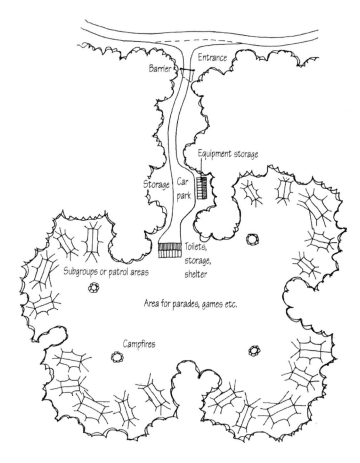

A layout for a youth camping area (suitable for scouts, church groups, etc.).

surfacing can look very intrusive in open sites, although this might be necessary to prevent too much site wear and tear.

Youth camping sites

These generally need more open space. If they are not of the primitive variety where the group rents a field from a farmer, digs its own latrines, and so on, then a central parking and administrative area with toilets and showers or several small units of these are provided. Larger spaces near these and separated from one another permit each patrol or other subgroup to pitch their tents in a cluster. A central larger area is needed for group activities. This should be arranged for easy access from tents, vehicular access and parking. With children participating in active games, good access for emergency purposes is essential. Spaces must have good separation between cooking fires and tents, which also allow the formation of large campfire circles for the evening storytelling and singing that is a tradition.

As large, relatively level open areas may be difficult to find in some places, it may be advantageous to develop and maintain permanent youth campsites in suitable locations.

Design of campsite utilities

Fire equipment, disposal points for water, chemicals and rubbish, maps of spur and numbering layout, phones, bulletin boards and other signs and artefacts are usually needed. All this can be unsightly if not designed to look simple, unified and in keeping with the setting. The sites for such artefacts should be chosen where they can be tied into the landscape. A clump of trees, a wall, a dense area of shrubs or a rocky bank can all provide suitable backgrounds. A fence or enclosing structure can help to integrate and screen many of the more unsightly facilities, while access to them is maintained.

Access for people with disabilities

Like other forms of recreation, as many camping areas as possible should be designed to be barrier-free and offer universal access. This is easy on flatter sites, where tent pitches or trailer-parking areas can be on the same level as the paths, picnic tables, fires and other facilities. On more sloping sites, a proportion of pitches should be levelled and have access paths that conform to the gradient requirement described in Chapter 9.

of doors on vehicles, spurs should have sufficient width for the vehicle to be parked more to one side than another for convenient access to surrounding and larger open spaces.

Each spur can be fitted with an electrical hook-up. The loop arrangements make cable routeing much easier than with more randomly spread trailer caravan sites. Increasingly, cable television and even internet access can also be provided at the same hook-up facilities. Grey water and chemical toilet disposal points can be located at the entrance to the trailer loop, where access is easier both for campers to pump out their units and for maintenance staff to pump out the collecting cisterns. The same criteria apply for rubbish disposal and collection.

Spur sites of all types are particularly well suited to wooded landscapes, where they gain most visual separation from one another, and where the forest floor is unsuited to free access by vehicle. The quantity of

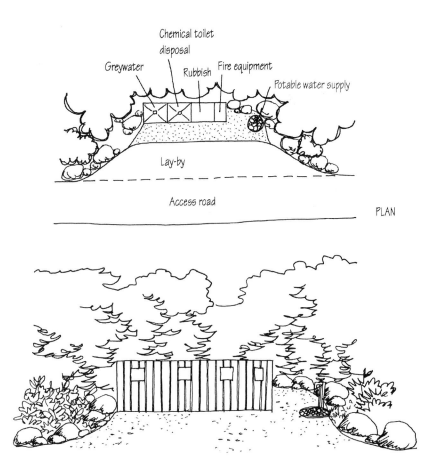

Chemical toilet disposal

Greywater

Rubbish

Fire equipment

Potable water supply

Lay-by

Access road

PLAN

A design for campsite utilities such as fire equipment, water, litter, grey water and chemical toilet disposal arranged into a neat enclosure provided with a lay-by and surfaced access. Trees and shrubs help to screen it, although the tidy design would also work in open sites.

A campsite with quite a lot of trees for shade but otherwise open underneath. The sewage disposal place can be clearly seen, not very well screened from view. Near Cap Ferret, Aquitaine, France.

A choice of experience should be offered, from the wildest to the best equipped, just like any other site. Parking spurs usually need more space around them to facilitate the manoeuvring of special equipment.

Other buildings

As well as the requirements for services described above, there may be other buildings needed on the campsite, such as entrance station and office buildings for administration, maintenance and fee collection. Occasionally shops, bars and restaurants are provided (often let to concessionaires). In all cases the layout of the site entrance should allow new arrivals to pull over to register, pay fees and collect information while permitting other campers to drive in and out. If there is more than one building, they should be grouped

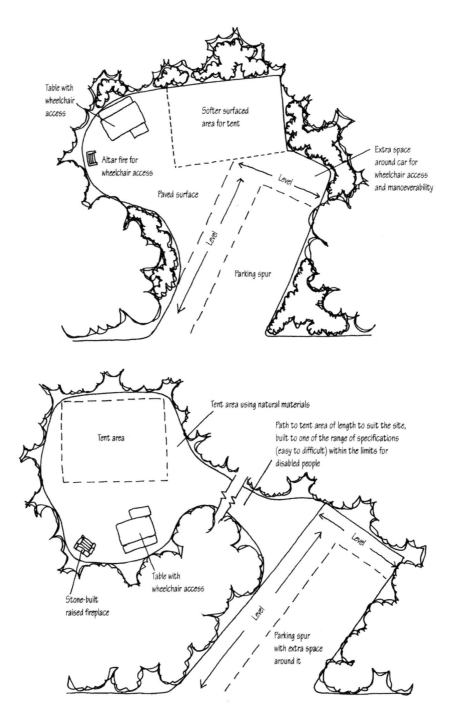

Table with
wheelchair
access

Softer surfaced
area for tent

Extra space
around car for
wheelchair access
and manoeverability

Altar fire for
wheelchair access

Level

Paved surface

Level

Parking spur

Tent area using natural materials

Path to tent area of length to suit the site,
built to one of the range of specifications
(easy to difficult) within the limits for
disabled people

Tent area

Level

Level

Table with
wheelchair access

Stone-built
raised fireplace

Parking spur
with extra space
around it

Some spur layouts to permit camping by people with disabilities:
(Top) A design for a campsite in a highly developed area.
(Bottom) A design for a wilder, remoter area with vehicle access.

and built to similar styles appropriate to the setting. If toilet, shower and laundry blocks are also provided, all the buildings on the site should be designed as part of a family, using the same kinds of form, materials and colours to ensure that unity is maintained. Trees, shrubs and other vegetation can be used to tie buildings further into the landscape.

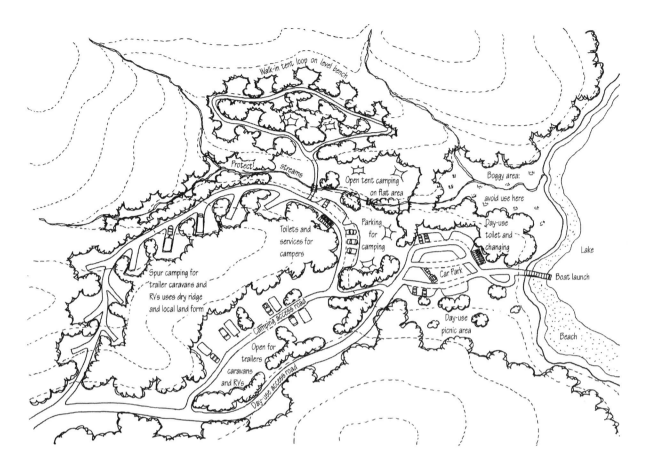

This design for a large layout shows how terrain and vegetation can be used to provide a range of open and wooded sites for caravans/RVs or tents, together with a day use area. Sensitive or difficult areas have been avoided, and circulation for pedestrians and vehicles has been organized.

Case study: Lost Lake Campground, Mount Hood National Forest, Oregon

In order to demonstrate some of the design concepts and principles described above, it is useful to look at a good example. Like so much recreation design in recent times, it involves major refurbishment and reconstruction rather than a completely new development.

Lost Lake Campground started life a long time ago in 1916. Prior to road access in the early 1920s, people took a train to the village of Dee, and then hiked 13 miles (21 km) to Lost Lake. In those days people sometimes drove cars, but more often they rode horses into the forest. As the location was relatively near the city of Portland with a growing urban population, and as road access improved, popular access to the recently established National Forest was in quite high demand. The campground originally comprised an access road with some fairly primitive sites for backwoods-type

camping. Fishing and boating on the lake provided the main attraction to both day visitors and campers.

As time went on, use gradually increased. Trailer caravans and RVs were introduced in the 1960s, and the number of pitches gradually grew. Nothing was consciously designed. Available areas away from the roads were developed into parking spurs with little thought for site degradation. The east lakeshore became overdeveloped and worn out by the early 1980s, with camping extending all along it. There were 87 pitches with still rising demand, while the concessionary site operator wanted more capacity to give better economic viability. As well as the camper use, there was increasing day visitor demand, which was mixed into the site and which needed some management. The US Forest Service realized that a major refurbishment was overdue, and a team of landscape architects and other Forest Service staff were appointed to the task.

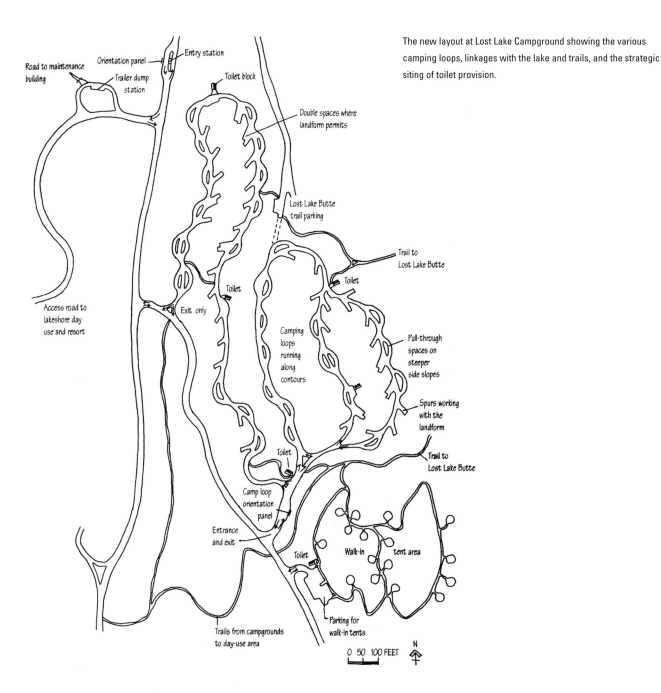

Road to maintenance building

Orientation panel

Entry station

Trailer dump station

Toilet block

Double spaces where landform permits

Lost Lake Butte trail parking

Trail to Lost Lake Butte

Toilet

Toilet

Access road to lakeshore day use and resort

Exit only

Toilet

Camping loops running along contours

Pull-through spaces on steeper side slopes

Spurs working with the landform

Toilet

Trail to Lost Lake Butte

Camp loop orientation panel

Entrance and exit

Toilet

Walk-in tent area

Trails from campgrounds to day-use area

Parking for walk-in tents

0 50 100 FEET

N

The new layout at Lost Lake Campground showing the various camping loops, linkages with the lake and trails, and the strategic siting of toilet provision.

The extent of the campground is limited. It is a generally forested area occupying a bench between Lost Lake and a volcanic cone (Lost Lake Butte). With variable terrain but a general 13 per cent side slope, the linear nature of the site parallel to the lakeshore provided challenges to the designers. The only really flat area is heavily forested with old growth cedar and fir, wet and unsuitable for development. Much of the area, particularly at lower levels, is fragile and easily eroded.

A survey of the site and an analysis of constraints and opportunities led to the crucial design decision to separate day use, concentrated on the lakeshore, from the camping by moving much of the latter up the slope away from the most fragile areas, which would be subsequently restored with native vegetation. The survey identified a paved, under-utilized logging road running along the slope some way above the original campground. This offered an opportunity to become the new main access road from which other loops for

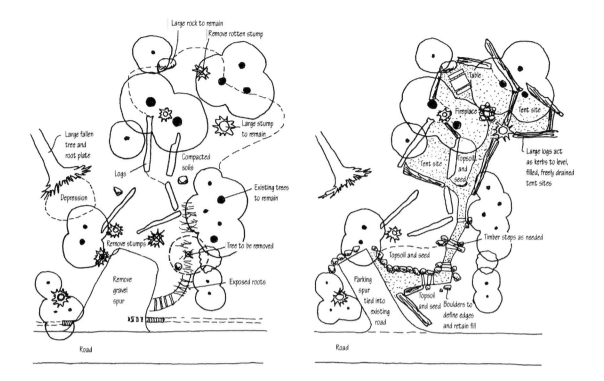

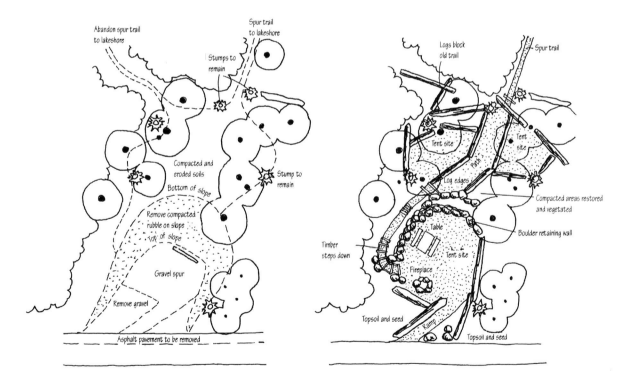

Spur designs at Lost Lake Campground: (Clockwise from top left – a) A typical spur before redesign, badly worn and ill defined. (b) The new spur above the road with the tent sites set above, surfacing bounded by logs and accessed by a short trail. Some areas have been restored to native vegetation. (c) A downhill spur before redesign, dominated by the compacted rubble used to build up the parking. (d) The new design removes the parking in favour of a walk-in spur, and provides several tent sites suitable for group use dispersed on two levels. Rocks are used to retain the slope, and logs provide edgings.

camping could be developed where the terrain and drainage permitted.

The design concept separated car-accessed tent camping from trailers and RVs, and these from walk-in or cycle-in camping. Loops were then designed for the different requirements and camping spurs fitted along each of them. The remoter area chosen to be developed was naturally more resilient than the original area but nevertheless drainage had to be carefully developed. To avoid disrupting the natural drainage pattern some of the roads were constructed on a permeable base on top of which was placed a filter fabric overlaid with gravel and asphalt. Thus, the water is able to percolate beneath the roads without having to be collected in ditches and culverted under them. This allows downslope trees to receive the same water as before construction.

A new water supply also had to be provided. The pipe layout generally follows the road system. Water is pumped from the lake, filtered and stored in a tank above the campground. Sewage disposal utilizes state-of-the-art SST facilities (sweet smelling toilets). These are simple vault toilets in which waste is collected in a holding tank, later being pumped into a 'honey' lorry for transport to the municipal treatment plant 24 miles (38 km) away.

As the access loops had to run parallel with the contours as far as possible, most of the camping spurs had to be built by cutting into or filling out the side slopes. Once the road alignments were marked out on the ground, the designers identified each spur so that the best fit into the landscape could be achieved. If the slope was too steep for a reverse-in spur, a pull-through one parallel to the road was used. Terracing retained with local rock and horizontal logs was used to reduce cut or fill for the tent bases and fireplace areas. For barrier-free spurs the flattest sites were chosen with the easiest grades. The goal was to have 25 per cent of campsites meeting barrier-free standards. Each spur site was carefully designed with details of retaining rockwork, paths and steps, trees and existing logs to be retained and fireplaces agreed before construction took place. Use areas were surfaced with compacted, fine gravel to prevent soil erosion.

Once the design for the layout had been finalized, the toilets were located, a path network for campers to the lake was slotted in, and a vehicle and pedestrian sign layout was executed to ensure that the minimum number of signs was used for the needs of the site. Signs were professionally designed, and constructed as routed letters in solid redwood panels, selected for their visual qualities and long life.

One of the redesigned sites at Lost Lake Campground, showing how the detailed aspects fit the site well.
Source: Courtesy Dean Apostol.

As well as the camp area construction, the abandoned spurs and access roads were restored and replanted using plants native to the site. Plants were salvaged from areas to be developed and stored on site in special 'capillary' beds. Other plants were propagated from cuttings or seed. In the day-use area, the eroding lakeshore was stabilized, along with other improvement measures. The design was constructed over several phases as new areas were opened and old ones were removed and re-vegetated. In 1994, the site was commended by the American Society of Landscape Architects.

Cabin sites

The next type of overnight accommodation to be considered is the cabin or chalet. Their layout and design should combine some of the elements of the various buildings so far discussed in this book together with many aspects related to campground design. This section will concentrate on the position and layout of a site, and the external form and design of cabins, rather than the internal design and detailed architectural aspects of construction.

Position

Whether one cabin or a series of cabins is built, their position in the landscape is of prime importance. The occupier of a cabin is likely to expect a view out onto the landscape. The wild and scenic qualities of the site may depend on the perceived lack of human intrusion, which the sight of groups of buildings might compromise. Service provision may be needed, which introduces other elements depending on the location.

A site containing several small timber cabins set around an open area. This is a high-density layout, which some people find acceptable. Amsterdamse Bos, Holland.

Siting of a single cabin: (From top – a) Shows the cabin near the water's edge, where it dominates the open space. (b) Shows how siting on the skyline creates a very focal view. (c) Shows an example set into the edge of trees so that it is much less intrusive, and does not dominate the landscape.

If a single cabin is considered, then the task is easier, The more primitive cabins, with no electricity, with a composting toilet and water obtained from a well, spring, river or lake, can offer a very significant contrast with the modern world. The location may depend on foot or boat access, and so a position should be chosen that makes use of the local terrain for shelter, sunshine, proximity to water and the access point while avoiding sensitive vegetation, or site excavation. This may entail a detailed search in the possible area. Local materials, together with some that are brought in, can be used to construct a cabin that should appear to be part of the landscape.

Many people's weekend cabins are likely to be more sophisticated. Running water will be needed. Vehicle access will be desirable for the delivery of equipment and stores as well as for emergency access if the location is an area of fire risk in dry conditions. All this implies a more developed site. Extensive use should be made of natural terrain and vegetation to screen and blend the cabin into the landscape. In most cases, a cabin position either parallel to or at right angles to the contour or landform will provide a satisfactory visual relationship. In damper climates, the cabin can be set among trees that are thinned to let light in but are kept close to the walls. In drier climates, a more open area is desirable to reduce the risk of fire.

If flush toilets are required, the location of sites for septic tanks needs to be identified (see Chapter 6). This may limit the choice of sites within the area.

Frequently people want to build their cabin close to a lake or the seashore. Shoreline vegetation, especially on sand dunes, tends to be extremely fragile, so that cabin construction, access tracks and disturbance of slow-colonizing plants can have a serious impact on the whole area. Sites should be chosen where the surrounding vegetation is robust and where the ground conditions are less likely to erode.

Site layout

Where several cabins are to be built as part of a commercial venture or where they are rented to people on holiday or vacation, their siting becomes more complex. A comprehensive site layout plan is needed. As with campgrounds, the cabins should normally be dispersed around the site and accessed from one or more loop roads. Short spurs can be made to a parking area next to the cabin, or small parking clusters can be provided from which paths lead to several cabins. This

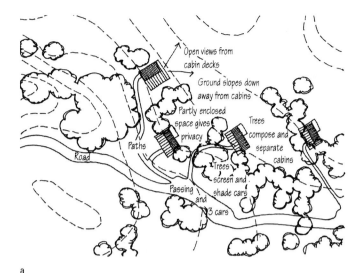

a

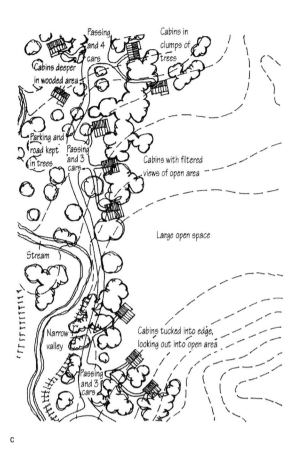

c

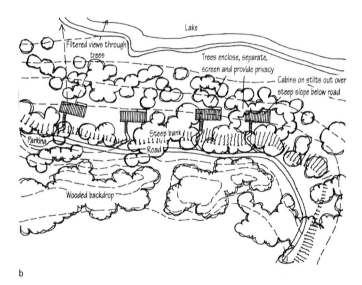

b

Three examples of cabin layouts taken from a design at Loch Aweside, Scotland, built by the Forestry Commission: (a) A cluster of cabins (three of one style and one of another) arranged asymmetrically among trees on a gentle slope. The parking and access are behind the cabins, and each cabin has an attractive view and a degree of privacy created by the orientation of the cabins and the use of trees. (b) A linear arrangement along a steep slope overlooking the loch (lake). The fronts of cabins are supported by stilts, giving them a dramatic location and spectacular views filtered through gaps in the trees. (c) Cabins arranged in loose clusters in or on the edge of woodland and a large open space. Some are right on the edge, some in the edge with filtered views, others more privately fitted in amongst the trees.

is convenient for services to minimize pipe runs for water, sewage and the number of septic tanks required. Electricity transmission lines should be underground wherever feasible.

In more open sites, scattered cabins can look chaotic, so a layout clustering them can resolve this problem. In addition, the position of the cabins relative to landform and to each other requires more use of architectural relationships in the grouping, angles, enclosure and regularity of the cabins, especially to improve views into the site from outside. To some extent, this may compromise privacy or a sense of wilderness.

Once the main functional and practical issues have been analysed, the site should be examined for the qualities that different spaces have to offer. Woodland or forest edge sites opening onto sunny areas may be popular. The woodland gives privacy and screening while the views out are open and the space offers opportunities to watch wildlife or for children to play. Places overlooking water are always attractive, so sites permitting views while also protecting the area (see above) should be chosen. Deeper woodland or forest might be the preferred choice of other people seeking

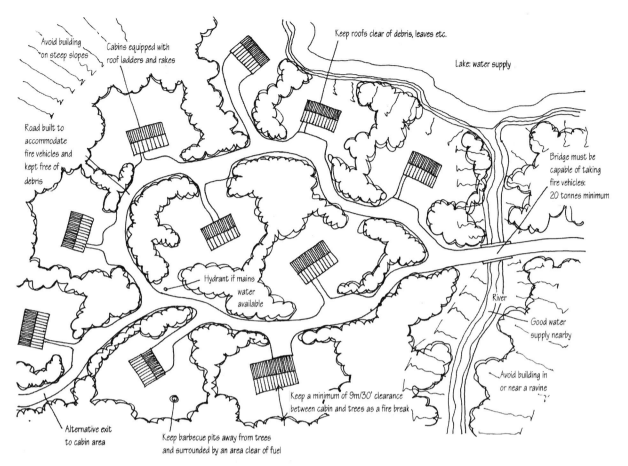

Avoid building on steep slopes

Cabins equipped with roof ladders and rakes

Keep roofs clear of debris, leaves etc.

Lake: water supply

Road built to accommodate fire vehicles and kept free of debris

Bridge must be capable of taking fire vehicles: 20 tonnes minimum

Hydrant if mains water available

River

Good water supply nearby

Avoid building in or near a ravine

Alternative exit to cabin area

Keep barbecue pits away from trees and surrounded by an area clear of fuel

Keep a minimum of 9m/30' clearance between cabin and trees as a fire break

This cabin site layout demonstrates the design and management requirements to minimize fire risk and to allow easy access to fighting any fires that do occur.

more solitude, so that the layout design should take the opportunity to provide as wide a range of locational experiences as possible.

The layout should be planned in such a way that vehicular access, parking and service requirements such as rubbish bins are behind each cabin and partly screened. This will ensure that views out are not impeded and that views into the site will not be spoiled by the clutter of cars or bins.

In dry forests or other places where fires are a hazard, the whole site should incorporate a range of fire prevention measures. These include the following:

- Access to a lake, stream or other water source should be provided for fire engines or tankers. This should be kept clear and not used as a boat launch or for car parking.
- Nearby day use areas and outdoor fireplaces at the cabins should be laid out so as to avoid the spread

of fire. A buffer zone free of flammable materials should be maintained around each cabin.
- There should be more than one access point in and out of the site; roads and bridges should be designed to take the weight of fire engines.
- A fire break around the perimeter of the cabin site area will help to reduce the risk of fires spreading in from outside. This should be a linear zone, which is shaded and kept clear of dead vegetation. Naturally non-flammable areas such as bare rock and water should be incorporated where possible. The cabins should incorporate non-flammable materials and be designed to limit the places where flammable debris can collect. Wood can be treated with fire retardant, although large-dimension timbers do not burn very quickly. Access onto the roof should be provided so that it can be swept and inspected, while chimneys should be fitted with caps and screens to prevent sparks escaping or birds from building nests in

them. A large barrel of water and a bucket should be provided as a useful emergency supply where no pressurized water is available.

Cabin design

Although detailed architectural issues are not being considered, the external appearance, style of building and use of materials are of interest in terms of the ambience created and the impact on the landscape. Most cabins will be made of natural materials, predominantly wood, perhaps with stone in places and other materials as appropriate.

There are two main varieties: log construction or frame construction.

Log construction

This type can range from the primitive pioneer-type cabin made of rough logs to more sophisticated versions where the logs are machined to fit together snugly and present a more finished and weatherproofed result. The rustic, primitive varieties will fit better into more remote, forested locations.

Logs can also be laid horizontally on top of one another, overlapping the ends of logs for stability, and intersected at the corners. This type of construction leads to a particular kind of structure with a horizontal emphasis, coarse texture and prominent corners formed by the intersections. They tend to have low-pitched roofs with wide overhangs, which cast deep shadows and help the cabin to hug the ground.

Because of its prominence the roof finish is often the most critical part of the design. Traditionally wooden shingles (shakes) or overlapping boards are used, and,

A well-designed traditional square log cabin built to modern insulation standards. It is equipped for use by people with disabilities, and has an access ladder to the roof in case of fire. It is set among a pine forest of open character and stained a dull colour in order to fit in visually. Ruunaa National Hiking Area, Finland.

if treated with preservative, these can last a reasonable time. Asphalt sheeting or tiles have a very smooth texture and can look too finished for the wilder locations, but profiled steel sheet with a dark colour is acceptable (see Chapter 6). Sometimes turf can be used, which gives a very interesting texture and colour.

Logs should be peeled, large in dimensions to reflect the scale of the landscape, and either allowed to weather to silvery grey or stained an appropriate colour. In Finland, logs from trees that have died, with the bark flaked off and the wood weathered silver, are highly sought after for cabin construction. Their texture and colour, as well as their stable, naturally dry condition, make them ideal for cabin construction.

The machined logs are modern versions of the traditional hand-squared logs used in many places. They give more regular dimensions, so that each cabin can be built easily and more cheaply – an important consideration at a commercial site. The timber can be treated for rot and fire, and even the jointing between logs gives a more weatherproof seal. The pattern created by the jointing of overlapping logs should have some regularity, as complete randomness causes visual confusion. The jointing patterns used in masonry, such as stretcher bond, can also be applied to log or sawn board walls. These designs are more appropriate in a less wild or rural area.

If the cabin is built on irregular ground, a level base will be needed. Natural stone should normally be used for this, rather than exposed concrete or brick.

A well-designed traditional log cabin in Trollheimen in Middle-Norway.
Source: Courtesy Jørund Aasetre.

Some examples of cabin designs including an attractive A-frame construction with large windows and a deck to give good light and a view over a lake and some mono-pitches with similar decks. Deerpark, Cornwall, England.

An unusual cabin built partly in a tree and partly on a frame. The Hermitage, Western Ghats, India.

Alternatively, a timber frame can be built on steeper ground to avoid cut or fill altogether and provide a more elevated view from the windows or balcony.

Frame construction

Frame construction using sawn timber clad onto a timber frame looks more finished than the machined logs and may fit some landscapes, such as in Britain, where log construction is not traditional. The design of the cabin need not follow a traditional or domestic form, and can be of more neutral, asymmetric forms such as intersecting mono-pitches. A-frames can also be interesting and contrast with everyday residential landscapes. Trees, landforms or other natural features can be the source of inspiration for their design. Overhanging roofs, balconies or decks, cabins on stilts jutting out over steep slopes or water are all features that can be accommodated in appropriate places.

The external finish of the cabin should, as above, reflect the textures and colours of the landscape so that their impact is lessened. Vertical board-on-board cladding of rough sawn, left-to-weather timber looks excellent. Clapboard is more traditional in some places but is normally painted or stained, not left to weather. Shingle or profile steel roofs also give texture.

Shadows cast by deep bargeboards and a dark stain for the roof help to give the cabin visual weight and reduce its apparent size and reflectivity, thus reducing its impact both on the site and in the wider landscape.

Window frames and doors can be given a brighter colour to provide an accent.

Frame cabins are an easier form of construction if large expanses of glass are wanted to let more light in, to give wider views out and to merge the inside with the outside. Fine mesh screens to all windows, doors and ventilation apertures should be fitted to prevent biting insects from flying in.

Decks, porches, balconies or other sitting out or eating areas can greatly increase the opportunities for inside/outside living, perhaps in conjunction with French windows, as suggested above. Given that many cabin sites are on uneven ground, one advantage is that this can be used for decks to protrude out over sloping ground. The landform and site can also be used to take advantage of breezes to help keep biting insects away, although in extreme conditions fans may be required to create a sufficient breeze.

Decking and handrails (if the slope is steep) should reflect the design of the rest of the cabin and take account of the safety issues described in Chapter 9. Access to the cabin and its deck by people with disabilities should also be a standard consideration. Access from behind the cabin should ensure a fairly level approach so that any landform falling away is taken up by the deck. Thus, taking advantage of scenery also provides a good barrier-free approach. Elsewhere, ramps may be needed if the cabin is raised on a stone under-building.

Cabins can also be built to reflect local styles and use of building materials, or to take advantage of unique features, such as trees, to make a tree-house or other form. There is no reason why only traditional forms should be used. A tree-house offers a special experience.

External finishes should avoid urban materials. Natural stone surfacing or timber decking should generally be used for paths to the access road, which should follow all the recommendations for car parking described in Chapter 5. Attention to detail in the finish of the areas immediately around the cabin is important, because many natural features can be disturbed or lost during construction.

It may be appropriate or necessary to provide some lighting for access to cabins at night. Rather than use urban types of lighting on high poles, it is much better to choose low-level lights set at waist height, which illuminate the path only. This reduces the overall effect of lighting and helps to maintain the atmosphere of remoteness so important for the quality of experience.

Sites for barbecues can be laid out near the cabin in an open area, safe from the spread of fire, together with picnic tables. Sometimes these are shared by several cabins in a large development and are placed a little way off so as not to be overlooked or invade the privacy of the cabins.

Signs, enclosures for rubbish bins, car park barriers, picnic tables, bridges, steps, gates and all the other artefacts that might be needed as part of the cabin development should be designed to reflect the idiom used in the cabins. If possible, litter bins should be incorporated into the exterior structure of the cabins.

A reception building, perhaps including public phones, television, a shop, indoor games, refreshments and laundry facilities, may be needed at larger sites. The design should also reflect the architectural style and construction of the cabins.

This is an example of a set of condominiums designed in clusters around the edge of an open space and set against a backdrop of trees. The location provides uninterrupted views from the units and conveniently screens cars and utilities from view as well as providing shade and shelter. Black Butte Ranch, Oregon, USA.

Condominiums

As well as single cabins to be occupied by one family, it is not infrequent for a single building to contain two or more units, or for cabins to be arranged in multiples. In North America, these are referred to as condominiums or 'condos' for short. The same design and layout criteria apply, however, because of the multiple occupancy, there is a greater density of facilities required, such as more car parking and services per unit. In some areas the denser clustering and greater density can solve problems by concentrating use into a smaller and less fragile area, or constructing fewer actual buildings. Nonetheless, there can be difficulties related to the privacy of shared decks or balconies. In other places the density can cause problems if the landscape is sensitive, such as greater visual impact, greater site disturbance and adverse effects on natural drainage. This means taking more care in site choice, layout and design as well as the design of buildings.

Thirteen

Interpretation

So far, this book has covered the practical needs of visitors to the outdoors so that they can fully enjoy the experience of scenery, wildlife and physical activity. It is vital to ensure that the special qualities and the spirit of the place are not overwhelmed by the facilities and artefacts provided for visitors, as well as by the people themselves. Some basic information and orientation will also have been provided to help them find their way around safely and with due respect for the environment. If visitors are to gain a greater understanding about the wildlife, landscape and its heritage that they are visiting, this can be provided through interpretation, which is the subject of this chapter.

What is interpretation?

Interpretation has a recognizable history going back to the eighteenth century, when particular people, mainly in Europe, guided visitors to places of natural wonder or ancient history and told them facts and fantasy about those places. The subject was put on a professional footing in the 1950s and 1960s by the US National Park Service, as part of the legacy of the 'Mission 66' era and it has continued to develop since that time.

Interpretation was defined by Freeman Tilden in 1957 for the US National Park Service as the work of revealing, to such visitors as desire the service, something of the beauty and wonder, the inspiration and spiritual meaning that lie behind what the visitor can with his senses perceive.

These concepts are embedded in the well-known series of booklets to be found at US national parks: *The Story Behind the Scenery*.

In Britain, the Centre for Environmental Interpretation offers a fuller explanation:

Interpretation is the art of explaining the meaning and significance of sites visited by the public. There are three key elements:

1. A specific site of natural, historical or cultural value is involved and is being, or will be, experienced at first hand by the visitor.
2. The visiting public, whether tourists, day visitors or local residents, are making a recreational visit.
3. The organization or individual interpreting the site aims to generate a concern for its conservation and/or to encourage an understanding of the processes and activities taking place.

In several countries, the subject has now gained its own profession of standing, such as the National Association of Interpreters, USA, who define the subject as 'A communication process designed to reveal meanings and relationships of our cultural and national heritage through first-hand involvement with objects, artefacts, landscapes and sites.' Therefore, it is clear that interpretation is a different process from that of supplying information and orientation, environmental education or propaganda. This is frequently misunderstood, to the detriment of the organization, the visitor and ultimately the site, as raising understanding about wildlife and landscape often provides the stimulus for conservation.

Supplying information and orientation is simply providing facts to assist visitors (covered in Chapter 4). It helps them to find their way around the site and avoid getting lost, and it advises them what they can and cannot do in safety.

Environmental education is similar to interpretation except that it deals with a much wider spectrum of the environment and its relationships with people of all ages and background – at work, in the home, at school and during leisure. That is not to say that interpretation has no educational content, nor that interpretation media cannot be used as part of an educational programme. However, interpretation tends to be more concerned with innovative and stimulating ways of explaining the key aspects of a particular site or issue.

Propaganda is the promotion of a particular point of view through the selective use of material that seems to be factual and which is presented in an enjoyable way. For example, visitor centres operated by organizations whose primary purpose is to exploit natural resources may aim to convey a message justifying those activities, even though they may be harmful to the environment.

Why interpret the environment to visitors?
Organizations usually have several reasons for engaging in interpretation:

- to increase the enjoyment that visitors gain from their experience, in the belief that an understanding of the landscape and aspects of natural and cultural heritage leads to greater pleasure;
- to increase understanding and appreciation of the area visited and of the great outdoors in general, to lead to a greater respect for it and recognition of the importance of conservation, protection and management (this arises from the first reason);
- to help managers at a particular place by influencing the patterns and habits of the visitors who use it;
- to convey a particular message relating to an organization or activities in ways that leave a good impression in the minds of visitors;
- to increase sales of souvenirs, literature or other merchandise or to recruit members of an organization.

Some of these reasons tend towards propaganda, but they are not inappropriate as long as they are secondary to the purpose of increasing enjoyment through understanding.

There is no doubt that large numbers of visitors to all kinds of natural, cultural or historical sites enjoy guided walks, visitor centre exhibitions, nature trails and enactments of historical events. Major centres can attract many thousands of visitors, and they can sometimes become visitor destinations in their own right. However, there are some central common elements to all these places:

- The place is special, for a reason that draws people to it. This might be a famous and important historical event, a natural wonder or a unique cultural site. These arouse people's curiosity and thus their appetite for finding out more about it.
- The people who go there tend to be interested in the subject, which is the prime reason for its attraction.
- The people who tend to gain most from their visit are those who are curious by nature and keen on finding out about the world around them at every opportunity.
- A greater understanding of the special qualities of the place may occur if there is engagement with it mentally as well as physically.
- Visitors making a special trip to the place, especially a first or an infrequent visitor, are more likely to want some interpretation than do regular, frequent visitors, who are more likely to have their own knowledge and different reasons for visiting.

In order to make the correct assessment of the interpretative content for an area, an overall strategy should be adopted. For example, Scottish Natural Heritage in Britain have produced one covering the sites they manage, National Nature Reserves in Scotland, and for general advice to other landowners.

What to interpret
As a rough guide, it is likely to be appropriate to develop interpretation programmes at sites if three basic conditions can be fulfilled:

1. The site or location has something special, which is outwith the general experience of most people.
2. There are substantial numbers of potential or actual visitors who wish to learn something about the area.
3. The site can accommodate the interpretative media to be used and possible visitor pressure.

The sort of place with potential for interpretation is one with unique physical, cultural, ecological or historical features, processes or associations that are sufficiently special to attract quantities of visitors to go there as a day out, as part of a tour or as a school trip. Examples include:

These giant sequoia trees are good examples of wonders of nature worthy of interpretation: for example, aspects of their age, their natural history and the fragility of their habitat. Mariposa Grove, Yosemite National Park, California, USA.

- **historic sites** such as Stonehenge in Wiltshire, England, Culloden in Scotland, Colonial Williamsberg in Pennsylvania, USA, or birthplaces of the famous;
- **wonders of nature**, such as the geysers and mud pools at Yellowstone National Park, Wyoming, USA, and Rotorua, New Zealand; rock formations such as Bryce Canyon, Arches National Park, Utah, USA, or Uluru (Ayers Rock), Australia; waterfalls of great splendour; groves of trees, such as the giant sequoias in California, USA, or the Major Oak in Sherwood Forest, England; habitats of rare or impressive animals;
- **places of great scenic beauty** connected with famous people, such as Wordsworth and the English Lakes, John Muir and Yosemite in California, USA, and Lewis and Clark's expedition across the USA to Oregon.

Small-scale interpretation may be appropriate at lesser, more localized examples than those cited above.

The degree of interpretation should match the status of the site, the numbers of visitors expected to use it, and the ability of the site to cope with the proposed level of activity. Large investments can be justified only for the most important and highly visited sites. Smaller places would be overwhelmed by sophisticated and large-scale facilities. It is most important that the interpretative media, especially visitor centres, do not become surrogates for the real experience gained from the landscape itself.

What to interpret, in terms of the choice of different themes or subjects, will depend on the characteristics of the visitors, such as their age range, socio-economic grouping, expected educational background and range of interests. It might be impossible to determine some of this for many sites so that a variety of topics might be chosen and presented in different ways.

Interpretative strategies

Before developing interpretative plans for individual sites, it is important to consider the overall strategy for the whole area under management. Such a strategy can ensure that interpretation at one site complements rather than duplicates that at another, and that opportunities for good stories are not missed. Such strategies can be developed by individual owners or agencies, or by consortia covering a much wider area.

A simple but clear example of a strategy is provided by the US Park Service at Craters of the Moon National Monument in Idaho. This area has a strong character because of its recent volcanic history. A drive takes visitors through it after an introduction to the subject at a small visitor centre. Along the drive are sites with walks of various length, which are interpreted in different but complementary ways. Some deal with different aspects of volcanoes, such as cinder cones, lava tubes or different types of lava, while others look at the ecology and wildlife living in such an inhospitable landscape.

Interpretation planning

Having gained a general idea of the potential of a place for interpretation, some planning will be necessary. This will ensure that the interests of the organization and of the visitor will be harmonized, and that the best methods are employed for the situation.

As in any plan, there must be some management objectives, expressed in terms of outcomes from the interpretation programme for the organization and for the visitor. These can be described in the following ways:

- **Behavioural**: what it is hoped the visitor will do as a result of participating in the programme. This might be to visit particular places, to show more care for fragile areas, to purchase a souvenir, or make a donation.
- **Learning**: what the visitor is expected to take away from the visit. This might be some salient facts about the place and its evolution or development, or events and personalities connected with it.
- **Emotional**: what it is hoped the visitor will feel as a result of their visit. This might be a belief that the place and associated features of wildlife should be protected, that management of special sites is a good thing, and that the organization is doing a good job.

Once the objectives have been established, the messages or stories that the interpretation should convey can be developed. There might be one message for a small site or several for a larger one. There is a risk that too many messages can cause confusion, so a single strong theme with a few variations is likely to be the most effective. This theme can be presented in different ways for different people, such as adults or children.

The message should be organized in a hierarchical way, with a main title or slogan that encapsulates the key elements with an issue or the character of the landscape. The main theme can be divided into subsidiary themes with appropriate titles and contents lists, each containing a summary part and a detailed part. In this way, whatever the medium employed to convey the message, its coherence will be maintained, and every visitor should be able to obtain as much or as little of the message as is desired, depending on the circumstances prevailing for a particular visit.

The objectives, message structure and content should be kept under review. Perceptions may change, knowledge may become out of date, and visitor characteristics may shift over time. It is important that the interpretation should meet its objectives and maintain its learning quality at all times.

The themes and the story-lines should be worked up into a script, much like an advertising campaign. Different media may be required for different sections of the script, depending on the most effective way of conveying a particular part of the message to particular audiences.

It is often helpful to plot the interpretative plan on a map, indicating the location for different stories with their associated media: in this way, the interactions of the interpretation can be monitored by the site managers.

There may be several stages in delivering the message, depending on how the site is expected to be visited. For example, at the entrance pay stations of US National Parks the visitor is handed a brochure. This introduces the park and provides some orientation. It also contains the basic story-line of what is special about the place, its history and the main interpretative themes.

Often one of the first places visited is the visitor centre, normally containing an exhibition devoted to the natural and cultural history of the site and its development, using well-designed display panels, models, artefacts and interactive displays with computer software or simple 'feely-touchy' samples. In addition, there will usually be one or more audiovisual shows, which provide a general introduction to the area using tape/slide, film, or, more usually nowadays, video. Breathtaking photos of the landscape over four seasons, the wildlife and human interaction and activities reinforce the quality, fragility and value of the landscape. Visitors are invited to explore it for themselves. A shop area full of books, pamphlets and souvenirs gives people a chance to purchase mementoes or useful articles such as maps, and finally some refreshments may be provided.

Once the visitor centre has been experienced (some parks have more than one, each dealing with a different part of the interpreted message), the visitors may follow the park road, stopping to look at the view (where interpretative panels explain what can be seen), to hike a loop trail (accompanied by a trail leaflet or stopping to look at signs by the route explaining the features of interest) or to picnic, swim, back-country hike or ride, camp or otherwise stay there. There could also be a programme of guided walks, where rangers will take people on varying lengths of hike on easy or difficult trails to see and learn about different aspects in detail.

Children will be provided with their own version of this menu at various points: parts of the exhibition, explanatory talks, a film or slide show appealing to them as well as adults, and the souvenir shop selling items attractive by design and price to different age groups.

People with disabilities will also be catered for, perhaps by barrier-free trails and, interpretative signs in three dimensions or Braille, or with audio facilities for people with visual impairments and hearing loops, subtitled presentations or deaf interpretation for people with hearing impairments.

Such an extensive menu of interpretation at a large site of national or international importance has more material than can be consumed during a single visit. Thus, repeat visits are encouraged to find something new, especially if temporary exhibits further expand the variety from time to time.

The menu described above introduces the main forms of interpretative media available to interpreters and graphic designers. It is important that the right media are chosen, and that simpler, rather than complex solutions are chosen. Not every site requires every medium to be used.

Interpretative media

The media available for conveying interpretation are:

- people telling the story;
- leaflets;
- portable digital recorders;
- on-site panels (including listening posts);
- exhibition areas;
- visitor centres.

People telling the story

For many sites, especially those with complex and detailed stories and where the audience is likely to be a curious one, people who can explain and answer questions are very effective, although costly. There is the added advantage that the landscape is not littered with interpretative panels or signs detracting from the enjoyment of those people who may find such devices intrusive.

Listening to an enthusiastic and knowledgeable guide can be very rewarding, and there is the added feeling of reassurance for those who are afraid of getting lost or misjudging how long it takes to follow a trail. The rangers who lead the walks can also monitor visitor activity, especially on the more popular parts of the area, and supervise behaviour when necessary.

Ideally, the ranger, interpreter and designer should collaborate in planning and designing the trails that lead to particular places of interpretative value for storytelling. This might include providing areas with benches where a larger group can be seated while the ranger tells the story. The surfacing, gradients, length of trail and the presentation of its features should be designed for the selected audience (see Chapter 9).

A recreation ranger explaining about tree roots to a party of visitors. Face-to-face communication with a knowledgeable and enthusiastic staff person is a very effective mode of interpretation.

At some visitor centres or at campgrounds in national parks and national forests, there might be a demand for outdoor lecture theatres. These involve tiers of seats set in an open natural hollow or amphitheatre with good natural acoustics, electrical provision for audio-visual projection and a screen, a campfire ring and perhaps a low stage or dais. The campers can sit around the fire to hear stories, sing songs or watch films or slide shows. Thus they can be entertained and informed at the same time.

The design of these amphitheatres should take into account the capacity of the campground and therefore the potential audience size, the type of weather (in rainy places the stage and screen might need shelter), and the type of design character that is appropriate. In some places (the more rural or urban ROS characters) more formal benches and harder surfacing might be appropriate, whereas in wilder areas logs or stone seating might suffice, or even a mown grassy bank for informal sitting on rugs or groundsheets.

A wooden stand with weather protection (glass-fronted box) for a projector together with an extending screen kept in another structure forming part of the stage or dais backdrop will be needed for regular slide shows. White screen surfacing must be maintained, and should not be kept out in the open air to become dirty, mouldy or sooty.

Deaf or hearing impaired visitors can also benefit from live presentations. Some people may be able to lip-read, others with hearing aids will benefit from a loop system and yet more will require a deaf interpreter

These brochures are a standard series, designed to a family 'style' and given to every visitor at the entrance to US National Parks. They are well designed and produced, and make an excellent collection.

A range of examples of interpretative leaflets from various places and produced by different organizations.

Leaflets

These are one of the most common and popular ways of interpreting the environment. They can relate to the whole area or to a part of it, perhaps to a single trail designed to follow a particular theme. Leaflets also provide a form of souvenir and something to refer to later.

The text of the leaflet can be related to points on the ground, such as plants, views or cultural artefacts, by means of photos or drawings that identify them, by points on a map of the route, or by numbered posts along the trail. The posts will have no meaning to visitors without the leaflet, and spotting the next post and interpreting what it relates to can become an exciting game for children.

The design of an effective leaflet is a specialist task, and it should be undertaken by a skilled graphic designer once the trail alignment, interpretative script and marker post locations have been decided. Special photographs, illustrations and maps might be needed for the leaflet. Some organizations maintain their own design teams, who can produce leaflets to a general house style but with localized characteristics. If external consultants are used, they need to be given a good brief on the interpretative design and requirements of the leaflet.

Versions of leaflets in large print, in Braille and in simpler language should also be considered to meet the needs of people with disabilities. A minimum of 12 point text size, sans-serif typefaces and high contrast between text and background are basic requirements for accessible leaflets.

Languages must also be considered. Making versions of leaflets available in several languages can be very important in tourist areas. Care is needed that the translations are good quality and that the right selection of languages has been made. English is inevitably a major language, either the first or certainly the second, given its universal use. French, German, Japanese and Spanish are also important, with Russian, Mandarin and other languages becoming more so.

Leaflets must be kept up to date, especially if the landscape changes suddenly, as happened after the forest fires at Yellowstone some years ago. The number of leaflets to be produced needs careful assessment; it is likely to be affected by several factors, such as the likely demand, the audience, the quality of the production, the shelf life and the budget available. Large print runs reduce unit costs but maximize overall costs. Therefore, for sites or trails with a low turnover, cheaper leaflets with a short shelf-life that can be easily revised and reprinted should be used, while glossier leaflets are likely to be confined to places with a high turnover.

Portable digital players

Another means of giving an interpretative message that can be up to date, and also reducing the number of artefacts on the area or the number of leaflets that have to be updated, is a portable tape or, more usual nowadays, the digital player of the Walkman, MP3 player or iPod variety. These might be available to rent from

The text continues with "using sign language. All these methods should be considered and staff in visitor centres should also receive training in deaf etiquette."

an information centre, and prompt the visitor to listen to sections in accordance with marked posts set along the trail. In places where foreign visitors are common, versions can be produced in different languages. The recorders do not interfere with other people walking the trail, and are also useful for blind or visually impaired people. The trail can be marked with a different texture to signify that the visitor has reached a point to listen to another instalment of the interpretative message.

On-site panels

In many areas, trails can have small signs or interpretation panels carrying short messages and pictures relating to features on the site. There are many types of structure:

- **Simple wooden posts** of substantial dimensions can be angled off at a convenient height to provide a surface on which to glue or screw small plaques with an interpretative message. The message can be engraved into material such as plastic or metal, or printed on materials encapsulated in plastic or resin. The posts should be placed so that they are orientated towards the point of interest. The plaques can be damaged accidentally or deliberately,

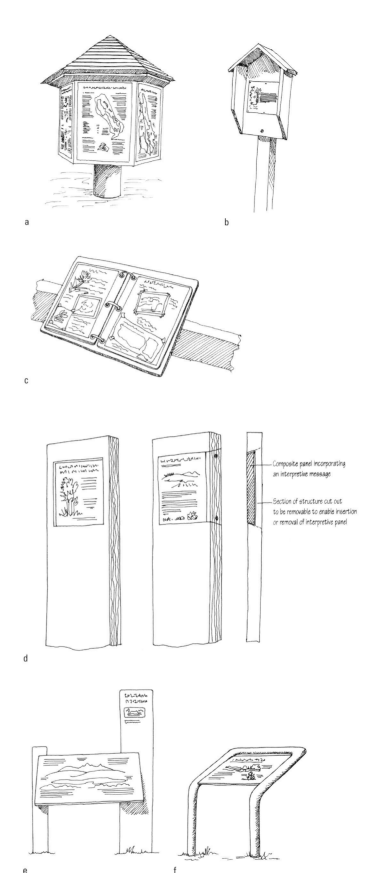

A range of both good and bad designs of interpretative signs used on along trails: (a) A fairly large multi-sided structure with A roof provides information and interpretation. Quite a lot of material can be presented, and several people can look at it at one time. This is more appropriate for the entrance to the trail. The roof is a fussy aspect of the design. Koli National Park, Finland. (b) A small panel screen printed on aluminium and housed in this little shelter is an overdone structure for a small amount of material. A fussy solution like this is also quite expensive to make. Dolly Sods Wilderness Area, West Virginia, USA. (c) An interesting and effective exhibit made of laminated sheets, which open like a book. The graphics are photographs of pages of a ranger's notebook, recording daily sightings of wildlife and descriptions of seasonal changes. Well presented and generally sturdy, although it can be damaged. Skunk Cabbage Trail, Glacier National Park, British Columbia, Canada. (d) Interpretative structures made from large slabs of timber. Laminated panels can be clipped into recessed sections, or a side-piece can be unfastened to allow a graphic panel to be slid in or out. Forest Enterprise, Britain. (e) A structure using a tall post carrying site and organizational information acts as part of a frame to an angled interpretative panel using laminated material. Scottish National Heritage. (f) For a vandal-prone area, tubular steel, either zinc coated or 'Cor-ten' rust patina steel, can be used to make a strong structure to hold a laminated panel fixed to flanges or cross-pieces.

An interpretative sign along a car drive in the bison reserve at the 'Land Between the Lakes' in Tennessee. The sign is mounted on a rock and has a sound system powered by solar energy. It plays wildlife sounds, making it useful for visitors with visual impairments.

so some maintenance and replacement will be required. Three-dimensional embossed pictures as well as Braille text can easily be provided as part of the design of the plaque.

- **Sawn slabs of wood** in single or multiple units can be used for larger panels. The artwork can be printed in the same way as for the smaller posts, but it can contain more information, pictures or even photographs. The materials and techniques described

Two examples of interpretative panels for different impairments: (Top) A set of listening panels with bird song, at a bird observation hide at Abriachan Community Forest in Scotland, which is good for blind or visually impaired people. (Right) A tactile sign on a botanical trail in the Great Smoky Mountains National Park in Tennessee, which is good for deaf or hearing impaired people.

in Chapter 4 for information signs can also be applied to interpretative signs. A useful design is one in which a recessed section is routed out of the face of a timber slab. The upper and lower edges of the recess should be angled to create a dovetail joint. A separate panel is slid into this and secured by a side piece fixed by recessed screws. The interpretative panel can be removed easily over the winter, or for repair or updating (see figure d on the previous page).

- **Metal-framed structures** can be used to carry plaques in places where vandalism is a problem. They can be galvanized, plastic coated, enamelled or made of 'Cor-ten' steel. They also fit into places with more buildings, where a more finished appearance is appropriate. The plaques can use the same materials as described above.
- **Small panels** in circular or oval shapes can be fixed to rocks, either where they occur naturally or placed there for the correct orientation. Where feasible, engraving using a sandblasting technique is the most effective method to give a legible message that blends in with an irregular surface.

A concentration of interpretative panels makes this almost an outdoor exhibition area. Pancake Rocks, South Island, New Zealand.

This structure provides a more ambitious yet still outdoor exhibition structure. It gives limited cover and protection against the weather. The neutral, almost sculptural form and natural finish work very well. Deschutes River, Oregon, USA.

- **Larger on-site panels** can also be used. These might be needed at a major viewpoint along a trail, at a wildlife observation area, or at an important cultural or archaeological site. The structures described for information panels could also be used in these circumstances, although the layout of text and graphics will be different.
- **Listening posts** are devices that contain a digital player which plays a message when a button is pressed. They can be powered by energy from solar panels, making them feasible in remoter areas. They are useful where blind or visually impaired people use the trail, or where the sounds of animals help to evoke the right atmosphere. The posts can be free-standing or incorporated into an interpretative panel containing written and pictorial material.

As in all types of structures used outdoors, panels should be subservient to the landscape, and should be chosen for form, size, colour and materials that will fit in with the local surroundings. Graphic techniques have to present a memorable message without this becoming intrusive. Bright colours and shiny finishes tend to look out of place, as do over-elaborate graphics. All structures must be carefully maintained and cleaned at least once a year before the visitor season.

Exhibition areas

A more developed stage of interpretation provision than leaflets or onsite panels is an outdoor exhibition area. A number of panels – which might include text, illustrations, photographs, interactive devices and 'touchy-feely' exhibits (tree cones, fur, antlers, stone, etc.) – are arranged in a sequence, perhaps near where trails start. The design of the panels can be an extension in structure and materials of the information panels (see Chapter 4), taking the information a stage further into interpretation. An enclosure formed from the panels and open to the air and natural light can also work quite well.

Alternatively, a shelter of the type described for picnic areas or an overlook platform can also be used to house the exhibition area, giving some weather protection and a vantage point to help relate the interpretative story to the landscape.

Visitor centres

The biggest and most comprehensive way of presenting interpretation is at a special centre. During the 1930s, before the term 'interpretation' was coined, the US National Park Service built what it called 'museums'. Some of the buildings were of outstanding design, and they still serve as models of the attention to detail for functional requirements and the harmonious visual relationships between the building and the surrounding landscape.

However, the visitor centre as a self-contained, multi-purpose building was a development of the 'Mission 66' era of the US National Park Service, although it has become more ubiquitous around the world. A visitor centre can be very expensive, and a fundamental first question is whether or not it is essential for the delivery of the interpretative objectives of the site: hence a careful economic appraisal of all the options should be undertaken to determine the most appropriate range of facilities to be provided, and the size of building in relation to the expected number of visitors.

Visitor centres usually combine some or all of the following:

- **A reception area and information counter** manned by staff, at least in the main busy periods. The staff are there to answer questions and manage the building.
- **An exhibition area** consisting of static displays, interactive or hands-on gadgets, dioramas, artefacts, computers and things to handle ('touchy-feely'). This may be similar to the outdoor display brought indoors, or may be more sophisticated, as the controlled environment and availability of power make it possible to use computers, web-cams to observe wildlife, action models, and so on. Web-cams are increasingly used to show features that may not be otherwise easily accessible, such as rare birds nesting or birds living on remote cliffs or islands. Increasingly, these interpretative resources are also accessible via the website of the organization and can be accessed before or after the visit (see Chapter 3).
- **An audiovisual area.** This might be a theatre where tiered seating creates the best views for a tape/slide, cinematic film or video, or a smaller, more informal area with fewer seats just for a video.
- **A souvenir and book sales area** where revenue can be made. Books on natural history, the history of the area, guides and maps, stories and other appropriate material such as posters or art prints are well-tried merchandise. Other items might include pens, pencils, badges (buttons), mugs, toys, games and crafts made from, labelled or otherwise identified with the area and its attractions.
- **A classroom or study area** for environmental education of both children and adults.
- Some **comforts** for the visitor, including toilets/restrooms, perhaps a café or restaurant, and spaces for lectures or talks (possibly the same area as for the audiovisual display).
- **Staff facilities,** including office space, toilets, storage and workshop areas.

The size of the various spaces required needs to be carefully assessed relative to the expected numbers of visitors at different times. The result can be a substantial building with the potential to make a significant impact on the landscape, and with high capital and running

This building, modelled closely on traditional vernacular architecture, houses an information and exhibition centre. It is not pretentious, and is well built with no fuss in its setting or surroundings. Ruunaa National Hiking Area, Finland.

costs. The design of such a building should be carried out by an architect. Different approaches can be taken to fit it into the landscape, which have been successful in various settings. The 'Mission 66' era visitor centres are mostly still in existence and functioning as intended, but the modernist architecture has received much negative criticism over the years. However, there are some aspects of the best of these buildings that should not be overlooked (see below). Some of the conceptual approaches are now discussed.

Traditional or vernacular

There may be strong reasons for using traditional or vernacular forms, materials and construction in an area. There may be other buildings nearby, and too much contrast could look out of place. In many wilder places, pioneer or homestead style, using local materials without a high level of finish, can be entirely appropriate.

Neutral or non-domestic style

Here the building forms are derived from the shapes and character found in the landscape, such as rocks, landform and trees. Vertical emphasis can be given to the building in a forest or where there are steep mountains, while a horizontal emphasis is more suitable to flatter land, or near a lake or the sea. In this way, the sculptural qualities of the building can reflect and interpret those found in the surrounding landscape. Some of the modernist buildings took this approach rather successfully, contrasting with what were often over-scaled large buildings of the 1930s.

This visitor centre, from the 'Mission 66' era is a simple form that blends well with the rocks above. Seneca Rocks, West Virginia, USA.

A scene in miniature of dwarves and their houses, illustrating the stories of Anna Brigadere, a Latvian writer. The carving of the figures and the construction of the small buildings demonstrates excellent traditional skills. Tervete Nature Park, Latvia.

The building should be set into the landscape so that its size does not dominate. This is difficult to achieve in smaller-scale landscapes, so external treatments such as earth mounds and tree-planting might be needed to reduce the apparent size and proportions of the structure. Heavy roofs that overhang, subdued neutral or earth colours and coarse textures all help to tie the building down into the landscape (see discussions of toilet block and shelter design in Chapters 6, 7 and 9). Continuing the path surfacing materials into the building also creates a sense of continuity with the rest of the site.

Every care should be taken to ensure that the visitor centre is not a surrogate for the real landscape, so the interpretation plan should stimulate the visitors' appetite to explore and spend time in the outdoors while respecting it.

The layout of the building with respect to the site should aim to present the landscape or feature of interest using the dramatic techniques described elsewhere – the centre building may screen the attraction as the visitor approaches, while itself being as modest as possible. On entering, the 'wow' factor can be invoked by a view through a large window, after which the visitor can make use of the various facilities. On leaving the centre towards the attraction, not back through the entrance, the building is left behind and the visitor, suitably prepared, can enjoy the visit.

Art as interpretation

If one of the aims of interpretation as described above is to help visitors understand something of the spiritual meaning of the place, then all the earnest facts and explanation may not achieve this. However, there are ways in which it might be conveyed through poetry, prose and painting about the area, and the use of these elements in the displays. Another way is to use sculpture out in the landscape. If visitors come across sculpture along a trail it can evoke all sorts of questions and responses, and can often prompt an understanding of the spirit of a place. The use of sculpture in forests was pioneered by the Forestry Commission in Britain over 30 years ago.

At Grizedale Forest in Cumbria, a partnership project was undertaken between the forest managers and Northern Arts, a government-funded arts promotion body. Together they were able to fund a series of residencies over the years for talented sculptors, who were able to explore the landscape through art and the use of local materials. Some of the sculptures are highly abstract evocations of the land, of water, of growth and decay, while others are more figurative. The use of sculpture in this way has been taken up elsewhere in Britain with some interesting results.

Other approaches use sculpture to invoke a specific theme and dramatic effect bordering on the magical, or use it as a way of introducing children to stories and legends. An interesting project that contrasts with the Grizedale model described above can be found at Tervete Nature Park in Latvia. Here, wooden sculptures and models have been used to bring to life the characters in a set of stories written for children by the Latvian author Anna Brigadere. The forest is large enough for areas to be set aside into different

The 'King of the Forest', another piece of sculpture from Tervete Nature Park, Latvia, this time invoking a different atmosphere.

Other art elements might include poetry – perhaps lines from a poem engraved into rock, on wooden posts or to be listened to from a sound post or from a portable digital player. Many poems have been written about landscapes, nature or cultural history and to read or hear them at the place about which they were composed adds a special aspect to both the place and the poem.

Other special, perhaps one-off techniques include sound and light shows held at night. In Scotland every year around Hallowe'en, an event called 'the Magical Forest' is held in a different forest area. Theatrical sound and light designers and technicians rig up outdoor theatrical lights among the trees, with sound accompaniment. Visitors walk along the trail in the dark to experience this, which is, as the name suggests, quite magical.

themed areas such as the 'Dwarves forest' of the 'Magical forest'. The sculptures are produced to a high standard of execution using traditional wood carving craft rather than the more consciously artistic approach at Grizedale.

However, there is a danger of overloading the landscape with sculpture, and it is important to view the sculpture as a means to an end and not as an end in itself. Ideally, the sculpture should emerge from and be part of the landscape to which it ultimately returns, thus demonstrating something of the cycle of creation, change and decay. In this scheme, the landscape is not a setting for a studio piece.

Fourteen

Comprehensive site design

We have now described the sequence of events, decisions, activities and facilities that make up a visit to the outdoors. It is essential that each component is fitted together properly through the design process. While thinking this process through from the perspective of the visitor it is still necessary to take a wider view of the recreation area from the point of view of the manager and designer. It is not possible to design a visit step by step unless a broad view of the area is gained, providing a context and purpose into which the chosen facilities are inserted. It is usually appropriate to consider the design at a number of scales:

- **The planning scale** (as described in Chapter 1) where the main issues about a large area are considered and general activity zones or ROS areas are defined.
- **Master planning** where the general layout and circulation of people in an area is developed from the planning scale according to zones or ROS categories or from landscape character areas (see below).
- **Site planning and design**, where the locations of different facilities have been decided by the master plan and the detailed layout is to be designed.
- **Detailed design** of individual elements such as signs, barriers, toilets, picnic tables and so on.

The brief

Site design at any scale needs to start with a brief. This contains a set of objectives, which should have emerged from the planning stage. It may identify who the expected visitors are likely to be, how many, over what time, and for what activities or else this type of survey may be part of the project. It will also identify planning of management issues that need to be overcome through zoning, by design, or by management.

The brief should also contain timescales, funding, financial performance targets, and the various approvals to be obtained before implementation can begin. A team of people bringing together the necessary skills should be assembled, including those who will be responsible for the management.

If the site is sensitive ecologically, culturally, politically or in other ways, a wider group of people may need to be consulted about the development of the design. These might include local residents, representatives of key user groups, especially the disabled community, local politicians, and agencies responsible for particular aspects of the resource, such as forest and wildlife services, highway authorities and water agencies.

The design team may consist of recreation planning specialists, landscape architects, engineers, architects and building surveyors, artists, ecologists and wildlife biologists, as well as accountants and economists. Each member should avoid taking up a narrow position with respect to their specific discipline and instead provide factual information at the survey or inventory stage, co-operating at the analysis phase, and remaining open-minded in order to contribute integrated and constructive ideas at the design phase.

Stages of design

Once the brief is agreed with the client or client body, the typical stages of design are as follows.

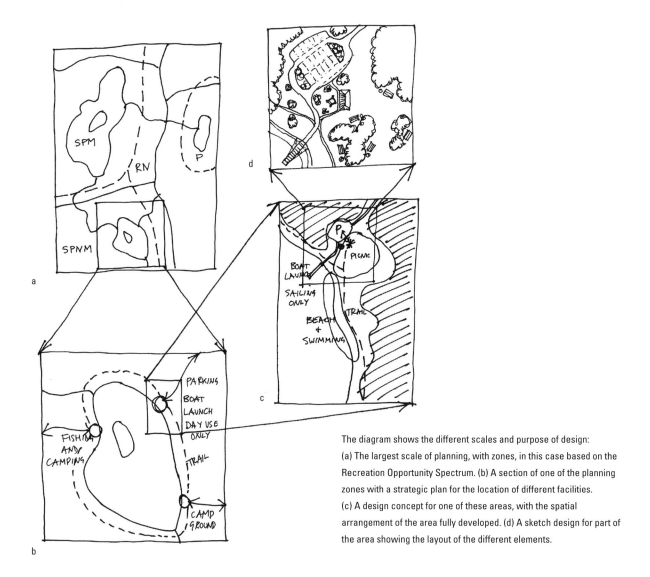

The diagram shows the different scales and purpose of design:
(a) The largest scale of planning, with zones, in this case based on the Recreation Opportunity Spectrum. (b) A section of one of the planning zones with a strategic plan for the location of different facilities.
(c) A design concept for one of these areas, with the spatial arrangement of the area fully developed. (d) A sketch design for part of the area showing the layout of the different elements.

Assessment of demand

It is usually a good idea to try to find out what the likely level of demand is for recreation in the area. If the area is already used and the design is more concerned with improvements or reconstruction, then monitoring of the visitors should be done by a combination of visitor counting, either manually or by automatic counters (magic eyes) and surveys to find out who visits, where they come from, their age and gender profile, their activities, perceptions and likes and dislikes. Since such surveys by their very nature only capture information about who visits but not about who does not and why they do not, supplementary surveys of the local or regional area that forms the catchment for visitors should be carried out. Surveys of users can be carried out using a face-to-face questionnaire or a survey sheet

that visitors are handed when they arrive and which they can send in to the manager of the area later.

For an area where the development is new, there may be only a few low-key local informal visitors. In this case a larger survey of the proposed catchment should be undertaken. Such a survey should collect a reasonably representative sample of age, gender, ethnicity, population distribution (by area) and socio-economic indicators (income level, educational achievement or occupation type). Face-to-face, telephone, postal or internet surveys using a mix of yes/no or scale answers (for example, level of agreement with a statement on a scale of 1–5) and straight factual choices (age range, gender, educational level and participation in activities) can be employed. These can be quite simple to administer yet straightforward to analyse using fairly simple statistics and they give a good picture which can be used for planning purposes.

By collecting demographic and socio-economic aspects it is then possible to determine some of the subgroups that make up the demand – activities for older people, for young professionals, for teenagers, for disabled people, and so on. If some attitudinal or perception questions are also asked, for example, about fear and safety, stress reduction, love of nature, the design can ensure that the impact of negative perceptions can be reduced and the positive aspects promoted to make the area as welcoming as possible.

Survey/inventory phase

First, information is collected on a number of different themes. This should be recorded on maps to a suitable scale, in notes and reports supplemented by photographs. Aerial photographs are very useful and base maps at least at the planning stages and larger scales are normally available from national mapping agencies at 1:50 000, 1:20 000 or 1:10 000. If a GIS (geographic information system) is available, this can be used so that later on layers can be combined for analysis purposes. The GIS can also produce maps at any scale so that when locations for a facility have been selected, the site can be mapped at a more detailed scale such as 1:2500 or 1:500, although accuracy probably will not be high enough for setting out a site and a more detailed topographic survey will be needed.

If a GPS (global positioning system) unit is available, the location of elements can be accurately identified and incorporated into the GIS plan. This is good for adding details not available on the base map provided by the national mapping agency. It can also be used to preparing the more detailed plan.

Compared with architectural and urban landscape, construction it is not necessary to have extremely accurate survey plans most of the time. This is because such surveys are never available and the designs are not usually prepared with such accuracy in mind. In fact, for most of the time setting out of a design will be done on site so that detailed aspects of the site can be taken into account (see below).

Types of survey/inventory

There are several layers of information that should be collected for an area. Some of these are more relevant at the larger planning or master plan stages as they are more concerned with the location of facilities rather than the layout or detailed design. All of these should be produced to the same scale for future overlaying and analysis:

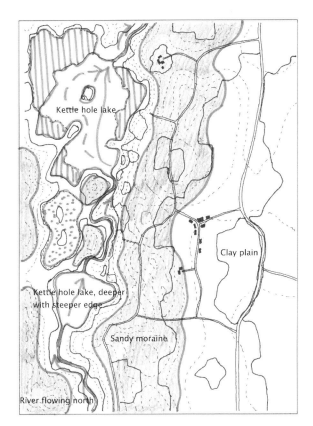

This plan shows an area to be developed for recreation. The survey layer is of geology, landform and hydrology. This information is needed to plan activities and to see where there are constraints due to soil or moisture conditions.

- **Physical aspects of the site**, such as landform, geology and soils; water movement; terrain slopes and stability. These are very important for planning an area. Landform may have a major influence on many activities that need slopes, elevation, cliffs, views and exposure or shelter from the elements. A basic contour map can be overlaid with other information from geological surveys, hydrological information and site survey. A map showing these aspects should be produced. Sensitive areas such as unstable slopes, boggy areas, deep, cold, fast-flowing water and sand dunes should also be identified and mapped.
- **Ecological aspects**, such as plant communities; wildlife use; sensitive sites; habitat dynamics, such as fire or insect attacks; pollution risks. This information can be compiled from aerial photographs, forest cover maps, habitat maps and field survey. A good way to present information is to use landscape ecological structures such as matrices, patches and

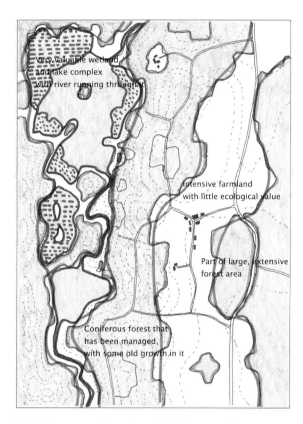

This plan is a survey of the main ecological elements of the area. These will be analysed further later on in the process.

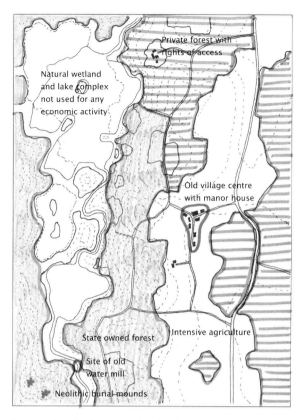

A survey plan of land use and cultural heritage. Private land is shown, which will create constraints later on, as do historical and archaeological features.

corridors (see analysis section) and to present these on a map. The location of key habitats, protected areas and sensitive areas should also be recorded.

- **Cultural aspects**, including traditional recreational uses and history; heritage and archaeological remains; previous land use. This can be mapped and sites and areas such as archaeological remains that are potentially sensitive not only to construction activities but to damage by visitors should be highlighted.
- **Recreational aspects**, such as the potential of the area; limitations on carrying capacity; safety issues; environmental education potential, including interpretation. Areas where different activities may be suitable should be mapped as areas, routes or points. Symbols can be used as well as annotations or colours/hatchings on the map.
- **Landscape character**, where the area is divided into areas with different character because of landform, vegetation, presence of water, historical aspects, qualities such as mystery and specific ways of

experience such as high elevation views. A map of these areas should be accompanied by photographs and short explanations added to the map.

Analysis phase

Here the implications of the information are tested. The maps and accompanying information are overlaid either manually, using tracing paper maps, or in the GIS where the interactions can be tested and resultant maps produced but where also some of the insights gained from poring over maps on a desk can be slow to come. This can be categorized into:

- **Landscape character, aesthetic qualities, views and eyesores**. The landscape character map, which at the survey/inventory stage is a record of areas should be evaluated to see which are the most attractive, which have aesthetic problems, which have special qualities such as a high degree of *genius loci* (spirit of the place), tranquillity, mystery, remoteness or disturbance. Later on, this map can

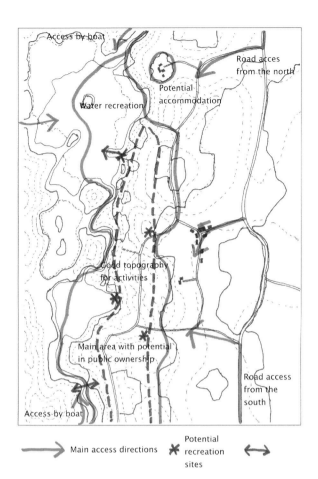

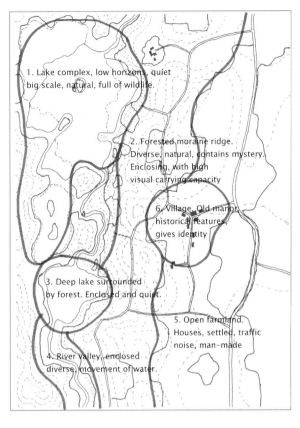

1. Lake complex, low horizons, quiet big scale, natural, full of wildlife.

2. Forested moraine ridge. Diverse, natural, contains mystery. Enclosing, with high visual carrying capacity

6. Village. Old manor, historical features, gives identity

4

3. Deep lake surrounded by forest. Enclosed and quiet.

5. Open farmland. Houses, settled, traffic noise, man-made

4. River valley, enclosed diverse, movement of water.

→ Main access directions   ✱ Potential recreation sites   ↔

Clockwise from top left

This map shows the assessment of recreation potential for the area, based on where there is access, suitable terrain, land use types, and so on.

This is one of the first of the analysis stages, looking at landscape character and quality. This will be used to try to ensure that recreational development both fits into and makes the most of the character and its qualities.

The map of opportunities and constraints, mainly those of a practical or legal nature. The idea is to make the most of the opportunities and to work around the constraints.

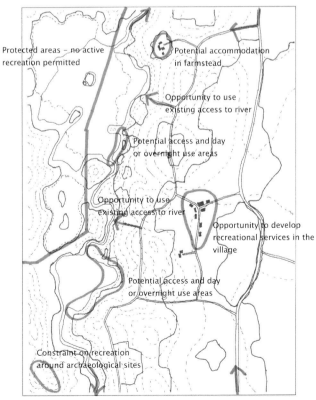

Protected areas – no active recreation permitted

Potential accommodation in farmstead

Opportunity to use existing access to river

Potential access and day or overnight use areas

Opportunity to use existing access to river

Opportunity to develop recreational services in the village

Potential access and day or overnight use areas

Constraint on recreation around archaeological sites

Complex made up of several different wetland patches and corridors

Forest matrix

Old growth forest

Early successional forest

← →   □
Animal movement corridor   Protected area

← →   ← - - →
Primary and secondary people movement corridors

The ecological analysis examines the vegetation patterns in more detail and also considers the movement of animals, considering possible conflicts that should be avoided. In this case, a protected area already exists which is a major constraint on recreation and creates a form of zoning between recreation and nature conservation.

be used to try to relate the planned recreational activities to the qualities of the landscape.

- **Constraints and opportunities** for recreation and environmental education including locational conflicts, site constraints. This is in many ways a very practical map, sieving from each layer those factors that constrain the development of different recreational activities and those where there are plenty of choices. Potential conflicts between recreational activities in a single area can be evaluated using a simple matrix.

- **Ecological analysis** of the likely changes to plant communities and wildlife uses by various activities which might be developed, their location, places to be avoided and management options to maintain biodiversity requirements. A simple landscape ecological analysis looking at the main wildlife movements (flows) in the area related to the different vegetation patches and corridors can highlight places where wildlife disturbance can be most likely. Special habitats may already be identified through the protected areas and these can be assessed for their sensitivity to certain forms of recreation, especially seasonal disturbance of nesting birds, for example.

Design phase

This is the creative phase, where the objectives and outcomes of the analysis interact. It requires imaginative, creative thinking to achieve an integrated and successful resolution of all the issues. The design team should consider a wide range of ideas in seeking both well-tried and original ways of solving problems and maximizing opportunities. The first level of design, below the planning level discussed in Chapter 1 is to develop a design concept or strategy at the largest scale, possibly the master plan for a significant land area that may contain several sites with different facilities as well as routes for different activities between them or radiating from them. Such a plan can be presented in a fairly diagrammatic way with nodes, symbols to signify different elements or activities and the route plan for the area. Zones related to landscape character should be used to unify the facilities, the activities and the experiences. For example, a walk along a deep valley aimed at creating a sense of solitude and finding mystery. The path should be routed and constructed to respect this and to enhance the experience (see Chapter 9).

From the master plan or design strategy, individual sites where visitors gain access, park cars, obtain information, have a picnic, embark on trails or other activities can be developed as a series of more detailed design projects. This includes the layout of different sectors within a site (parking, picnicking, play, etc.) and the circulation of vehicles and people. Another important aspect of the design concept is the design idiom for all the necessary structures such as signs, bollards, barriers, benches, bridges, toilets, picnic tables, and so on. This is very important as it gives the feel for the place. Designing elements to be custom-made may be expensive but worthwhile.

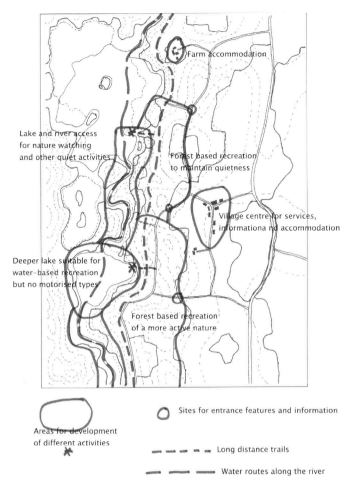

Areas for development
of different activities

Sites for entrance features and information

— ·· — ·· — ·· — Long distance trails

——— ——— ——— Water routes along the river

Based on all of the former analysis, an overall strategy is developed
which matches the landscape character to recreational opportunities
and takes into account the constraints imposed by the various factors
identified from the survey stage.

It may also be the case that the standard designs
developed by the landowner, for example, a national
park service, will be used. In any case a sense of unity
between each constructed element and the landscape
is essential. The philosophy presented in Chapter 2
should be considered here. The concept should make
the most of what the site has to offer, and reflect the
spirit developed in the strategic plan. Concepts are
gradually refined into initial sketch design options. The
landscape architect may work up the concepts into
feasible and costed layouts.

Once the initial design phase for a site has been
concluded, it is important to test how it is likely to
work for the prospective visitor. This can be done by
the design team using a checklist based on each stage
of a visit, or by asking people less familiar with the
design to imagine a visit, using the same checklist. In
this way, an indicative quality of the visit, which is the
main determinant of the success of the design, can be
assessed, and the layout and design can be refined
as required. Questions of safety, barrier-free access,
vehicular and pedestrian circulation and information
provision can be answered in a similar fashion.

Once the design has reached this stage, it must
be offered to the client and any consultees for their
assessment and approval. It may also be helpful if they
use a checklist similar to that derived from the stages
of the visit. This enables the client to ensure that the
overall objectives have been met. Consultees with
disparate interests can more easily offer comments
or require changes to particular aspects without
compromising the whole design. The process of
consultation and approval is likely to require several
iterations of refinements to be incorporated into the
overall design and objectives, and this has to be built
into the project lead-time.

The needs of the prospective manager are important
when testing the initial design, and it should be fully
tested by simulating the various maintenance and
management tasks at specified intervals: for example,
daily, weekly, monthly or annually. It is useful to prepare
an outline maintenance and management plan at the
initial design stage so that the client is clear about the
obligations and resources that are likely to be needed.

Finally, an important aspect of the design phase is
to communicate with the local community about the
project. They might be sensitive about changes to their
environment, particularly if they are established users
of an area that is about to be changed. Consultation
should start at an early stage and continue up to and
including the construction phase.

Detailed design

Once the sketch design has been accepted and the
design idiom agreed with the clients, more detailed
design is needed in order to make everything work
together properly. If unique design elements are to
be used, prototypes may need to be made and placed
in the landscape to see how they will look in terms of
scale, materials, colours, and so on. Special graphic
elements such as site symbols or logos will need to
be developed. At this time a draft interpretation plan

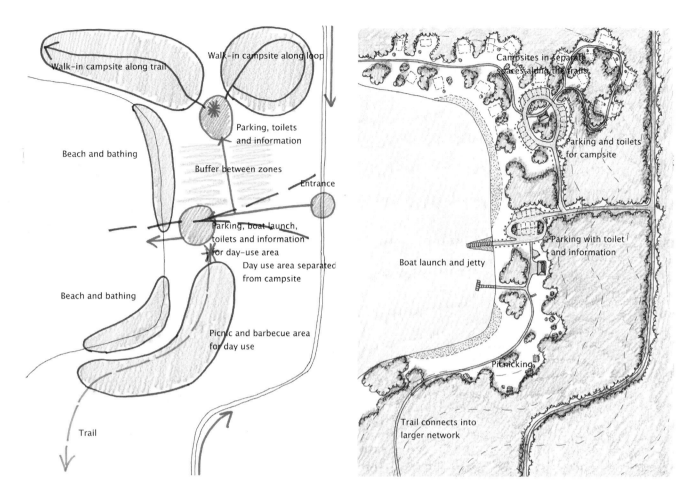

The next step is to descend a level of scale and work on the design of one of the sites identified at the strategy stage: (Left) A concept plan which takes an areas and developed a spatial layout for day and overnight recreation. The goal is to keep them separate and to fit the development into the landscape, making the most of the lake environment. (Right) The sketch design development showing in detail the layout of roads, paths, parking, toilets, information, picnicking, camping and boat launch. This is a complex task requiring detailed knowledge of the site.

should be drawn up if interpretation is to be an integral part of the project. It may be necessary to check out the sources of materials if they are not to be locally obtained, to ensure that colours and textures are right.

Construction phase

Once approval for the project has been received, it moves into the construction phase. Specifications and detailed drawings are prepared to form the sketch plans and developmental detail designs to enable contractors to estimate prices, and for construction to take place. In the outdoors, especially in wilder places, the site survey information collected at the survey/inventory phase may lack precise detail. Hence there may be

a need for some flexibility in the construction layout when compared with the design. For this reason, all setting out of the design on the site should be closely supervised by a member of the design team, and only approved when the desired quality is achieved.

Site protection measures, especially when working in sensitive areas, must be adhered to. These should be clearly stated in the project specifications and closely monitored. Trees near construction areas such as road excavation need to be well protected – fences set out along the drip line of the tree canopy will protect most trees from damage by machinery and equipment.

In some circumstances, construction may be carried out by volunteers or other less skilled people. This is

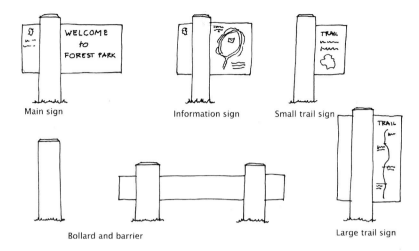

Main sign

Information sign

Small trail sign

Bollard and barrier

Large trail sign

The design of details needs to be carefully thought out and coordinated. Here a set of details such as signs, barriers and bollards has been developed which have a unity of design in the use of the main structural element and construction technique. This means that when seen together, they appear to belong to the group rather than being an ad hoc collection of different designs.

common in small-scale projects on sites managed by the voluntary sector, such as local nature reserves, parks and trails. Quality of construction can be more difficult to achieve. The simplest designs and construction techniques should be used, and all workers should be supervised by someone with construction expertise, good knowledge of the site and an ability to read drawings and plans.

Quality control is essential if the design is to become a part of the landscape and also as functional as possible in terms of the design of the visit. Correct positioning of signs and other artefacts, restoration of scars of excavation, re-vegetation of bare or worn areas and installation of art work or interpretative media are vital and need someone of the design team on site almost continuously towards the end of the construction phase. Final checking of things (snagging) is necessary before the project is handed over to the client by the contractor and any missing or defective items fixed.

Bibliography

The following list of references is related to the chapters where they are most relevant. It will be noted that there is a substantial body of work on recreation planning, quite a lot on interpretation but much less on design. Access for people with disabilities is also well covered. Many of the design references are in the form of handbooks, manuals or design detail sheets produced by various agencies for their own purposes.

Introduction

Carr, E. (1998) *Wilderness by Design*. Lincoln, NE: University of Nebraska Press.

Cordell, H.K. (Principal Investigator) (1999) *Outdoor Recreation in American Life: A National Assessment of Demand and Supply Trends*. Champaigne, IL: Sagamore Publishing.

Cordell, H.K. (2004) *Outdoor Recreation for the 21st Century: A Report to the Nation: The National Survey on Recreation and the Environment*. State College, PA: Venture Publishing.

Driver, B.L., Brown, P.J. and Petersen, G.L. (eds) (1991) *Benefits of Leisure*. State College, PA: Venture Publishing.

Edington, J.M. and Edington, M.A. (1986) *Ecology, Recreation and Tourism*. Cambridge: Cambridge University Press.

Gray, D. and Pellegrino, D. (1973) *Reflections on the Recreation and Park Movement: A Book of Readings*. Dubuque, IA: Brown.

Hill, H. (1980) *Freedom to Roam: The Struggle for Access to Britain's Moors and Mountains*. Ashbourne: Moorland Publishing.

Human Kinetics (2006) *Introduction to Recreation and Leisure*. Champaigne, IL: Human Kinetics.

Jensen, C.R. and Guthrie, S.P. (2006) *Outdoor Recreation in America*, 6th edn. Champaigne, IL: Human Kinetics.

McLelland, L.F. (1998) *Building the National Parks*. Baltimore, MD: Johns Hopkins University Press.

Muir, J. (1901) *Our National Parks*. Boston, MA: Houghton Mifflin Co.

Parry Jones, W. (1990) 'Natural landscape: psychological well being and mental health', *Landscape Research*, 15(2): 7–11.

Rohde, C.L.E. and Kendle, A.D. (1994) *Human Well-Being, Natural Landscape and Wildlife in Urban Areas: A Review*. Peterborough: English Nature.

Thomas, K. (1984) *Man and the Natural World*. Harmondsworth: Penguin.

Wilson, A. (1992) *The Culture of Nature*. Oxford: Blackwell.

1 Recreation planning

Baud-Bovy, M. and Lawson, F. (1998) *Tourism and Recreation: Handbook of Planning and Design*. London: Architectural Press.

Bromley, P. (1994) *Countryside Recreation: A Handbook for Managers*. London: E & FN Spon.

Buechner, R.D. (ed.) (1971) *National Park, Recreation and Open Space Standards*. Washington, DC: National Recreation and Park Association.

Check, N.H., Field, D.R. and Burdy, R.J. (1976) *Leisure and Recreational Places*. Ann Arbor, MI: Ann Arbor Science Publishers.

Christiansen, M.I. (1977) *Park Planning Handbook*. Chichester: John Wiley & Sons, Ltd.

Clark, R.N. and Stankey, G.H. (1979) *The Recreation Opportunity Spectrum: A Framework for Planning Management*. Portland, OR: USDA Forest Service, Pacific Northwest and Range Experiment Station.

Clayden, P. and Trevelyan, J. (1983) *Rights of Way: A Guide to Law and Practice*. London: Ramblers Association.

Cole, D.N. (1994) *The Wilderness Threats Matrix: A Framework for Assessing Impacts*. Ogden, UT: USDA Forest Service, Intermountain Experiment Station.

Coppock, J.T. and Duffield, B.S. (1975) *Recreation in the Countryside*. London: Macmillan.

Countryside Commission (1995) *Growing in Confidence: Understanding People's Perception of Urban Fringe Woodlands*. Cheltenham: Countryside Commission.

Curry, N.R. (1991) *Countryside Recreation*. London: E & FN Spon.

Curry, N.R. (1994) *Countryside Recreation: Access and Land Use Planning*, 2nd edn. London: E & FN Spon.

Driver, B.L. (ed.) (1974) *Elements of Outdoor Recreation Planning*. Ann Arbor, MI: University of Michigan Press.

Eagles, P.F.J., McLean, D. and Stabler, M.J. (2000) 'Estimating the tourism volume and value in parks and protected areas in Canada and the USA', *George Wright Forum*, 17: 62–76.

Fog, G.E. (1975) *Park Planning Guidelines*. Washington, DC: National Recreation and Park Association.

Forestry Commission (1993) *Forest and Recreation Guidelines*. London: HMSO.

Gartner, W.C. and Lime, D.W. (eds) (2000) *Trends in Outdoor Recreation, Leisure and Tourism*. Oxford: CABI Publishing.

Ghimire, K.B. and Pimbert, M.P. (1997) *Social Change and Conservation: Environmental Politics and Impacts of National Parks and Protected Areas*. London: Earthscan.

Gilg, A. (1980) *Countryside Planning*. Norwich: Geo Books.

Glypsis, S. (1991) *Countryside Recreation*. London: Longman.

Henley Centre/Headlight Vision (2005) *Paper 2 Demand for Outdoor Recreation: A Report for Natural England's Outdoor Recreation Strategy*. London: Henley Centre/Headlight Vision.

Kajala, L., Almik, A., Dahl, R., Dikšaite, L, Erkkonen, J., Fredman, P., Jensen, F.S., Karoles, K., Sievänen, T., Skov-Petersen, H., Vistad, O.I. and Wallsten, P. (2007) *Visitor Monitoring in Nature Areas: A Manual Based on Experiences from the Nordic and Baltic Countries*. Copenhagen: TemaNord.

Knopf, R.C. (1983) 'Recreational needs and behavior in natural settings', in I. Altman and J.F. Wohlwill (eds) *Human Behavior and Environment 6*. New York: Plenum Press.

Liddle, M. (1999) *Recreation Ecology*. London: Chapman and Hall.

Lieber, S.R. and Fesenmaier, D.R. (eds) (1983) *Recreation Planning and Management*. London: E & FN Spon.

Litton, R.B. Jnr (1968) *Forest Landscape Descriptions and Inventories*. Berkeley, CA: USDA Forest Service, Pacific Southwest Forest and Range Experiment Station.

Manning, R.E. (2007) *Parks and Carrying Capacity: Commons without Tragedy*. Washington, DC: Island Press.

Miles, C.W.N. and Seabrooke, W. (1993) *Recreation Land Management*. London: E & FN Spon.

National Academy of Sciences (1975) *Assessing Demand for Outdoor Recreation*. Washington, DC: US Bureau of Outdoor Recreation.

Newsome, D., Moore, S.A. and Dowling, R.K. (2002) *Natural Area Tourism: Ecology, Impacts and Management*. Clevedon: Channel View Publications.

Patmore, A. (1993) *Recreation and Resources*. Oxford: Blackwell.

Scottish Natural Heritage (1994) *Sustainable Development and the Natural Heritage: The SNH Approach*. Battleby, Perth: Scottish Natural Heritage.

Shivers, J.S. (2002) *Recreational Services for Older Adults*. Madison, NJ: Fairleigh Dickinson University Press.

Stankey, G.H., Cole, D.N., Lucas, R.C., Petersen, M.E. and Frissell, S.S. (1985) *The Limits of Acceptable Change (LAC) System for Wilderness Planning*. Ogden, UT: USDA Forest Service General Technical Report INT-76, Intermountain Forest and Range Experiment Station.

Tait, J., Lane, A. and Carr, S. (1988) *Enjoying the Countryside*, CCP 235. Cheltenham: Countryside Commission.

Torkildsen, G. (1986) *Leisure and Recreation Management*. London: E & FN Spon.

USDA Forest Service (1982) *ROS Users Guide*. Washington, DC: USDA Forest Service.

USDA Forest Service (1988) *The National Forests: America's Great Outdoors: National Recreation Strategy*. Washington, DC: USDA Forest Service.

USDA Forest Service (1990) *ROS Primer and Field Guide*, R6-REC-021–90. Portland, OR: USDA Forest Service.

US Department of the Interior, Bureau of Outdoor Recreation (1977) *Guidelines for Understanding and Determining Optimum Carrying Capacity*. Bethlehem, PA: Urban Research and Development Corporation.

Van Dorens, C.S., Lewis, J.E. and Priddle, G. (1979) *Land and Leisure: Concepts and Methods in Outdoor Recreation*. Chicago, IL: Maaroufa Press.

Van Lier, H.N. and Taylor, P.D. (1993) *New Challenges in Recreation and Tourism Planning*. Oxford: Elsevier.

Veal, A.J. (2002) *Leisure and Tourism Policy and Planning*, 2nd edn. Oxford: CABI Publishing.

Wurman, R.S. (1972) *The Nature of Recreation*. Cambridge, MA: MIT Press.

Wyman, M. (1985) 'Nature experience and outdoor recreation planning', *Leisure Studies* 4(2): 175–88.

2–14 General references

American Society of Landscape Architects Foundation (1975) *Barrier Free Site Design*. McLean, VA: ASLAF.

Anstey, C., Thompson, S. and Nichols, K. (1982) *Creative Forestry*. Wellington: New Zealand Forest Service.

Beazley, E. (1969) *Designed for Recreation*. London: Faber & Faber.

Bell, S. (1993) *Elements of Visual Design in the Landscape*. London: E & FN Spon.

British Trust for Conservation Volunteers (various dates) *Handbooks on Hedging, Footpaths, Walls, Fencing*. Wallingford: BTCV.

Bunin, N., Jasperse, D. and Cooper, S. (1980) *Guide to Designing Accessible Outdoor Recreation Facilities*. Ann Arbor, MI: USDI Heritage Conservation and Recreation Service.

Burnett, J.A. (ed.) (n.d.) *Park Practice Design*. Washington, DC: National Park Service, Park Practice Program, Division of Federal and State Liaison.

Campbell, A. (1987) *The Designer's Handbook*. London: Orbis Books.

Countryside Commission (1980) *Recreational Cycling*, Advisory Series No. 8. Cheltenham: Countryside Commission.

Countryside Commission (1981) *Informal Countryside Recreation for the Disabled*, Advisory Series No. 14. Cheltenham: Countryside Commission.

Countryside Commission for Scotland (1981) *Information Sheets: Equipment and Materials* (2 vols), Battleby, Perth: Countryside Commission for Scotland.

Forestry Commission (1990) *Recofax: Recreation Planning, Design and Management Information Sheets*. Edinburgh: Forestry Commission.

Goldsmith, S. (1976) *Designing for the Disabled*. London: RIBA.

Good, A.H. (1990) *Park and Recreation Structures*. Boulder, CO: Graybooks.

Hultsman, J., Cotterell, R.L. and Zulis-Hultsman, W. (1987) *Planning Parks for People*. State College, PA: Venture Publishing.

Kidd, B.J. and Clark, R. (1982) *Outdoor Access for All: A Guide to Designing Accessible Outdoor Recreation Facilities*. Melbourne: Department of Youth, Sport and Recreation.

Ministry of Energy and Natural Resouces (1983) *Recreation Design and Construction Standards and Guidelines Manual*. Alberta: Forest Service.

Pigram, J. and Jenkins, J. (1999) *Outdoor Recreation Management*. London: Routledge.

PLAE, Inc. (1993) *Universal Access to Outdoor Recreation: A Design Guide*. Berkeley, CA: PLAE Inc

Pomeroy, J. (1964) *Recreation for the Physically Handicapped*. New York: Macmillan.

Reis, M.I. (1991) *Design Standards to Accommodate People with Disabilities in Park and Open Space Design*. Madison, WI: University of Wisconsin.

Rutledge, A.J. (1971) *Anatomy of a Park*. New York: McGraw-Hill.

USDA Forest Service (undated) *Recreation Facilities Design Catalogue*. Washington, DC: USDA Forest Service.

USDA Forest Service (1987) *National Forest Landscape Management: Recreation*. Vol. 2. Washington, DC: USDA Forest Service.

US National Park Service (1935) *Park Structures and Facilities*. Washington, DC: USDI, National Park Service.

5 Parking the car

Brierly, J. (1972) *Car Parking and the Environment*. London: The Institution of Municipal Engineers.

British Parking Association (1977) *Parking in Relation to Recreational Needs*. St Albans: British Parking Association.

Countryside Commission (1981) *Surfaces for Rural Car Parks*, CCP 45. Cheltenham: Countryside Commission.

McCluskey, J. (1987) *Parking: A Handbook of Environmental Design*. London: E & FN Spon.

Volmer Associates (1965) *Parking for Recreation*. Wheeling, WV: American Institute of Park Executives.

6 Toilet facilities

Countryside Commission for Scotland (1985) *Lavatories in the Countryside*. Battleby, Perth: Countryside Commission for Scotland.

Forestry Commission (1991) *Forest Toilet Design Manual*. Edinburgh: Forestry Commission.

7 Picnicking

USDA Forest Service (1937) *Camp Sites and Fireplaces*. Washington, DC: USDA Forest Service.

8 Children's play

Consumer Product Safety Commission (1991) *Handbook for Public Playground Safety*. Washington, DC: US Government Printing Office.

Countryside Commission for Scotland (1984) *Providing for Children's Play in the Countryside*. Battleby, Perth: Countryside Commission for Scotland.

Moore, R.C., Goltsman, M. and Iacofino, D.S. (eds) (1992) *Play for All Guidelines: Planning Design and Management of Outdoor Play Settings for All Children,* 2nd edn. Berkeley, CA: MIG Communications.

Potter, D. (1997) *Risk and Safety in Play: The Law and Practice for Adventure Playgrounds*. London: E & FN Spon.

Thompson, D., Hudson, S.D. and Olsen, H.M. (2007) *S.A.F.E. Play Areas: Creation, Maintenance and Renovation*. Champaign, IL: Human Kinetics.

Wellhousen, K. (2002) *Outdoor Play Every Day: Innovative Concepts for Early Childhood*. New York: Delmar/Thompson Learning.

9 Trails

Countryside Commission for Scotland (1981) *Footbridges in the Countryside*. Battleby, Perth: Countryside Commission for Scotland.

Fieldfare Trust (2005) *Countryside for All*. Fife: Fieldfare Trust.

Lundgren, Y. (2005) *Access to the Forest for Disabled People*. Rapport 1-2005. Stockholm: Jönkoping i Skogsstyrelsen.

Paths for All Partnership (2001) *Lowland Path Construction: A Guide to Good Practice*. Alloa: Paths for All.

Paths for All Partnership (2003) *Sign Post Guidance*. Alloa: Paths for All.

USDA Forest Service (1990) *Trails Management Handbook*, FSH 2309.18. Washington, DC: USDA Forest Service.

10 Water-based recreation

Nordhaus, R.S., Kantowitz, M. and Siembieda, W.J. (1984) *Accessible Fishing: A Planning Handbook* Albuquerque, NM: Development Division, New Mexico Natural Resources Department.

Wilson, K. (1991) *Handbook for the Design of Barrier Free Recreational Boating and Fishing Facilities*. Washington, DC: States Organization for Boating Access.

11 Wildlife viewing

Natural Resources Canada (1994) *Non Consumptive Wildlife Recreationists: A New Constituency for Forest Managers*. Forest Management Note 59. Ottawa: Natural Resources Canada.

12 Design for overnight visitors

Countryside Commission (1975) *Transit Sites for Mobile Campers*, CCP 57. Cheltenham: Countryside Commission.

National Caravan Council (1970) *A Manual of Caravan Park Development and Operation*. London: National Caravan Council.

Wagner, J.A. (1966) *Campgrounds for Many Tastes*. Ogden, UT: Intermountain Forest and Range Experiment Station, USDA Forest Service.

13 Interpretation

Aldridge, D. (1975) 'Principles of Countryside Interpretation and Interpretative Planning', in *A Guide to Countryside Interpretation*. Edinburgh: HMSO.

Barrow, G. (1988) 'Visitor centres: an introduction', in *Environmental Interpretation*. Manchester: Centre for Environmental Interpretation.

Countryside Commission (1979) *Interpretation Planning*. Cheltenham: Countryside Commission.

Gross, M., Regnier, K. and Zimmerman, R.C. (1992) *The Interpreter's Guidebook: Techniques for Programs and Presentations*. Stevens Point, WI: College of Natural Resources, University of Wisconsin.

Ham, S. (1992) *Environmental Interpretation: A Practical Guide for People with Big Ideas and Small Budgets*. Golden, CO: North American Press.

Lewis, W.J. (1981) *Interpreting for Park Visitors*. Philadelphia, PA: Eastern Acorn Press.

Pennyfather, K. (1975) *Guide to Countryside Interpretation*. Part 2. Edinburgh: HMSO.

Piersenne, A. (1985) 'Planning, scripting and siting panels', paper presented at Environmental Interpretation conference, Centre for Environmental Interpretation, Manchester, 8–11 June.

Sharpe, G.W. (1976) *Interpreting the Environment*. New York: John Wiley & Sons Ltd.

Tilden, F. (1957) *Interpreting Our Heritage*. Chapel Hill, NC: University of North Carolina Press.

Uzzell, D. (ed.) (1989) *Heritage Interpretation*, vol. 1, *The Natural and Built Environment*. London: Belhaven Press.

Ververka, J.A. (1994) *Interpretive Master Planning*. Helena, Montana: Falcon Press.

Index

Page numbers in italics denote an illustration

Abercromby River National Park (New South Wales) *74*, *87*
Abriachan Community Forest (Scotland) *72*, *88*, *94*, *204*
'Adirondack Shelter' 182, *182*
adrenaline sports 13
agelessness 10
air travel 5
Akasamylly (Finnish Lapland) *77*, *90*
Alberta Forest Service *158*, *165*
all-terrain cycle trails 153–4, *153*
Alps 27
altar fireplaces 86, 88–9, *88*
amphitheatre 201
Amsterdamse Bos (Holland) 21, *21*, *151*, 191
animals
　attacks by 23
　play equipment based on 102–3, *102*
　see also dogs; horses; wildlife
arch bridges 130, 133, *133*
archaeological sites 110
area car park 55–6, *56*
Arizona *78*
arrival at destination 42–3
art as interpretation 207–8
asphalt 59
assault courses 101, *102*
Australia 28
Austria 138

backpackers 173–4
Baikal, Lake (Siberia) *2*
bark 104, 123
barriers
　for controlling vehicles *see* vehicle control devices

bathing areas 159–62
　changing-rooms *159*, 160
　lake 161
　river 161–2
Baxter State Park (Maine) *62*, *181*, *182*
beam bridges 130, 131–2
beehive shaped shelter 147–8, *148*
benches
　picnic 82–5, *83*, *85*
　on trails 139–41, *140*
Benchmark in Britain 141
Berlin urban car park *59*
bicycle racks 154, *154*
bicycles
　all-terrain cycle trails 153–4, *153*
　cycle tracks 34
Black Water of Dee (Scotland) *160*
Blue Mountains (New South Wales) *2*
Blue Ridge Parkway (Virginia) *36*, *144*
boardwalks 118–20, *118*, *119*, *120*, 157
boating facilities 162–6
　boat launches 162–4, *163*, *164*
　jetties 164–6, *165*
bogs 15
box culvert 114, *115*
brainstorming 18
brick 78
bridges 130–6, 151
　abutments 135–6, *136*
　arch 130, 133, *133*
　beam 130, 131–2
　cantilevered beam 130, 133
　handrails 136, 151
　log 131, *131*, *132*
　maintenance of 136
　sawn timber 132, *132*
　siting of 135–6
　steal beam 132
　suspension 131, 133–5, *134*

taking horses across 151–2
trussed beam 130, 133, *133*
brief, site design 209
British Forestry Commission *see* Forestry Commission
Budderoo National Park (New South Wales) *146*
built facilities 16, 27 *see also* individual types

cabin sites 190–6
　fire prevention measures 193–4
　lighting and access to cabins 196
　position 190–1, *191*
　site layout 191–4, *192*, *193*
cabins 174, 194–6
　frame construction 195–6, *195*
　log construction 194–5, *194*
campfires 86, *87*
camping shelters 182, *182*
campsites/camping 4, 173–90
　design of utilities 184, *185*
　and disabled visitors 184–5, *186*
　layout design 179–82
　Lost Lake Campground (case study) 187–90, *188*, *189*, *190*
　open sites 174–6, *174*, *175*, 180–1, *180*
　other buildings 185–6
　parking 180, 182
　and pedestrian circulation 176, *178*
　provision of facilities 177–9
　spur sites 176–7, *176*, 181–4, *182*, *186*
　variety of layouts 174–7
　walk-in/boat-in/fly-in 177
　youth 184, *184*
Canada 3
canopied views 143, *143*
cantilevered beam bridge 130, 133
Cap Ferret (Aquitaine) *63*, *120*, *185*

car parks 10, 31, 53–67
  and campsites 180, 182
  construction 61
  design of spaces 57, *58*
  and disabled visitors 59
  factors to be taken into account in design of 53
  number of spaces 53–4
  payment collection 66
  safety and security 66–7
  surface marking 65
  surfacing materials 59–61
  and trees 57
  types of layout 54–6, *55*, *56*
  vehicle control and management 61–5
carrying capacity 15, 16, 22, 23–4
  ecological 16
  limitation in original concept of 22
  social 16
cars 23
  dimensions of *57*
  ownership 4, 5
  use of to travel to destination 34
Cary (North Carolina) *103*
Cascade Mountains 16
Cassandra Peninsula (Halkidiki) *120*
causeway construction 117–18, *117*
Centre for Environmental Interpretation 197
change, limits of acceptable 22
changing-rooms *159*, 160
charcoal 88
charges, visitor 14
chemical toilets 73, *73*
children 13
  protection concerns 93
  and youth camping sites 184, *184*
children's play 93–104
  advantages and opportunities provided by outdoors 95–8, *96*
  and play theory 93–6
  stages of 94–5
  types of 94
children's play areas 32, 98–104
  design 98–9
  and disabled children 103, *103*
  materials and construction 103–4, *104*

safety issues 99, *99*, 104
selection of 98, *98*
themed 100–3, *102*
zones for different age groups 98
cinderblock 78
city
  contrast between wilderness and 25–6
  escape from the 1, 3, 5–6, 26
Civilian Conservation Corps (CCC) 2, 4, 27, *27*, 78, 92
clays 16
climate 16
  impact on surfacing materials 59
  and picnic sites 81
coach trips 10
code of conduct 45
cognitive play 94
colour-coding, trails 137
comments, visitor 48
commercialization 13–14
community buildings 177, 179, *179*
'community forests' 9
composite materials
  and sign structures 52
composite wood panels 49
composting toilets 71–2, *71*, *72*
concrete 29, 104
  abutments for bridges 136
  and boat launches 164
  used for picnic furniture 84
condominiums 196, *196*
constraints and opportunities, mapping of *213*, 214
construction phase 216–17
consumer empowerment 12
corrals 152, *152*
corrugated iron 77, *77*
Country Code 45
Countryside Commission for Scotland 93
Cradle Mountain National Park (Tasmania) *133*
Craters of the Moon National Monument (Idaho) 199
cross-country ski trails 154–5, *155*
cultural aspects, mapping of 212, *212*
culverts 114, *115*, 129
cut-off drains 113–14, *114*
cycles *see* bicycles

Dalbeattie Forest (Scotland) *153*
Dalby Woods (Sweden) *101*
dams 170, *171*
David Marshall Lodge (Scotland) *141*, *158*
deaf visitors 201–2
Deerpark (Cornwall) *195*
demand, recreation
  assessment of 9, 14–15, 210–11
  trends in 10–14
    changing perceptions of risk 13
    commercialization 13–14
    demography 10–11
    environmental concerns 14
    health issues 13
    increase in ethnic diversity 11
    and internet 13
    lifestyle changes 12
    and polarization of income 12
    social changes 11–12
    specialized tastes 12–13
demography 10–11, 14
Denmark 9, 34
Deschutes National Forest (Oregon) *59*
deserts 16
design concepts for outdoor recreation 25–32
design phase 214–15
design, site *see* site design
direction signs 46
disabled visitors 15, 16, 23
  and campsites 184–5, *186*
  and car parking 59
  and children's play area 103, *103*
  and hide design 167–8
  and interpretation planning 200–1
  and picnic tables 83, *83*
  planning a visit 33
  providing information for 32
  toilet facilities for 70–1, *70*
  and trails 106, 110, 112, *112*, 141
dog fouling 150, *150*
dogs
  and trails 150–1, *150*
Dolly Sods Wilderness Area (West Virginia) *203*
drainage
  and campsites 179
  path 113–15, *113*, *114*, 116
  and surfacing of car parks 60–1

drinking fountains 91
drinking water 91
drystone walling 78
Dune de Bouctouche, La (New Brunswick) *120*

earth mounds *61*, 62, 64
Eastern Europe 4–5, 28
ecological analysis 17, 214, *214*
ecological mapping 211–12, *212*
enamelled steel 49
Ennerdale Forest (Lake District) *149*
entrance, site 31, 38–41, *39*, *40*
    congestion issues 39–40
    payment for parking at 66
    pedestrian 40-1, *41*
    security requirements 39
    signs 31, 38, 41, 45
entrance, trail 138
environmental concerns 14, 24
environmental education 24, 198
ethnic diversity 11
exhibition areas 205, 206
existing facilities/sites, refurbishing 7

faggots 117, *117*
families 11
fascines 117, *117*
feature views 144
fences
    as vehicle control device 64, *64*
fibreglass 103
    signboards 49, *49*
    used in play areas 103
filtered views 143, *143*
fingerposts 139, *139*
fire prevention measures 193–4
fire risk warnings 38
fireplaces 86–9, 158
    area around 89, *89*
    campsites 190
    fuel for 88
    low-level campfires 86, *87*
    waist-high or altar 86, 88–9, *88*
fish cleaning stands 159
fishing 3, 157–9
fitness (or trim) trail 149–50, *150*
focal views 143–4, *143*
fords 129–30, *129*
Forest Code 45

Forest of Dean *54*
    Beechenhurst *61*, *85*
    Cannop Ponds *77*
Forest Enterprise *85*
Forestry Commission 93, 112, 207
forests 9, 15
    and car parking 54
    frightening aspects of 6
    picnic areas 80
    play areas 100, *101*
    toilet block design for 74, *74*
    trails in 141–2, *142*, 145–6
    vegetation 16
framed views 143, *143*
Franz Josef Glacier (New Zealand) 30–1, *30*

gabions 136, *136*
Garmisch Partenkirken (Bavaria) *174*
gates 149–50, *149*, 153
Gauja National Park (Latvia) *153*
genius loci 17, 30, 42
GIS (geographic information system) 211
Glacier National Park (British Columbia) 91, *203*
glades 168–9
Glen Affric (Scotland) 50, 54, *140*
Glenmore Forest Park (Scotland) *39*
Glenveigh National Park (Ireland) 29–30, *29*
Goat Fell (Arran) *130*
GPS (global positioning system) 211
grassland 15
gravel 78
gravel workings 170
Great Smoky Mountains National Park (Tennessee) *4*, *204*
Grizedale Forest (Cumbria) *102*, 207
guttering 78

Haldon Forest (Devon) *101*
handrails 151
    bridge 136, 151
    trails 127, *128*, *129*
health
    benefits of nature 5–6, 13
health concerns 13
hedges
    used as barrier *63*, 64
Helsinki Central Park (Finland) *150*

Helsinki City Forest (Finland) *101*
Hermitage, The (India) *195*
hides 167–8, *168*, *169*
High Tatra Mountains (Slovakia) *28*, *47*
historic sites 199
home working 12
horse trails 151–3, *151*, *152*
household types 11
hunting 3, 4, 16

identification signs 46
income, polarization of 12
Industrial Revolution 3
information, visitor 32, 45–52, 197–8
    leaflets 48, 202, *202*
    medium 48–50
    message 46–8
    on-site panels 203–5
    planning a visit and 33
    requirements needed 45–6
    signboards *see* signboards
internet 13
    and planning visits 33
interpretation 197–208, 215–16
    art as 207–8
    features of sites with potential for 198–9
    meaning 197–8
    media available for conveying of 201–6
    planning 199–201
    reasons for 198
    strategies 199
interpretation signs 46
inventory 17–18, 211–12
Iriomote National Park (Japan) *28*
Irving Nature Park (New Brunswick) *73*, *123*, *129*, *145*

Japan
    recreation design 28
    sign from *46*
jetties
    boating 164–6, *165*
    fishing 157-8, *158*
    for pond dipping 172, *172*
journey to destination 31, 33–43
    arrival 42–3
    entrance 31, 38–41
    planning and anticipation 31, 33–4

journey to destination (*continued*)
on the road 34–5
roadside landscape design 37, *37*
threshold signs 35–7, *36*, 41
wayfinding 35, *35*
wind-down stretch of road 41–2, *42*

kissing gate 148–9, 154
Kokanee Glacier Provincial Park (British Columbia) *147*
Koli National Park (Finland) *140*, *203*
Kolka (Latvia) *50*
Krkonoše National Park (Czech Republic) *124*

ladder stiles 148
lake bathing areas 161
Lake District 26
Ennerdale Forest *149*
lakeshore protection 160, *160*, *161*
laminated materials
used for signboards 50, 52
land base 15
landform 211
landscape
appraisal of 17–20, *18*
beauty of 25
changing of during route to destination 34–5
inventory/survey of 17–18, 211–12
range of opportunities for recreation in 16–17, *17*
roadside 37
as a setting for recreation 15–17
variety of 15–16
visitor impact on 22
zoning 19–20, *19*
landscape character map 212, *213*, 214
languages
diversity of 11
and leaflets 202
Lapland 91–2, *155*
Lapp shelters 91–2
laundry facilities 177
leaflets 48, 202, *202*
on places to visit 33, *34*
lecture theatres 201
life-rings 158
lifestyle changes 12

lighting
and access to cabins at night 196
and toilet blocks 75
limits of acceptable change 22
linear car park 55, *56*, 57
Lionthorne Wood (Falkirk) *142*
listening posts 205
Listvyanka (Siberia) *89*
litter, picnic sites 89–91, *90*
litter bins 89–90, *90*
local materials, use of 29
Loch Aweside (Scotland) 192
log barriers 62–3, *63*, 64
log bridges 131, *131*, *132*
log cabin construction
and toilet block 76, *77*
log cabins 194–5, *194*
log posts 63–4, *63*
logs
used as picnic furniture *84*
lone parents *see* single parent families
loop layout for car parks 54–5, *55*, 57
lost, worry about getting 22
Lost Lake Campground (Mount Hood National Forest, Oregon) 187–90, *188*, *189*, *190*

Mabie Forest (Scotland) 141, *154*
'Magical Forest' event (Scotland) 208
Manchester 3
maps
site area 46, *47*
survey/inventory 211–14
marshes 15
materials
use and appropriateness of 24, 29–30
matrix technique 18
meadows 15
media, interpretative 201–6
exhibition areas 205
leaflets 202, *202*
on-site panels 203–5, *203*, *204*
people telling a story 201–2
portable digital players 202–3
visitor centres 205–6
mental health
benefits of nature to 6, 13
merchandise, selling of 206

metal
used for picnic furniture 84, *84*
used for sign structures *51*, 52
midges 176
migration 11
Mission 66: 4, 27, 28, 197, 206
mobile phones 13
Mother Walker Falls State Park (Maine) *125*
motor play 94
motorhomes 173, 174 *see also* trailer caravans
Mount Baker-Snoqualmie National Forest (Washington) *60*
Mount Hakkoda National Park (Japan) *122*
Mount Orford Provincial Park (Quebec) *87*, *128*
Mount Revelstoke National Park (Canada) *49*
Mount St Helens (Washington) *145*
mountain biking 10, 153–4
mountainous areas 15, 16
Muir, John 3, 5
music
in play areas *101*

National Association of Interpreters 197
national parks (United States) 3, 4, 27, 200 *see also* US National Park Service
natural materials, use of 27
nature
health benefits of 5–6, 13
Netherlands 21, 34
networked society 13
New England 16
New Forest (Hampshire) 4, *5*, 176
New Zealand 16, 28, 30
non-renewable resources, wise use of 23
North York Moors National Park *60*
Nuuksio National Park (Finland) *126*

obesity 5, 13
Okanagan region (British Columbia) 174
older people 10–11
O'Neill, Tony 29

open campsites 174–6, *174*, *175*, 180–1, *180*
orientation signs 31, 45, *46*
outdoor recreation
    history of 3–5
    importance of 1
    trends in demand for 10–14
overnight visits 173–96
    cabin sites 190–6
    condominiums 196, *196*
    desirable qualities for 173–4
    see also campsites/camping

Pacific Crest Trail 108
Pacific Rim National Park (British Columbia) *43*, *132*
paintball 104
Pancake Rocks (New Zealand) *129*, *205*
panels, interpretative on-site 203–5, *203*, *204*
panoramic views 142, *143*, *144*
parking *see* car parks
pasture grass 16
paths *see* trails
pay-and-display machines 66
payment
    for parking 66
    for visiting site 40
Peak District 16
peat 16
    paths across 116–17, *116*
    techniques for crossing 117–18, *117*
pedestrian circulation
    and campsites 176, *178*
pedestrian entrances 40–1, *41*
Pennine Way 108
Perspex signboards 50
picnic furniture 82–5
picnic sites 32, 79–92
    behaviour of people in open space 79–80
    drinking water 91
    fireplaces 86–9
    layout of 80–2, *80*, *81*
    litter management 89–91, *90*
    regional differences in use of 79–80
    shelters 91–2, *91*, *92*
picturesque movement 3
'pinch point' 37

pioneer way of life 4
pipes, drainage 114
planning, recreation 9–24, 209
    appraisal of opportunities 17–20
    assessment of demand 14–15, 210–11
    landscape as a setting for recreation 15–17
    levels of 9–10
    measuring and responding to changes 22
    and Recreation Opportunity Spectrum (ROS) 20–2, *20*
    reducing of negative factors and perceptions 22–3
    and sustainability 23–4
    trends in demand for outdoor recreation 10–14
planning a visit 31, 33–4
plastic 29
    used for picnic furniture 84
platforms, viewing 145, *145*, 168
play
    adult 104
    co-operative 94, 95
    constructive 94
    functional 94
    role 95
    symbolic 94
play areas *see* children's play areas
play theory 93–6
play trails 98–9, *100*
plywood 49
poetry 207, 208
pond dipping 172, *172*
ponds 170, *170*, *171*
portable digital players 202–3
pre-arrival signs 46
precautionary principle 24
primitive settings 20, 21, 22, 106
propaganda 198
public transport 14, 34
publicity 15

quality control 217

rafting 117, *117*
railway sleepers 125
railways 4
ramps, trail 124
rangers 201, *201*

Recreation Opportunity Spectrum (ROS) 20–2, *20*, 26–7, 53, 137, 173
recreation planning *see* planning, recreation
recreational aspects, mapping of 212, *213*
regulation signs 46
renewable resources 23
Ringwood Forest (Dorset/Hampshire) *102*, *146*
risk, changing perceptions of 13
river bathing areas 161–2
roaded natural setting 20, 22
roadside landscape design 37, *37*
rocks 16
    opportunities for play 97
    painting of 138
    used for boat launches 164
    used for campfires 86, *87*
    used as picnic furniture 84, *84*
    used for trail benches *140*
    used as vehicle control device 62, *62*, 64
rockwork walls
    and lakeside protection 160, *160*
role play 95
roofing
    log cabins 194
    toilet blocks 76–7, *77*, 78
ropes 104, *104*
routing 49
rule games 95
rural setting 20, 22
Ruunaa National Hiking Area (Finland) *194*, *206*

safety issues 13, 22–3, 38
    car parks 66–7
    play areas 99, *99*, 104
    see also security issues
Samarskaya Luka National Park (Russia) *46*
sand 104
sand dunes 15, 16
sandblasting 49
Scotland 16, 23–4
    and 'environmental justice' 12
Scottish National Heritage *203*
Scottish Natural Heritage 23, 51, 198
Scouts 174

screen printing 49
sculpture 207–8
seasonal changes 16
seasonal zoning 19
security issues 23
     car parks 66–7
     site entrance 39
     see also safety issues
semi-primitive setting 20, 21–2
Seneca Rocks (West Virginia) *207*
Sheffield 3
shelters
     camping 182, *182*
     picnic 91–2, *91*, *92*
     trailside 146–8, *147*
showers
     and campsites 177
signboards 48–52, *50*, 203–5
     metal 49, *51*, 52
     stone 50–1
     wood 48–9, 51–2, *51*
signs 31, 45
     entrance 31, 38, 41, 45
     fastening of to trees 138
     function of various 44, *45*
     interpretative 203–5
     orientation 31, 45, *46*
     threshold 35–7, *36*, 41, 45, *46*
     vehicle management 45, 64–5, *65*
     warning 31, 38
     wayfinding 35, *35*
single parent families 11–12
site design 209–17
     brief 209
     stages 209–17
          analysis 212–14
          assessment of demand 14–15,
               210–11
          construction phase 216–17
          design phase 214–15
          detailed design 215–16
          survey/inventory 17–18, 211–12
site plans 10
ski trails 154–5, *155*
skylights 75
sloping ground, trails on 120–3, *121*
Slovakia *46*
soakaway 73
social changes 11–12
social play 94
soil 16

sound and light shows 208
Soviet Union 4–5, 12, 28
specialized tastes 12–13
spur campsites 176–7, *176*, *186*
     for tents 181–2, *182*
     for trailer caravans 182–4
stainless steel 29, 103
steal beam bridges 132
steel pedestal fire 88, *88*
step stiles 148
stepping-stones 130, *130*
steps
     trail 124–7, *124*, *126*
     and viewing towers 144–5
stiles 148, *149*, 154
stone 29
     used for fireplaces 86, 88, *88*
     used for litter bins 90
     used for signs 50–1
     used for toilet block construction
          78, *78*
     used for trail steps 125, *125*
stone abutments 135–6, *136*
stone paving 123–4, *123*, *124*
stone-walled shelters 147, *147*
stream crossings 129–36
     bridges *see* bridges
     fords 129–30, *129*
     stepping-stones 130, *130*
stress 5, 6
SUDS (sustainable urban drainage)
     systems 60
surfacing
     beneath play area structures 104
     car parks 59–61
     fitness trails 150
     horse trails 151
     impact of climate on materials
          used 59
     and trails 115–16, 122–3
surveys
     of area 211–12
     and assessment of demand 14,
          210–11
suspension bridges 131, 133–5, *134*
sustainability 14
     and drainage 60
     and recreation planning 23–4
SWOT analysis 18–19
symbols 48
     trail categorization *111*

tables, picnic 82–5, *82*, *83*
Taeveskoja Forest (Estonia) *133*
Taman Negara National Park
     (Malaysia) *146*
Targhee National Forest (Idaho) *88*
tents
     open campsites for 180, *180*
     spur sites for 181–2, *182*
Tervete Nature Park (Latvia) 27, 39,
     99, *135*, 207–8, *207*, *208*
Thingvellir National Park (Iceland)
     49
three-dimensional maps 46
threshold signs 35–7, *36*, 41, 45, *46*
ticket machines (car park) 66
tiles 78
timber 29
     as fuel for fireplaces 88
     preservation and treatment of 52,
          119–20
     used in boardwalks 119
     used for boat launches 164
     used for cabin frame construction
          195
     used for litter bins 90
     used for picnic furniture 84–5
     used in play areas 103
     used for sign structures 50–1
     used for toilet block construction
          76–7, *77*
     used for trail steps 125, *126*
timber abutments 136, *136*
timber benches *140*
toilet facilities 31–2, 69–78
     building construction and materials
          used 76–8
     and cabin sites 191
     campsites 177
     car numbers and provision of *71*
     design of block 74–5, *74*
     and disabled visitors 70–1, *70*
     factors to be taken into account
          when deciding on 69–70
     hand washing 75
     interior materials and finishes 78
     light and ventilation 75, *75*
     lobby area 75
     scale of provision 70–1
     types of 71–3
          chemical 73, *73*
          composting 71–2, *71*, *72*

flush 72–4
vault (pit or big drop) 72–3, *72*
and vandalism 76
year round use 76, *76*
Tongariro Crossing (New Zealand) 108
tourism agencies 14
traditional architecture 206–7
traffic jams 14
trailer caravans/tent-trailers
open sites for 180–1
spur sites for 182–4, *183*
trails 23, 32, 105–55, 214
benches 139–41, *140*
and boardwalks 118–20, *118*, *119*, *120*
categorization of 110–12, *111*
construction principles 110---13
construction and surfacing of path 115–24
cross-country ski 154–5
design of route 106–10
lengths of trail 107–8, *108*
sequences of experiences 108–10, *109*
survey of landscape 106, *106*
and disabled visitors 106, 110, 112, *112*, 141
and dogs 150–1, *150*
drainage 113–15, *113*, *114*, 116
entrance 138
fitness or trim 149–50, *150*
handrails 127, *128*, *129*
horse 151–3, *151*, *152*
information on 32, *111*, 203–4, *203*
play 98–9, *100*
purpose of 105–6
sloping ground 120–3, *121*
star rating system 112
steps, ramps and changes in level 124–7, *124*, *125*
stiles and gates 148–9, *149*
and storytelling 201
stream crossings 129–36
trailside design and management 141–2, *141*, *142*
trailside shelters 146–8, *147*
tree-top 145–6, *146*
viewpoints 142–5
waymarking *see* waymarking
zoning of 19

travelling to destination *see* journey to destination
tree-top trails 145–6, *146*
trees
and campsites 177, 179
and car parks 57
fastening of signs to 138
opportunities for play 97
painting of with markings 138
and picnic areas 81–2, *82*
Trollheimen (Norway) *194*
Troodos Mountains (Cyprus) *79*
trussed beam bridges 130, 133, *133*
tundra regions 16
turnstiles 148
typeface
leaflets 202
threshold signs 36
webpages 33

United States
Interstate system 4
Mexican immigration 11
national forests 21
national parks 3, 4, 27, 200 *see also* US National Park Service
strategic planning 9
urban setting 20–1, 22
urbanization 3, 5
US Forest Service 19, 27
US National Park Service *34*, 50, 197, 205

vandalism 52
and toilet blocks 76
vault (pit or big drop) toilets 72–3, *72*
vegetation 16
and campsites 179
trailside management of 141–2
types of 15
and wildlife management 169
vehicle control devices 62–4
earth mounds *61*, 62, 64
fences 64, *64*
hedges *63*, 64
log barriers 62–3, *63*, 64
log posts 63–4, *63*
rocks 62, *62*, 64
walls 64, *64*
vehicle management 64–5

vehicle management signs 45, 64–5, *65*
vehicle dimensions *57*
vernacular architecture 206–7
viewing platforms 145, *145*, 168
viewing towers 144–5, *144*
viewpoints, trail 142–5
canopied 143, *143*
feature 144
filtered 143, *143*
focal 143–4, *143*
framed 143, *143*
panoramic 142, *142*
visitor centres 4, 42, 199, 200, 205–7, *207*
visitor charges 14
visitor information *see* information, visitor
visitor monitoring 210
volcanic lava 16

walls
rockwork 160, *160*
toilet block 78
as vehicle control device 64, *64*
Walls of Jerusalem National Park (Tasmania) *127*
warning signs 31, 38
water
attractiveness of 15
and children's play 97, 101–2, *102*
crossing of *see* stream crossing
drinking 91
water-based recreation 157–72
bathing areas 159–62
boating facilities 162–6
fishing 157–9
lakeshore protection 160
site layout 157
wayfinding 35, 43
waymarking 22, 23, 45, 136–9, *137*
and cycle trails 154
fastening signs to trees 138
painting rocks 138
painting trees 138
posts 138, *138*, *139*
weather *see* climate
web-cams 206
websites 33–4
Westskoven (Copenhagen) *88*
wetlands 170, *170*

Whistler (British Columbia) *160*
wilderness
    contrast between city and 25–6
wildlife
    and ecological analysis 214
wildlife viewing 98, 110, 167–72
    design of wildlife areas 169–72,
        170, *171*
    hide layout and design 167–8, *168*
    protecting of wildlife 167
Williamson Lake Provincial Park
        (Alberta) *159*
wind-down stretch of road 41–2, *42*
windows
    in hides 168
    in timber cabins 195
    in toilet blocks 75
wood *see* timber
wood chips 104, 123
wood stains 52, 85
wooden bridges 131–2

wooden posts
    used for on-site panels 203–4
    used for waymarking *138*, 138,
        139
wooden signboards 48–9, 51–2, *51*
work patterns 12
Working Time Directive 12
Wyoming *4*

Yosemite National Park (California)
        3, *199*
youth camping sites 184, *184*

zoning 15, 19–20, *19*
    and children's play areas 98
    lakes 161
    and Recreation Opportunity
        Spectrum 20–2
    rivers 161
    seasonal 19
    trails 19